A PSYCHIATRIST'S GUIDE TO SUCCESSFUL RETIREMENT AND AGING

A PSYCHIATRIST'S GUIDE TO SUCCESSFUL RETIREMENT AND AGING

Coping with Change

H Michael Zal

ROWMAN & LITTLEFIELD
Lanham • Boulder • New York • London

Published by Rowman & Littlefield
A wholly owned subsidiary of the Rowman & Littlefield Publishing Group, Inc.
4501 Forbes Boulevard, Suite 200, Lanham, Maryland 20706
www.rowman.com

Unit A, Whitacre Mews, 26-34 Stannary Street, London SE11 4AB

British Library Cataloguing in Publication Information Available

Library of Congress Cataloging-in-Publication Data

Names: Zal, H Michael, author.
Title: A psychiatrist's guide to successful retirement and aging : copying with change / H Michael Zal.
Description: Lanham, MD : Rowman & Littlefield, 2016. | Includes bibliographical references and index.
Identifiers: LCCN 2015039792 | ISBN 9781442251236 (cloth : alkaline paper) | ISBN 9781442251243 (electronic)
Subjects: LCSH: Older people--Psychology. | Retirement--Psychological aspects. | Aging--Psychological aspects. | Change (Psychology)
Classification: LCC BF724.8 .Z35 2015 | DDC 155.67--dc23 LC record available at http://lccn.loc.gov/2015039792

Printed in the United States of America

A special thank you to Katherine E. Galluzzi, D.O., CMD, FACOFP dist., who is professor and chair of the Department of Geriatrics at the Philadelphia College of Osteopathic Medicine, for writing the foreword. She is also director of Comprehensive Care at PCOM, as well as being well known for her research, teaching, and writing on gerontology. Her words add a new dimension to my work.

This book is dedicated to Buba Paul,
my maternal grandmother

CONTENTS

AUTHOR'S NOTE

When I retired as a psychiatrist, I thought that I would miss the work, the activity, the intellectual stimulation, the educational aspects, and the ability to help others. I did miss these things. Particularly, during the first three months, I missed being a physician and a psychiatrist, which was such a big part of my identity for so many years. However, in reality, I did not miss having to deal with the tension, the constant need to learn about new medications, deal with billing issues, and patients, who thought that their problems were unique and overwhelming, but whose trials and tribulations really were quite average and repetitive. It was a pleasure not to have to deal with the long hours, the financial restrictions set by insurance companies, prior authorizations, and attorneys, who tried to influence your professional opinion.

It was delightful not to have to put up with medical records, patient reports, and time pressure. I no longer had to second guess patients, who dealt with their emotional pain with veiled or sometimes more overt suicidal threats. I no longer had to decide if a patient was indeed suicidal or just angry and wanting attention. It was wonderful not to have to work so hard to get patients to gain insight or accept outpatient psychiatric care and psychiatric hospitalization when necessary. People think that a psychiatrist's job is easy. It is indeed very tiring and emotionally draining. Actively listening to patients and finding just the right response to be helpful to them is hard work.

Most of all, I found that what I really missed were the people. My patients, office personnel, and the other physicians in the suite had offered me companionship and personal interaction. There was always someone around to talk to briefly, joke with, discuss the ball game with, or share life events. Earlier in my career, I, as a solo practitioner with no office help, had been in the office alone all day. I had handled the isolation by being sure to go out of the office at least once a day and talk to others: other physicians, whom I knew in the building, hospital or nursing home staff, or even the restaurant personnel at lunch. The pharmaceutical representatives were knowledgeable and friendly. If all else failed, there was always the mailman. Part of the advantage of sharing office space with others during the last fourteen years was that I was not constantly by myself.

I gradually realized, however, that, most importantly, I missed my patients. During my work day, many of them, particularly those whom I saw once a week, every two weeks, or once a month had become "professional friends." Many I knew over the course of several years. I had met their family members and children in the waiting room and during family consultations. In some cases, I ended up seeing a husband and wife, their parents, and sometimes even their older children for therapy or consultation. Several times during my career, I had three generations of the same family coming to see me, separately, for professional care. They were an integral part of my life, since they fulfilled many of my needs, such as providing company. Now, I missed the stimulation and I felt alone. This was the first time since first grade that I was in this position. During the first few months of retirement, the obvious gradually dawned on me. Although my wife and I had a good relationship and many friends outside of work, my patients had added a lot to my existence.

I now live in a fifty-five and older community of four hundred families, most of whom are retired or about to retire. The average age is about seventy years old. For the most part, the residents are vital, active individuals, who are enjoying a whole host of social activities and hobbies. They face their lives with gusto. They are forming new friendships, volunteering, traveling, and even starting new careers. Behind this beautiful façade is the reality that, as we retire and grow older, we also have to deal with physical illness and our own mortality. Life is both bitter and sweet. Many people who live in our community have pacemakers, neurological illnesses, and suffer from hypertension, arthritis, lung disease, and diabetes. Memory problems are common. Hearing aids are not unusual. Community gossip is often filled with reports that so and so is sick or in the hospital. People die. Often the front gates are left up so that visitors can enter to make a Shiva call or visit relatives after a wake.

However, for the most part, the people in this community deal with life proactively. They travel and try to stay active. They exercise and go to the gym. They attend planned social, cultural, educational, and charity events. I hope that you, like them, will enthusiastically embrace the possibilities of your new life as you retire and age. Express gratitude for what you have achieved and what you do have. Do not dwell on the negative aspects of aging. Take charge of your emotions, embrace change, and actively engage with your new life. If you follow through, you may find that retirement and aging offers many new and exciting opportunities and experiences.

Although long-awaited, adjusting to and coping with retirement is not always easy. It is helpful if you plan ahead, not just financially but also emotionally and behaviorally. This involves investing in new relationships to compensate for the loss of people from work. If married, your retirement will affect issues of time and space and perhaps a re-working of your respective roles. Your expectations of your spouse or significant other when you retire may also be problematic. You may have to consider current health and wellness issues as well as deciding where you will live. Unexpected events such as new health issues, divorce, or widowhood may complicate the situation. Your attitude throughout, particularly if it is positive, will also play a part in being successful. You may want to look at your spiritual or religious affiliations. They often can provide support and something to hold on to during the storm. This book will deal with these issues.

It is also very important in retirement to stay engaged in the outside world or else you can end up feeling isolated, lonely, and even depressed. This may also require some planning. You will want to establish some specific, possible goals. As I pointed out in my last book, *Ten Steps to Reduce Anxiety*, the best approach to life is to take a problem-solving approach to its problems. Be active and not passive. Do not let negative feelings and fear stop you. Take charge of your life. Examine your assumptions. Get information that you need to find out the possibilities. Ask for help and suggestions from friends, mentors, and others. Avoid avoidance. These suggestions are helpful in reducing anxiety but also in dealing with retirement, aging, and life in general.

Be realistic in your expectations. Your spouse or partner cannot fulfill all your needs; nor can friends. So many people look for constant happiness. This is not possible every day. Life is chaotic with many unknowns that are not under our control. I suggest that you seek contentment. Be happy with who you are, your lot in life, and what you have achieved. Throw away old regrets and old jealousies and animosities. Life is short. We only go this way once. We are all the same, regardless of the wrapping paper. We all have needs for acceptance and approval, honesty and trust, respect and dignity, hope, freedom from pain, emotional support, intimacy, affection, and tenderness. Most of all we all need love.

This book makes use of a composite fictional couple, Harold and Vivienne, that I invented and will use throughout, as a hook to facilitate and illustrate the material. They will serve as one example of what can really happen initially after you retire. You will see how retirement and aging affected them in various aspects of their life and how they initially coped with the change and loss. You will also see what they did to help themselves move forward in a more positive way.

Life passes quickly. I remember one day my daughter, who was walking behind me commented, "Dad, when did you get so old?" In Helen Simonson's novel, *Major Pettigrew's Last Stand*, the major's son expresses the same sentiment when he visits his father in the hospital. "You gave me a fright, what can I say? . . .You've always been an unmovable rock in my life and suddenly you're an old man wearing tubes. Quite nasty."[1]

GUIDELINES FOR SUCCESS IN PREPARING FOR RETIREMENT AND AGING

1. Begin planning early
2. Take an active approach
3. Define your lifestyle
4. Stay calm
5. Try not to procrastinate
6. Have a support system

7. Be patient
8. Seek out community resources
9. Consider all personal variables: finances, health status, personality traits and emotional needs, coping history, ability to sustain relationships, spiritual and religious beliefs.

As you can see there is a lot to consider when planning for retirement and aging. The process can be overwhelming. However, planning ahead and considering all of the factors noted above will help put things in perspective and give you a road map to follow as well as a safety net. As an unknown author once said, "It pays to plan ahead. It wasn't raining when Noah built the ark."[2] Planning ahead will not guarantee perfection or absolute success. However, it will allow you to have more input about your future and feel more in control of your destiny. It will give you a leg up in dealing with your upcoming retirement life and prevent you from forgetting about the important issues and other personal variables noted above that need to be considered. All of these things will play a part in your ability to plan for a more contented retirement, maintain success during the transition period, and be a winner in your new life.

I have written this book to help you prepare for and successfully navigate retirement and aging, the last phase of life. So many authors have focused just on the financial planning aspect of retirement. When I researched the topic on the Internet and in the library, I found that the same was true in reference to book topics on retirement and aging. Most dealt only with financial planning. This topic is important. However, as noted, it also is helpful to consider many other issues, including emotional and psychological adjustment, in preparing for and living out your remaining years. Many books on retirement and aging give an idyllic view of the "golden years" as a wonderful time filled with relaxation and fun. Adjusting to decreasing physical strength, declining health, the death of loved ones, loneliness, and establishing new relationships is not easy. Although there are many positives, this time of life is not always so great or pleasurable. I hope that this book will fill the void and give you a more balanced view that will be helpful to you. With the baby boomers entering their retirement years, it is important to have a guide covering all of these topics. Once you have some ideas and some suggestions on how you can start your journey, it is up to you to follow through and bring them to fruition.

A Psychiatrist's Guide to Successful Retirement and Aging: Coping with Change will deal with preparing and coping psychologically. It will also talk about the physical changes that occur as you age and the influence of these changes on your emotions. It will deal with marriage and other relationships and show how they are affected by retirement and the aging process. To retire successfully, it is important to plan ahead and insert new activities and people into your life. It is helpful to start some of these behaviors prior to stopping work, so that the transition is smoother and not abrupt. This book concludes with a philosophical discussion of the meaning of life and other wisdom gleaned from getting older. This book is meant for future and current aging retirees, such as the baby boomers (born from 1946 to 1964), those who are already in this new phase of life, the silents (born before 1946), as well as the old-old generation (those over age eighty-five). It will also be helpful to their family members, friends, caregivers, and others who want to understand and support them. It will be of interest to mental health professionals, medical audiences, and retirement service organizations. I hope that this book will help you set realistic goals and obtain success in your journey.

FOREWORD

Katherine E. Galluzzi, D.O.

"If you fail to plan, you are planning to fail." This statement, attributed to several thinkers but possibly originating with Benjamin Franklin, epitomizes the underlying message of *A Psychiatrist's Guide to Successful Retirement and Aging*. Written by another lifelong Philadelphian and observer of the human condition, H Michael Zal, D.O., this book affords readers the opportunity to reflect on how they might best plan for what many hope to be the best, if last, of life's chapters.

Dr. Zal presents an overview of what to expect during "The Golden Years;" this is in essence a practical and detailed reality check about what lies ahead. A retiree himself, Dr. Zal's long career in psychiatry has afforded him an insider's view of the physical, emotional and existential issues faced by aging individuals. His candor and insight allow us the opportunity to recognize that the years following the end of our work life will require as much thought and planning as we invested in planning our families and work lives. Further, during the tumultuous years of work and child-rearing, we may have had precious little time to reflect on how we would spend our time in retirement. Leisure time, a fondly-held goal, may actually leave us adrift and isolated. Once the demands and anchors of family life and career are gone we may lose our sense of belonging, our sense of self. Dr. Zal cautions that without having meaningful relationships, established hobbies or activities that are sustaining and enjoyable during our worklives, we may find in retirement that life lacks focus; in fact, what we had viewed as treasured leisure time may devolve into boredom and loneliness.

All is not doom and gloom, however. After providing a realistic view and practical advice for a full life in retirement, Dr. Zal shares his unique perspective, based on his decades of psychiatric observation, on what it is that gives meaning to life. His heartfelt and honest insights are extremely useful.

Much of what has been written about retirement focuses on financial preparedness, lifestyle options and living considerations. In contrast, *A Psychiatrist's Guide to Successful Retirement and Aging* is a compassionate and thoughtful look at aging through the lens of our emotional and "people" needs. With its easy-to-read format, this book should be part of everyone's library and the "go-to" for needed advice and wisdom during the challenging years of retirement and into the emotionally difficult choices we will all face at the end of our lives.

INTRODUCTION

Psychological Aspects of Retirement and Aging

According to the US Census Bureau, the average retirement age in the United States today is sixty-two years old. Modern medical advances allow us to live longer. The average length of retirement is eighteen years.[1] You will have a lot of time to deal with this new, different, and, at times, trying stage of life. These years have the potential to bring with them new psychological challenges. Therefore, it is particularly important to prepare for getting older, not just financially, but also emotionally and physically. This book, written from a psychiatrist's perspective and covering the period of time from retirement until the end of life, will increase your awareness of potential mental health problems, as well as some of the behavioral, physical, and spiritual issues that you may encounter down the road.

For some, late adulthood can be difficult, bringing with it a whole range of emotions. Social and physical losses can cause feelings of loneliness, frustration, and helplessness. Along the way, you may have to deal with mental health problems such as stress and anxiety, grief and depression, drug and alcohol abuse, changes in your marital and sexual relationship, and memory loss and Alzheimer's disease, as well as elder abuse. Are you ready? How will you cope with the psychological changes in yourself or a family member? This book will not only increase your awareness and help you get ready but will also aid you in dealing with the common mental health issues that may arise along the way. It will offer treatment options, suggest coping skills, and even deal with the emotional concerns that occur at the end of life. Let it be your guide and light your way.

Reporter Eric Adler, in the Sunday, February 1, 2015, issue of the South Florida *Sun Sentinel*, "Special Section—Health Report," tells us that each day ten thousand baby boomers turn sixty-five years old.[2] As the baby boomer generation becomes senior citizens and enters into the last stage of life, a new definition and set of expectations for retirement and aging are evolving. This is not your father's way of being an older adult. Forty years ago, as a person aged, they slowed down, sat in a comfortable chair, read the newspaper, watched TV, or played tennis or golf, and waited to die. People today tend not to retire in this traditional way. They bring a new dimension to this period of life. They see no need to follow a progressively downhill course. They envision getting older as bringing with it a challenge to stay active and engaged, reinvent themselves, and reach for new goals.

The advent of over-fifty-five communities for active adults has reinforced this philosophy. However, we have no true role model or guide on which to base this new lifestyle. That is why I wrote this book. Most books on retirement focus only on finances; however, there will likely be changes in health, marriage and other relationships, housing, and other aspects of life. Few authors talk about coping mechanisms for all of these issues or suggest ideas to put this new style into action and allow it to be purposeful. Few help you prepare emotionally. More information is needed. The first three to twelve months are the hardest and are a true period of adjustment. Each individual handles this period differently.

How will you fill your new free time? This book will educate you in how to invest in relationships with friends and family, redefine your marital or partner relationship and broaden your horizons. There are many with things that we cannot control. However, *A Psychiatrist's Guide to Successful Retirement and Aging: Coping With Change* addresses the biopsychosocial aspects of retirement and aging, including the final phase of life, and will point you in a positive direction. This book will allow you to plan ahead and take charge of your life as you age and not just let it happen to you. Feeling more in control will allow you to see the whole picture and realize what is really important in life.

Inspirational author Catherine Pulsifer tells us, "retirement may be an ending, a closing, but it is also a new beginning."[3] She is right. Retirement today is a time of multiple possibilities to feel vital and embrace a new life filled with new hobbies, social interaction, and relations. It can be a time of passion and purpose. It can even be a time to start a new career. In fact, author and Harvard Business School professor Rosabeth Moss Kanter tells us, "The boomers' biggest impact will be on eliminating the term 'retirement' and inventing a new stage of life . . . the new career arc."[4] It is never too late. Pulitzer Prize-winning author, Frank McCourt wrote his first book at age sixty-five. Astronaut John Glenn orbited the earth at age seventy-seven. In his eighties, British leader Winston Churchill completed the four-volume *A History of the English-Speaking Peoples*. Renaissance artists Michelangelo and Titian worked until they were nearly ninety. Heart surgeon Dr. Michael DeBakey practiced medicine, lectured, and wrote well into his nineties. Grandma Moses began painting in her nineties.

However, experiences during this time vary. For some the transition is not so easy or natural. In the 2002 film, *About Schmidt*, the main character, Warren Schmidt feels adrift after retirement from his job as an actuary. He sees an advertisement for an organization that aids African children. He eventually finds solace in providing financial support and writing letters to Ndugu Umbo, the Tanzabi boy he sponsors.

Retirement may be a true test of our resiliency. A surprising number of people are retired at any one time. Statistics show that between 92,000 and 120,000 people between the ages of fifty-five and sixty-five years old retire each year.[5] This amounts to 333 people a day. Stopping work doesn't happen in a vacuum. Often, it parallels another challenging life change, called getting older. Over ten thousand people in the United States will turn sixty-five years old on any given day.[6] For some these two changes can be a double whammy. We all move into this senior citizens phase of life on different biological, sociological, and psychological tracks. No matter how or when we arrive at its front door, getting older isn't always fun. During this period, we are confronted with new emotional and physical demands and challenges. Retirement often accentuates these issues and brings them into sharper focus. How will we handle this change? What will we do with the years remaining in our life? What happens to us will depend on the tone and achievements of prior developmental phases. We have spent our lives learning and adapting.

According to psychologist and psychoanalyst, Erik Erickson, the challenge of getting older, roughly after age sixty-five, or the final stage of man is "integrity versus despair."[7] Emotional integrity is derived from an individual's overall satisfaction with life. If, for the most part, you have no regrets over the past and view your life as meaningful, you potentially can accept the future with equanimity. If, on the other hand, you see life as a series of missed opportunities, you are likely to be discontented and despair over the realization that it is too late to start over. You are acutely aware that the clock is ticking. The way to resolve this crisis is to accept the fact that death is relatively near and review your life with satisfaction. Successful resolution brings with it the development of wisdom.[8]

Other things that you need to do as seniors include adjusting to physical aging, such as decreasing physical strength and declining health. You will need to adjust to living on a fixed and often reduced income. Some people may have to cope with the death of a spouse and other loved ones. Many will sell their family home, downsize, and establish new living arrangements. This may include fifty-five and older communities or other senior housing developments. Here, for the first time in years, you may have to work at establishing new relationships with people of a similar age. Everyone differs in their ability to adapt to these challenges. It is difficult to change or undo a lifetime of habits and personality traits. Every journey begins with the first step. The first test of your resiliency may be retirement. For some it can be a time of growth and contentment. For others, it can tip the scales in a negative direction.

How will you know when you are ready to retire? The answer depends on socioeconomic and physical circumstances. Some will be forced into retirement due to company policies, physical and mental disability, or other health issues. Those who have more flexibility will sense when they are ready. For years you have loved doing what you did for a living, but suddenly you find that the work is no longer fun and seems routine. You are doing things by rote and not from passion, and you find it more tedious than before. Unexpectedly, you start to find that your patience is wearing thin. You are not as tolerant with your customers and clients. You watch the clock more and look forward to closing time. You know that you are ready for a change.

Everyone dreams of retiring someday, so that they can do whatever they want. They daydream about this new and more perfect life. Your fantasies about what it will be like are always beautiful, happy, and splendid. In the reverie, you always seem young and robust. You see yourself traveling to warm weather and exotic places, entertaining friends and laughing frequently with a glass of wine in your hand. Your spouse or significant other is also young and passionate. You see yourself doing useful things and people appreciating you for your endeavors. The options are limitless. Some prepare for retirement; while others just fall into it in time. In either case, the reality is usually not as marvelous as anticipated in dreams.

Harold and Vivienne are an imaginative composite couple that I invented and will use throughout the book, as an example of what can really happen initially after you retire. Here is how they looked when Harold first retired.

Harold had looked forward to retirement for many years. The long-awaited day finally came. His goal was to do nothing for the first three months of his new life. For a while, he was happy with his newfound freedom. He did what he wanted to do. He took walks, read his newspaper, and watched TV. He could sleep late and did not have to deal with schedules, company meetings, and the constant tension of the large manufacturing plant that had been his life for thirty-three years. Now several months into retirement, he noticed that everything seemed to have changed. He got the feeling that his wife, Vivienne, resented his presence in "her house" and his small demands on her time. She constantly pestered him about putting his things away and keeping the house clean.

He avoided getting out of bed in the morning and looked forward to going to sleep at night. The day seemed long as he moped and puttered in his garden. He had no friends or acquaintances outside of work and few hobbies or interests. Somehow, he missed the hustle and bustle of his old job. No one came to him for decisions any longer. He had always been a good provider. Now he worried about being able to exist on a fixed income. He felt diminished. His body seemed to hurt in new places. He felt isolated, alone, and rudderless. He started to reflect on the past and thought about all the things he had wanted to accomplish, but had not. After so many years of looking forward to being retired, he could not understand why he was not happy or content.

Vivienne also was experiencing the challenges of getting older and of living a full life after sixty. She had no guide or role model. Her mother lived to an older age but never worked outside the house or even wore slacks. She lived in a different world. Vivienne had concerns about finances, keeping the family together, and maintaining a relationship with their two children. In her mother's world, the children lived close by and were available for support and companionship. Today their son lived in Dallas, Texas, and their daughter lived in New York, many miles from their home in southern New Jersey. Sometimes they were lucky if the children called once a week. This confused and angered her, because she felt that she had given them so much of herself while they were growing up. She also worried about her health and could see her body declining.

Since her retirement from teaching third-grade elementary school last year, she saw her main vocation as keeping her house clean and making nice meals for Harold. Somehow, he kept putting his finger-print on the plan and messing it up. She had two girlfriends to whom she spoke on the phone. Going food shopping on Wednesday was the highlight of her week. Like Harold, she had few hobbies or interests outside the house. She tended to focus her disappointment in life on Harold's failures. Her feelings of frustration and irritability were build-ing. Vivienne also is going in the wrong direction. She always prided herself on being open and verbal. However, somehow, she just doesn't get around to talking with Harold about their present situation. They could benefit from better communication and a good sharing session.

Harold and Vivienne's situation and feelings are not unique. Many people have trouble coping during this period of transition. Like other men, who no longer feel in charge of their lives, Harold tends to with-draw into himself, feel sorry for himself, and avoid the world. He is going in the wrong direction. He needs to come out of himself and focus on others and the outside world. He needs to fight against his feelings of loss and depression and focus on others and his relationships. Vivienne is trying to deal with this big change in her life by focusing on her household duties. She also needs to reach out more and try new things. Elisabeth Kübler-Ross wisely comments in her book *Life Lessons*: "Love has nothing to do with knowledge, education, or power; it is beyond behavior: It is also the only gift in life that is not lost. Ultimately it is the only thing that we can really give. In a world of illusions, a world of dreams and emptiness, love is the source of truth."[9] Paying attention to each other more could be Harold and Vivienne's first positive step in their new life journey. They could each use a hug, a kind word or someone to show them attention. Perhaps, then, they would be more willing to change their behavior from negative to positive and take the important and healing step of reaching outward and refocusing on others.

Retiring isn't always easy. Many like Harold and Vivienne will experience emotional pain and frustration due to their difficulty in dealing with change and the accentuation of negative personality traits and poor coping skills. For some, work or family is the only investment that they have made in life. When they are out of these arenas, they feel out of control. The addition of physical illness and lowered economic status makes them feel helpless and useless. For those who have planned ahead by developing other interests and hobbies, the later years can be a time of pleasure and contentment. People who have a self-assertive problem-solving approach to life do best. Some may just enjoy eating a good meal, visiting friends, or reading a good book. For others, retirement can be a time to expand life in new directions and develop new outlooks and interests.[10] There are no rules. The goal is contentment.

If you do not know what to do, just try something that you haven't done before. Columnist, Darrell Sifford, in his June 28, 1990, article, "Mining the Pleasures of the 'Golden Years,'" in the *Philadelphia Inquirer*, tells us

> The key to a successful retirement is to "stay involved." It is important to have something to get up for in the morning and something to look forward to. Keep busy. Continue to learn and grow. Continue to share your knowledge and teach the younger generation. Look at the future with optimism. Retain your previous passion for work in other projects. Continue to invest yourself in others. This will help you to continue to feel needed and alive and fill your life with meaning.[11]

These are some of the things that Harold and Vivienne need to learn to have an easier transition and obtain a more contented retirement.

Initially, retirement can be a difficult bridge to cross. As with many life changes, be patient with yourself and have realistic expectations.

Regardless of your native ability, any significant change usually takes at least three to twelve months for you to adjust and feel comfortable. If you have been retired for six months or more and you are still feeling alienated, unhappy, and uncomfortable, perhaps it might be the time to talk to someone who is trained to deal with such problems, who knows your individual emotional and physical history. You do not have to do it alone. Your family physician may be the place to start. Maybe your spiritual advisor has been trained as a counselor. A mental health worker or psychiatrist may also be a possibility. Help is available. Please reach out and ask for it.

A *Psychiatrists Guide to Successful Retirement and Aging* will elaborate on each of the issues noted above. We will see how Harold and Vivienne do as they learn new coping skills and add more depth to their retirement lives. This book will also deal with the topics of emotional and physical awareness, the common mental health problems that may show themselves as we age, mental health in the final phase of life, psychiatric treatment options, and coping skills that will help you be successful. It will conclude with a chapter on aging wisdom and the meaning of life. I suggest that you do not make big decisions during the initial transition period of retirement. There are often too many losses for you to think clearly about and what is best for your future. The advice and suggestions in this book are not meant to be substitutes for professional care. However, I hope that this information will help you navigate the journey ahead in a more positive way, and help you adjust and survive retirement intact and with a smile on your face. Good luck.

I

Getting Ready: Awareness

I

EMOTIONS

People spend years worrying about having enough money saved to pay their bills in old age. Preparing emotionally for retirement and getting older is as important as financial planning; however, few give any thought to getting ready psychologically for this major lifestyle transition from midlife to late life. Thus, many people may feel overwhelmed and have difficulty handling this change. Accustomed to the structure, comfort, and status that they felt in the workplace, they are not aware that they may soon find themselves dealing with feelings of loss, loneliness, guilt, grief and depression, and nervousness, as well as anger and frustration.

No longer feeling that they have a definite role, some may go through an identity crisis and have to redefine themselves and their purpose in life. Opening the door to retirement often makes them more aware of the physical and mental changes of aging that they are experiencing. The aches and pains and other physical impairments that they ignored while working now seem to stand out in sharp relief, adding to their feelings of frustration and discomfort. Their occasional memory loss of recent events may add to their dissatisfaction.

Disappointed that their fantasy expectations are not being met and that their needs are not being fulfilled may cause them to feel irritated, abandoned, and helpless. If not prolonged, many of these emotions are normal. Awareness that these feelings may occur and can be transitory can be helpful in preventing catastrophizing and withdrawal, and allows retirees to spend their energy navigating new territory and seeking positive solutions.

In 2006, the Winnipeg, Canada-based investors group, Decima Express polled six hundred employed Canadians over age forty-five. A third of those polled said that they were well-prepared financially for retirement; however, only 4 percent said they felt prepared for the emotional transition to retirement life.[1] The sheer numbers, involved as the baby boom generation ages and moves into retirement, make it even more important for people to be aware of the emotional issues that they may experience during this period of adjustment.

Although I advise you to start working on your emotional readiness now, remember retirement and aging are gradual processes. Things will not just take care of themselves the first day that you stop working and stay home. Like many things in life, it takes thought, hard work, and practice to retire and age successfully. Give yourself time to adjust. However, if three to six months have gone by since you retired and you are still emotionally under the weather and floundering, talk to someone that can be objective about your condition. This can include a trusted friend, your rabbi or priest, or a mental health professional.

The vignette below uses a couple, who are a composite of many of my patients, whom I have treated through the years, to illustrate some of the emotions and issues that you may encounter when you first retire and start to age.

Harold quickly turned over and went back to sleep. He had already woken up twice, not counting two trips to the bathroom to urinate. He had no desire to get out of bed and begin his day. He felt like crawling back into a dark cave. When he opened his eyes again, he saw that the red LED screen on his nightstand clock said 11 AM. Instead of getting up, he laid in bed thinking. "What will I do today? I'll eat breakfast, read the newspaper, look at the computer, eat lunch, pay some bills, get the mail, read a few pages of a book, take a nap, eat dinner, watch some television, and be happy to go to sleep for the night. This is not the way for a grown man to spend a day. I hate retirement. I hate getting older."

Feeling irritable and disgruntled, he felt that it almost was not worth getting up. He didn't like his new routine: sleeping, vegetating, eating, and sleeping again. He didn't like being at his wife's beck and call. He particularly did not like accompanying her on shopping trips where he felt that she wasted so much time touching everything. He felt tense and alone. He missed the stimulation and positive feedback that his job had offered him. He missed the company of his co-workers. He missed the work that had made him feel useful.

He had not envisioned retirement or getting older in this way. In his pre-retirement fantasy, he had felt alive, vital, and in control. Instead, he felt helpless and old. His arthritis pain seemed worse than usual and he was more aware of his slow-moving, aging body. He had thought that it would be great to have nothing to do. It seemed enticing to be able to just sit back, watch sporting events on television whenever he wanted, and drink a beer now and then. He now knew that he was wrong.

In reality, he felt sad, discouraged, and adrift. His new routine, following retirement, soured very quickly. He had not anticipated that he would experience such a "loss" when he left his job. He did not realize that he would miss the work routine and the people so much. However, Harold had not planned ahead. He felt that it would just all work out on its own. He had no plan B. He began to realize that American basketball coach, John Wooden, was right when he said, "Failing to prepare is preparing to fail."[2]

His wife, Vivienne's story was different, but yet the same. She also had not planned emotionally for the future. When she retired one year ago, after twenty-five years as a third-grade teacher, she had anticipated that she would be content just doing the other things that she had always done without having to be at school. She thought, "Gee, it will be nice not to have to go to work each morning, not to have to deal with the paperwork or my boss, the principle. It will be nice just to relax and leisurely do my chores, shop, and meet my friends for lunch." It didn't quite work out that way.

Although she was busy, she was not happy. Something was missing. Although Harold was in the same house, he seemed miles away, lost in his own thoughts. She had anticipated that she and Harold would travel and spend more quality time together. However, she had not communicated these ideas to her husband. She had not planned ahead. Now she felt betrayed, mildly depressed, and very irritable. She felt frustrated that Harold had not magically anticipated and fulfilled her needs.

LOSS, LONELINESS, AND GRIEF

Ending your career, even if done voluntarily, may result in feelings of loss and grief. Although you may not have realized it, work satisfied many of your needs. Going to work gave you a reason to get up in the morning. It gave you feelings of respect and self-esteem and satisfied your needs for companionship and belonging. Those living alone, such as single, widowed, or divorced retirees, may find that they feel isolated and lonely. These feelings can lead to depression. John Murray underlines the fact that "the pain of retirement means loss."[3] Face these losses directly. Admit them, allow yourself to grieve, and then let these issues go. It is often helpful in letting go to talk to someone about how you are feeling and not hold it all inside. Then, you will be better able to find new ways to fill the void.

During the first three months of my own retirement, although I was busy and active, I did not quite feel myself. I knew that I had made the decision to retire on my own and felt that it was the right and appropriate choice. I had planned ahead of time by adding a few new activities to fill my time. My wife and I also had made plans to do some traveling. I thought that everything would run smoothly; however, life did not follow my plan. I found that I felt irritable and mildly depressed. Gradually, I realized that I was experiencing feelings of loss related to the fact that I missed the people that had been involved in my career as a psychiatrist.

I missed the patient interaction. Some patients I had seen weekly, some every two weeks, and some once a month for many years. Some had become professional friends. I realized that at the office I had other physicians and office staff to talk to during idle moments. Now, on most days I was alone much of the time. I admitted this to my wife and several friends. I restarted an old coping mechanism that I had used when in the office alone in solo practice. I made sure that I went out of the house, even for a little while, each day. I made conversation with those that I met. I began to feel better.

GUILT

Guilt is another feeling that is often prevalent at the beginning of retirement, particularly if your parents raised you to believe that it is always important to be productive. You may feel uncomfortable when you have more time to relax. A recent article spoke about the "workaholic withdrawal syndrome." It said, "Since the time our ancestors were hunters and gatherers men have been pre-programmed to be the defender and provider. Men who retire often feel guilty that they are not 'out there in the hunt.'"

You may feel as though you are not serving your family well by not working. You may feel that you should be on the job being productive, instead of enjoying a walk in the park during the afternoon.[4] Sir J. Lubbock, British political leader and scientist, got it right when he said, "rest is not idleness, and to lie sometimes on the grass on a summer day listening to the murmur of water, or watching the clouds float across the sky, is hardly a waste of time."[5]

Depression can be seen as anger turned against the self. The hidden message is often, "I am a bad person." This can be expressed in the form of dejection, self-depreciation, and physical disturbances. Depression also involves unconscious guilt, arising from interpersonal issues, perhaps from unconscious ambivalence and hostility with resentful and aggressive impulses directed toward persons who are the objects of an undesired obligation or toward persons on whom one is dependent for security. These hostile impulses, which are originally directed against others, but become directed against one's self, can express themselves, only a little disguised, as repetitive complaints of feeing inferior, hopeless, and worthless. Tearfulness sometimes just announces, "I am feeling angry." Depression is adaptive. It keeps the person in contact with their environment and prevents an even deeper regression to a more serious mood disorder. By their incessant complaints, the depressed person stimulates his relatives and friends to counterbalance his feelings of inferiority, unworthiness, and hopelessness by providing reassurances that these negative images are not true. In therapy, psychiatrists often try to get a handle on what a patient is feeling angry, resentful, and guilty about. Verbalizing these issues and putting them in perspective can often help elevate your mood.

At work, you had clear-cut goals and tasks. Your energy was outer-directed. When you retire, your time becomes inner-directed. You alone must plan your day and week.[6] To be successful will require a problem-solving approach to your situation, where you are proactive and take charge of your dilemma. Be creative. To fill that empty space in your life, focus on the opportunities that still exist to invest yourself in life in new ways and perhaps with new people. Try to find some things about which you feel passionate that can give you new emotional rewards. Embrace change and stay engaged.

WHO AM I?

For many, employment defines their lives and offers social interaction and a reason to get up in the morning. The retiree will have to find new ways to inject passion and purpose into their life. Many people tend to define themselves based on their occupation, profession, or major job. For some, work or family is the only investment that they have made in life. As you near or enter your retirement years, you may have to alter how you view and describe your identity. Plan ahead. Do not wait until the last minute.

The question, "Who am I?" will have to be redefined and not just be based on what you did for a living. Without your job title, you may feel inadequate, helpless, and useless. You will have to broaden your concept of yourself and take into account who you are as an individual. Remember, being a husband or wife, mother or father, grandparent, and friend are all also part of your identity. You can also define your identity by giving yourself credit for your positive characteristics. Are you helpful to others? Are you organized and resourceful? Are you friendly and outgoing? Are you a good spouse, parent, or friend? These qualities are also part of who you are.

Counselor, Elizabeth Holtzman, in her paper, "Emotional Aspects of Retirement" warns,

> Making the transition from work to retirement involves sharp and abrupt changes in what is expected of you and what you expect of yourself. Your role as a worker may be over or reduced, but your role as a spouse, partner, parent, or friend doesn't stop, and neither do other multiple roles you play. . . . People who are unable to let go of

the role provided by their work may find it difficult to enjoy their retirement years.[7]

There is more to life than your employment or professional status. In retirement, it is helpful to define yourself by other parameters. In explaining to others who you are, focus on your family and other relationships. Tell others about your activities and explain how you reach out to others and the world. Be proud to say, I am a grandfather; I am a writer or artist; I do volunteer work to help the needy or the disabled; I am taking courses at the community college to learn new things; I am challenging myself to continue to grow and expand my life in new directions. Robert Holes, PhD, rightfully tells us, "People who survive and who thrive in retirement are those who are flexible, and those who know that they are more than what they do."[8]

ANGER AND FRUSTRATION

The best laid plans of mice and men oft times go astray. Your expectations help define your attitude about what happens in life. If you come into this post-work phase of life expecting that your life will be a daily picnic filled with pleasure, prosperity, and adventure, you will be disappointed and may even feel frustrated and angry. Some men will be disgruntled, not having a post-retirement life of their own: They find themselves caught up in their wife's schedule and life. I have seen some patient's express these feelings in therapy by becoming tearful when talking about their present life. They have no idea that their behavior is giving me a clue that they are feeling angry about how things are going. Although there is more time to do fun things, the normal routine of life goes on. We still have to pay our bills, go to the doctor, clean our house, do the wash, and go grocery shopping. As I am apt to tell my patients, things in life are not black and white but rather gray. Gray can be a good color.

In doing therapy, I often find that patients have feelings which they sense inside themselves, but do not have the words to describe them. This is particularly true of the feelings of frustration and anger. Harold and Vivienne certainly did not realize how angry they felt. People often feel that they "should not" have such feelings and therefore do not want to admit to feeling them. The therapist often has to put words on their feelings so that patients can better articulate them. This ventilation is often helpful, frees up energy, and can offer some relief. Initially, the patient may only be able to deal with the word upset or annoyed. It may take them some time for them to own up to the more emotionally charged word, "anger."

CONTENTMENT

People come into retirement thinking that now that they are no longer under the restraints of the workplace and can do whatever they want, within reason that they will be happy all the time as they age. They soon learn that no one is constantly happy. Physician, author, and natural-remedy guru and champion of integrative medicine, Andrew Weil, MD, in a newspaper interview in the *Philadelphia Inquirer*, suggested that a more realistic expectation is to seek contentment, which is an inner sense of fulfillment that is relatively independent of external circumstances.[9]

I certainly agree with this premise. If you can be at peace with yourself, the people in your life, the hand that you have been dealt, and the road that you have chosen, you will feel more in control of your world and ultimately be happier more often.[10] Remember what novelist, journalist, and Pulitzer Prize-winner Anna Quindlen says in her book, *A Short Guide to a Happy Life*, "Life is made up of moments of small pieces of glittering mica in a long stretch of gray cement."[11] Seek contentment and not constant happiness. The best way to increase your pleasure and enjoyment, increase your feelings of contentment, and reduce your feelings of frustration is to live in the present. We now call living in the moment, mindfulness.

Perfection is an unrealistic goal. Many things are not under our control. Life is full of unknowns and surprises. It can change in a moment. Try to look at the whole picture and be thankful for what is going right. I hope that you are able to gain a new clarity about what is important in life. I hope that you gain a new appreciation of how lucky you are if you have good health, are free from emotional and physical pain, and have meaningful relationships. I hope that the wisdom borne of life experiences will help you gain a perspective that will allow you to maintain a positive attitude.

This chapter has dealt mainly with the possible pitfalls and negative feelings that you might encounter starting your journey on the road through retirement life and aging. I have also noted various ways that you can deal with these emotions. Although I do not want to sugarcoat the difficult reality that some people encounter entering this phase of life, I felt that it would be helpful and more balanced to end on a more positive note. At one extreme, there are some individuals who cope with retirement and aging with adolescent-like turmoil, filled with emotional labiality, confusion, and identity issues. At the other end of the spectrum, people transition into and cope with late adulthood without significant emotional problems. From what I have seen in my professional capacity as a psychiatrist, most people are in the middle, in the "gray area." They tend to experience both positive and negative feelings during their journey.

I hope that this chapter has increased your awareness of the emotions that you might meet in your final years. This knowledge can increase your ability to adjust, to mourn your losses, to seek mental health treatment if necessary, and continue to grow so that in your final years, you live up to your full potential. It helps to accept that which we cannot change and have realistic expectations. Positive emotions, such as pleasure, joy, love, and contentment are possible if you work at it. Retirement and aging can be a time of new opportunity and self-fulfillment. The next chapter will deal with the negative behaviors that can also impede success in adjustment.

2

NEGATIVE BEHAVIORS

Retirement and aging require that we deal with the stress of loss and change. This is a difficult task. Some try to cope by making use of negative behaviors that are counterproductive and only make life harder. They might find themselves overeating, smoking too much, gambling, or becoming dependent on drugs or alcohol. They may experience marital relationship problems, have outbursts of temper, and overreact to minor issues. They may compulsively shop, surf the Internet, and increase their sexual activity. They may compulsively clean or over exercise.

These activities take on the coloring of an addiction, although they do not meet the true definition of being psychological and physically dependent on something and experiencing withdrawal symptoms if you stop. They are really technically closer to compulsions, which are urges that evoke anxiety if they are resisted. However, anxiety is not a factor if these negative behaviors are resisted. The term "behavioral addictions" may be a good compromise label.[1] Biological and environmental factors may play a role in causing these activities. Seeing a parent use similar behaviors may cause you to try the same techniques. There may be a genetic (inherited) propensity. Behavioral addictions may trigger the pleasure centers in the brain, allowing you to feel better in the short run.

Although not effective, these negative behaviors do serve a purpose. They are an attempt to cope and feel better emotionally. Compulsive behaviors can be a temporary way to hide and override feelings of anxiety and depression. Sexual acting out, for instance, may be a way to make contact with another human and escape depression. Drug abuse may be another method of trying to deal with underlying depression. Behavioral addictions may be an attempt to meet unmet needs for love and security. They may be an attempt to deal with a chaotic world that often makes people feel helpless (see "the void" in chapter 7). They may be the person's way of trying to feel better about themselves. Overall, their purpose is to make us feel happier and more in control.

Author and researcher, Karley Randolph Pitman, teaches a course called "When Food is Your Mother" to illustrate the connection between compulsive eating and the persons unmet need for love. She maintains that overeating is emotionally driven behavior, that it is not logical or rational, but that it is rooted in deep, unmet attachment needs. Attachments meet needs for love and belonging. The key is to replace attachments to food with a positive attachment to oneself and others through increased self-esteem, by loving others, and, for spiritual people, with God or life itself. Positive attachments allow people to feel safe and secure and supports the growth process that helps them outgrow compulsive food behavior and allows them to use food in a healthier manner.[2]

Psychologist and researcher, Ryan T. Howell, PhD, talks about the cause of compulsive shopping in his blog for *Psychology Today* magazine. He states that 10 percent of adults in the Western world are shopaholics. They keep spending in spite of harmful financial, emotional, and social consequences. His research found that compulsive buying is caused by poor credit management and a belief that new purchases will produce a happier life. "Compulsive shoppers report that they bought items to get a buzz or put themselves in a better mood. They also believed that purchases could change their life . . . by transforming their appearance, self-confidence, reputation and relationships."[3]

Many people like to shop for multiple presents during the holidays and often overspend. Some like to keep their house or apartment immaculately clean and neat. Many adults and children use their electronic devices constantly. They love to play "candy crush" or "farmville." How do you know when you have crossed over the line from pleasant diversion to a compulsion or behavioral addiction? Psychiatrist and psychoanalyst, Gail Saltz, MD, in her *Woman's Day* article,[4] suggests that we watch for the following clues:

1. You are preoccupied with planning and doing the behavior.
2. The behavior negatively affects one or more areas of your life.
3. You are secretive about the behavior most of the time.
4. You have tried your best to stop the behavior but couldn't or stopped for a while but soon restarted.

What can we do about these potentially destructive behaviors? How do we regain our confidence, quell our anxiety, and stop feeling overwhelmed without them? How do we chase away the negativity and the fear that something worse will happen? How can we feel more in control of our new situation and start moving forward? There are three basic alternatives to any stress situation—such as entering retirement or dealing with new physical problems involved with aging. We can do something to change the situation; we can get out of it; we can change ourselves so that we can live more comfortably with the state of affairs. Sometimes, it is only the third alternative that we may be able to control.

Dr. Saltz suggests the following four things that you can do to help yourself deal with these negative behaviors.[5] She states:

1. Admit that you have a problem.
2. Think about what's driving the behavior.
3. Try to interrupt or at least postpone the behavior.
4. Change the way that you do it.

Things you should *not* do to try to cope with the new situation, because they will only increase your stress and are not helpful in moving forward in your new stage of life, include:

- *Procrastinate*: Procrastination is the habitual and intentional putting off of action. This may be because the project will take a lot of time, it is a task that you do not like to do, or perhaps you have a need for perfection and feel that you will fail. A parallel issue may be low self-esteem. Two ways to help yourself would be to put the task at the top of your to do list rather than at the bottom or break the task down into pieces, which may feel less overwhelming.[6] Some live by the maxim: "If it weren't for the last minute, nothing would get done."[7] However, I do not recommend taking this too seriously. Procrastination can only increase your stress and lead to feelings of guilt and depression.

- *Avoid*: Avoidance is the way that people keep themselves from doing a task, attending a function, or reaching out to others. It is fueled by feelings of anxiety and fear, self-doubt, and inferiority and concerns about what others will think. It is a negative attitude that assumes failure. The truth of the matter is if you take a risk and do the task, things usually work out better than you would have expected. Harold, for instance, found that when he took his friends suggestion that they go bowling, he actually found that he enjoyed it, as seen in the next chapter. This is why I always told my patients, "Avoid Avoidance."
- *Catastrophize*: This involves over estimating the likelihood of negative events and underestimating one's ability to cope. Some people have a tendency to have what I call "all or nothing (black and white) thinking." They believe that things will either be wonderful or terrible. There is no gray area in their mind. In cognitive behavioral therapy (CBT) this is called cognitive distortion. This thought pattern can escalate the cycle of fear and anxiety, causing one to feel that something terrible is going to happen and that they are going to lose control.
- *Hibernate and mope*: This tends to be more of a male characteristic. John Gray, PhD, explains in his book, *Men Are from Mars, Women Are from Venus*, how men and women deal with stress differently.[8] He maintains that men become quiet and go into their caves to mull things over and problem solve. Harold clearly showed this negative behavior when he initially spent his time moping in his vegetable garden. Women, on the other hand, seek out someone they trust, and talk about their problems and concerns. Men also could benefit by talking about their worries and distress. As I have often seen in doing therapy, it may take men longer to open up, but they also will feel better if they share their feelings and trepidations in a safe, accepting, and trusting environment.
- *Keep it all inside*: Holding your feelings in can eventually lead to emotional or physical problems. My hope in doing therapy is that if people can learn to talk it out in my consultation room, in individual or group psychotherapy, they will eventually be able to

do the same in other settings. However, this action requires tact and selectivity. It is not a good idea to walk in and tell your boss exactly how you feel about him. Many married people feel that they can say anything to their spouse. Remember, your spouse or significant other is a human being. You will need to have respect for their feelings and their ability to deal with anger or criticism. When you want to share, keep in mind that some people are limited in this area and may just throw your words back at you and go away angry.

- *Focus on the negative*: It is true that different people see things differently because of their personalities. Some see the glass as half empty and others look at the same glass and describe it as half full. Many have been brought up with negativity. Focusing on the negative can only be destructive and nonproductive. Even if you are not sure that things will work out, it is better to say, "I will try my best to make it happen," rather than proclaim, "It will never happen." Praise can help a person blossom. A compliment can raise self-esteem. A positive problem-solving approach will always be the better road to follow. A positive attitude often engenders success. Author, William James wisely said, "The greatest discovery of any generation is that a human being can alter his life by altering his attitude."[9]

- *Ruminate about the past*: Newspaper columnist, Darrell Sifford, in his *Philadelphia Inquirer* column, on October 17, 1983, defined the "midlife crisis" as "the nagging pain of unfulfilled dreams and the agonizing confrontation with discrepancy-facing squarely the gap between how we thought our lives were going to be when we planned them and how we now know they really are. . . . A time when we see life as it really is-full of its ups and downs."[10] Many, as they retire or start to age, go through the same process. Nobody has fulfilled all of their dreams. Tormenting yourself about what you have not achieved in the past can only engender feelings of guilt and frustration. Both these feelings are counterproductive to moving forward, and creating and enjoying the next phase of your life. No one can take away your prior achievements. Be proud of them. Use your energy constructively and build on what you have.

- *Worry*: Worry is an avoidance response that anxious people use to cope with threats in their world. It can interfere with concentration and decision making. It can interfere with functioning and inhibit life, by using up energy that could be used more fruitfully. Don't just assume a negative outcome. Edward M. Hallowell, in his book *Worry: Controlling It and Using It Wisely*, suggests that worrying can provide stimulation and excitement for those who are bored. It can also precipitate secondary problems such as depression, social anxiety, and demoralization.[11]
- *Blame others*: Take responsibility for your own actions. Apologize if you have to, but do not just put the blame on others. I have seen over and over again, in doing therapy, that every relationship problem is fifty-fifty. It is not always the one making the most noise that is causing the most problems. Many years ago, I attended a lecture where the speaker defined emotional maturity as being able to tell someone that you love them (positive feelings) or are angry at them (negative feelings). It also involves being able to accept these two feelings when they are aimed at you. Many individuals, even though they are behaviorally mature and can take care of their responsibilities, have difficulty verbalizing and or accepting these feelings.
- *Lash out at others*: Dumping your anger on someone else may allow you to feel better momentarily. However, it is an immature coping mechanism and can be very hurtful and disrespectful to the other person. In therapy, I will at times ask a person to write a letter to someone that they resent or toward whom they have a lot of pent up anger. Putting pen to paper can be very therapeutic. I ask them not to mail the letter, but rather to bring it into their next therapy session. There we can use it as grist for the mill and help the patient talk about their negative memories and rage. Releasing these pent up negative emotions can make you feel a lot lighter emotionally and more content.

Things that you *should* do. There are many other techniques that you can use to take control of your situation and reduce the stress caused by loss and change:

- *Refocus*: Concentrate on the here and now. Meditation and mindfulness (focusing on the here and now) are often helpful in promoting this goal. Distract yourself. Focus on something beautiful in nature, a baby's smile, or the aroma of your spouse's cooking. Concentrate on being helpful to someone. Throw away those negative feelings. Do not take it all so seriously. Lighten up, smile, laugh, and enjoy the moment. As you will see in chapter 20, laughter is often the best medicine. Give yourself permission to relax and have fun. Even if you are retiring tomorrow, you will not be taking out all your savings in one day. Do not live in the past constantly ruminating about what should have been, what you didn't accomplish or what you would have done differently. Use your energy to grow and move forward.

- *Express your feelings*: People who value control over sharing their feelings are more likely to show signs of stress. One of the worst things that you can do is to hold it all in and mope. Suppressing negative feelings can contribute to anxiety and may eventually cause you emotional or physical problems. You are not alone. We all need someone to listen to us sometimes. Talk out your problems and share your feelings with someone you trust. The support of your friends and family is crucial. You will find many people who can commiserate and understand. It is easier to go through a tough time with others who are having similar experiences. Ask for reassurance and even physical comfort if you need it. A hug goes a long way toward allowing a person to feel supported and safe.

- *Take care of yourself*: Take care of yourself physically and mentally. Find ways to work off your feelings of frustration and excess aggressive energy. Exercise works for many. It is the best method to quell anxiety. It is particularly important for those that have a chronic illness. In that situation, it is essential not to allow your muscles to atrophy or your body deteriorate. It is important to stay positive and try not to sink into depression. Activity, whether it is a brisk walk, swimming, or even thirty minutes at the gym, is one of the best ways to reduce stress and is also good for your physical health. Sex and affection are also great stress busters. Sex causes the brain to release endorphins, which are hormones that can reduce feelings of pain and anxiety.

- *Give yourself time and permission to relax.* Some people grew up hearing the message that they must constantly produce. Now that they are older and retired, it is often difficult for them to change their behavior. However, they can easily learn relaxation techniques and gradually allow themselves the freedom to just "be still" and appreciate their surroundings. I often give my patients the assignment to "follow their nose." This entails taking a free four-hour block of time and doing whatever they want. There is no assigned task. Most find this liberating. Take care of your physical health. Watch your diet. Avoid excessive caffeine. Go for regular checkups with your physician. Get your flu and pneumonia shots. Try not to do things that increase a negative mindset. Don't watch negative news reports or focus on stories about violence and despair.
- *Take a problem-solving approach*: Take action. This is one of the best ways to stop the cycle of anxiety and worry. Take charge of your life. Check out your assumptions and accept your own limitations. Ask for what you want. Do not assume that others can read your mind. For some people, work and family are the only investment that they have made in life. Look for new activities that may also fulfill your needs. Thinking about and developing new interests ahead of time will help bridge the gap to retirement and aging.
- *Talk to your accountant and your financial advisor about financial worries.* Talk to a mentor who can give you a point of view and perspective and suggest some activities. Rather than feeling overwhelmed by health or other worries, get the information that you need to put things in perspective, put you on a more positive road, and make yourself feel more in control. People who have a self-assertive, problem-solving approach to life do best when they retire and age. Avoid avoidance. Try new things. Review the things that you wanted to do earlier in life that you could not accomplish due to work and family responsibilities. Some of these ideas can still bear fruit and revitalize you.

Another factor that can cause problems when trying to adjust to retirement and aging are expectations. Newspaper, magazine, and television ads make it look like all senior citizens are relaxing in the sunshine, moving to beautiful retirement homes or facilities with theater and art classes, and traveling to wonderful exotic places. Some do. However, older people mostly live normal lives, filled with mundane tasks such as doing housework, going to the cleaners, and food shopping. For entertainment, they watch TV or perhaps go to the movies or visit relatives and friends.

Your expectations in a situation are important. It is not the external circumstances that cause stress, but rather the way that a person deals with problems. Too often, we follow the maxim that if we do everything right, everything will work out all right. Life does not always fall so easily into place. Remember, life doesn't come knocking on your door. Usually, you have to decide what you want and go out and look for it. Unrealistically high expectations can start you off on the wrong foot and negatively influence your perceptions of your situation. On the other hand, confidence, in perspective, is important. Writer Henry David Thoreau tells us, "If one advances confidently in the direction of his dreams, and endeavors to live the life which he imagined, he will meet with a success unexpected in common hours." [12]

Time is another factor to consider when trying to reduce stress and take charge of your life. On the one hand, don't sleep your life away. Staying in bed until eleven and taking a long afternoon nap is not the way to solve problems. On the other hand, when you retire, there may be new time demands made on you. Your children may suddenly ask you to babysit more often. I am not against this often pleasurable activity. However, if it is interfering with your having your own life, it is time to set limits and say no. It is okay to save time for yourself. This is not selfishness, but rather self-preservation. Those who recognize and accept their limitations and take a problem-solving approach to life will do better in dealing with retirement and aging.

It took Harold and Vivienne a while to learn the benefits of practicing the above philosophy. Initially, they wasted much valuable time using unproductive approaches to their new situation and practicing ineffective coping mechanisms. When they finally started to engage more in the outside world and share their feelings with their friends and with each other, their life in retirement changed for the better. The guidelines above will also help you circumvent the negative emotions and behaviors often encountered when you retire and as you age.

If you have tried these suggestions and they are not working or if you are still floundering and unhappy, perhaps it is time to seek outside help. This is particularly appropriate if your behavior is prolonged and interfering with your life. Do not be afraid or ashamed to ask for help. It is available. Remember, even normal, average people react to stress. Even very smart and successful people need support at times. Everyone wears blinders when it comes to their own behavior. Sometimes, it is helpful to have someone else hold a mirror up to your negative behavior. Pick up that phone and make that call.

Reinforcing your relationships outside of work and forming new relationships will help your life be more enjoyable and content as you retire and age. The next chapter will look at this important aspect of your life.

3

RELATIONSHIPS

Relationships with people are one of the primary keys to dealing with retirement and aging. Start building a new support network of social connections, outside of work, now. It will help fill the void once occupied by people at your job. Keep up with your old friends and make new contacts. They will improve your life by providing both practical and emotional support. New hobbies, including continuing education, can bring new people into your life. Volunteering or doing charity work with causes that interest you will help expand your horizons and meet new people. A Pew Research Center report shows that friendships rank with sound health and finances as the factors most likely to boost happiness and contentment in retirement.[1]

During this time of life, our bonds with family members, including our spouse or partner, our grown children and grandchildren, and our extended family take on a more important role and serve to nurture us and give us joy more than at any other age. You still have a lot of love to give, which will be reciprocated. In her book, *My Time: Making the Most of the Bonus Decades after 50*, Abigail Trafford maintains that we need to develop a social network capable of sustaining us through our senior years.[2] In an article on About.com, Sharon O'Brien says, "A measurement of whether people are successful at retirement living is the strength of their social network."[3] Let us look at the various components of this group and see their significance during our final years.

FRIENDS

Friends are important at every stage of life. What is a friend? Ralph Emerson said, "A friend is a person with whom I may be sincere. . . . Friendship is composed of truth and tenderness. . . . The glory of friendship is not the outstretched hand, nor the kindly smile nor joy of companionship; it is the spiritual inspiration that comes to one when he discovers that someone else believes in him and is willing to trust him."[4] As they say, people come into this world alone and go out of it alone. Friends break down natural isolation. They are often a reflection of humanness and help one realize that they are not the only one experiencing life's trials and tribulations. Friends cannot fulfill all needs but they can be companions, provide emotional sustenance, and bring fun and laughter into quiet lives.

A good friend is someone with whom you have a deep connection. They are someone with whom you feel comfortable, who can accept you as you are, and who will be there when you need them. A friend is someone with whom you can relax and be yourself. An unknown author once said, "Everyone hears what you say. Friends listen to what you say. Best friends listen to what you don't say."[5] The Mayo Clinic elaborates further. They say that "Friendships enrich your life and improve your health. . . . Friends can help you celebrate good times and provide support during bad times. They prevent loneliness, increase your sense of belonging and purpose, reduce stress, and improve your self-worth."[6]

Some animals travel in herds for protection from danger. People join groups for companionship and security. Human beings are naturally social, gregarious creatures. Although people no longer travel in clans like the Bedouins or belong to tribes, like Native Americans, they still need to interact with others outside the nuclear family. Today, people are becoming more and more isolated. An increase in electronic devices and the advent of social media has caused a decrease in face-to-face communication and an increase in superficiality. People text in shorthand and keep away from a deeper exploration of feelings and sharing personal thoughts. In this day and age of often-meaningless contact, true friendships become even more essential and precious. People still need friends and relationships to give balance to their lives.

Friends and relationships are particularly important in retirement when it is helpful to stay active and engaged. When work relationships end, you may feel rejected and lost, which may cause you to grieve. These feelings may increase as you find your world getting smaller, particularly as friends move away to live near their children or in a warmer climate, or are less available due to health concerns or even pass away. David C. Borchard and Patricia A. Donahoe, in their book *The Joy of Retirement*, tell us that "the workplace fulfills many important relationship needs. . . . [It] offers a base for social interaction . . . saying goodbye to these relationships for the last time, when we retire, can be nostalgic but also disorienting. At a deeper level, we may find that leaving these associations behind also leaves us without a way to satisfy many of our needs for affiliation."[7]

When you were in school or newly married, it may have seemed that it was easier to meet people and make new friends. In school, everyone is in it together and in close proximity. As parents, you met other parents through your children. You made friends at work and through social clubs or networking. People were all going through the same thing for the first time and were more willing to reach out and relate. In middle age, as you became more involved in your career and children's lives, friendships took a backseat to other priorities. As time went by, you became isolated by concentrating more on upward mobility and work and seemed to have fewer opportunities to meet new people. In retirement, everything changes. Suddenly, there is a new need for people in your life. However, the same social opportunities are not there and interacting with new people seems harder to do. You are out of practice. You may feel that you no longer have the social skills or confidence to make a new friend. The good news is that most seniors are in the same boat and are open to new friendships. Here are some things that may help you bring new people into your life. It is not easy and you will have to work at it:

- Take a problem-solving approach to life
- Show a genuine interest in others
- Smile more
- Be complimentary
- Be accepting—no one is perfect
- Every friend does not have to fulfill all your needs
- Join a group that does things that interest you: athletic teams, performing arts organizations, volunteer for organizations dedi-

cated to causes that you believe in, alumni organizations, charitable organizations, environmental groups, service organizations, political organizations, avoid avoidance, say yes to all invitations, go to school to explore a new topic or learn a new skill, involve yourself in religious or spiritual congregations.

It took Harold and Vivienne some time to realize that they needed more in their life and that it was essential to increase their relationships outside the house. I would suspect that they each expected the other to fulfill their socialization needs during retirement and were resentful that this was not happening. Vivienne had some girlfriends with whom she communicated. Occasionally, they went out to lunch. One day, at lunch, she suddenly started to cry and shared her frustration with her friends. They listened quietly and told her that they understood, but that she was being unrealistic to assume that Harold would fulfill all of her needs. One friend suggested that she come to church more often. Another suggested that she apply to be a grandmother aide at a local school, helping the teacher with difficult pupils. She promised that she would look into it.

It took Harold longer to find some solutions to his dilemma. Even when he saw his wife going out more, he continued to mope around the house and play the victim; however, someone was looking out for him. Several weeks later, the phone rang. It was a man with whom he had worked years ago, who had moved out of town. Apparently, he did not like the new area and decided to move back. He asked Harold to have lunch with him on Saturday. At first, Harold gave excuses saying that he was not feeling well and was not up to socializing. However, his friend was persistent and Harold finally agreed. As is often the case when you finally say yes and follow through, the lunch went well. Harold enjoyed seeing his old friend. They agreed to go bowling the following week. Finally, Harold had made a first step, by chance, to break down his isolation and move in a positive direction. Luck pushed him out the door toward the start of a new life in retirement.

Retirees that live alone, such as widows and divorcees, are even more in need of social support. They are more dependent on their friends for survival. It is true that if you live alone, when you shut the door of your house or apartment, there is no one else there but you. I suggest to my patients that when they are feeling lonely they should just pick up the phone and call someone. There is no need to say, "I am calling because I am lonely," just say hello. In addition, I tell them to be sure to keep up contact with their friends by calling at least one each week. People want to know that you are interested in them. In retirement communities, large apartment houses and even single housing communities, women particularly tend to take care of and look after each other. They will often have a "buddy," who calls each morning to check on them. They are sure to include each other if they go to the movies, out to eat, or play card games. It is harder for men to form such relationships in that they tend to be less communicative and have less experience in admitting their emotional needs to peers. To do well in retirement, men need to learn to reach out more, to be more giving and more nurturing. For single people, such as widows and widowers, friends offer companionship and can add a sense of security and safety and help reduce anxiety.

You may be surprised to learn that mature widows, widowers, and divorcees, those over age fifty-five, are searching for companionship on the Internet and through dating services. Companies such as ourtime.com, seniorfriendfinder.com, youngatheart.com, and silversingles.com all target older people. Even more conventional sites such as ChristianMingle.com and JDate.com have had a tremendous increase in older registrants. Pepper Schwartz, AARP's "love and relationship ambassador" tells us that about half of singles over age fifty-five have tried online dating compared to about 10 percent ten years ago. A Pew Research Center poll showed that people older than age sixty-five are now twice as likely to think that online dating was a good way to meet people.[8] Baby boomers who have lost a partner to divorce or death continue to look for companionship. They seem to be unwilling to give up love, sex, and romance.[9]

Friends and relationships are important at every age but in retirement, they are imperative. With time on your hands, it is easy to start to vegetate and get into a routine of getting up late, reading the newspaper, doing a few chores, and suddenly the day is gone and it is time for dinner. If this is how you want to spend the rest of your life, so be it; however, I do not advise it for good mental health. Isolation can only lead to depression. It is always helpful, when going through a new phase in life, to know other people who are also navigating similar waters.

Remember, when the children were young how good it felt to realize that other parents were experiencing the same trials and tribulations.

It is always helpful to have a friend or two to broaden and enrich your life. Mutual support is beneficial. Remember, you will be helping them, too. You will both appreciate the interaction and the depth that relationships can bring to your life. It is nice to hear the phone ring, and have someone offer an invitation to a social gathering or ask you to join them to go out for a meal. It feels good to have someone accompany you to a sporting event or movie, if you live alone or if this particular event does not appeal to your spouse or significant other. This is particularly important to widow or widowers. If you are married, or a committed couple, going out with another couple can also be fun, allow you to gain new helpful information, and sometimes give you a chance to share your similar life experiences. There are so many things to do in the world. Certainly, some you can do with your spouse or significant other. Others things may be fun to do with a friend. Aging can be a lonely road to travel on your own. Having friends will enhance both their lives and add texture to yours.

FAMILY

Just as family is of primary importance during childhood, it becomes equally important as you age. Family bonds, including those with siblings, aunts, uncles, and cousins, as well as children and grandchildren, can provide essential support and a sense of belonging during this challenging period of transition. A Humana/National Council on Aging survey of 1,500 seniors indicated that some seniors' health and well-being may actually depend, in part, on how much time they spend with their extended families.[10] We are fortunate that even if family members live elsewhere, in this day of technology, we can keep in touch via Skype, Face Time, and e-mail.

Different cultures have different attitudes toward the elderly, which can influence their quality of life. The Chinese revere their elders for their wisdom and experience. In India, people have a tremendous sense of duty and responsibility toward their relatives. They honor their elderly as symbols of humanity and divinity and thus hold them in highest esteem.[11] In the United States, we tend to worship youthfulness, health, and vitality. Thus, we often forget and ignore the needs of senior citizens. What a shame. The elderly have so much to offer. Their personal memories and histories can be so informative and educational. Their recipes are delicious. Their love and tenderness can add so much to your life. Carrying on their traditions, from one generation to another, will add connection and security to your world. Best of all, seniors are appreciative of any attention or kindness offered by others. Let them into your life.

Adult Siblings

> For older adults, relationships between siblings are unique and important. Often, this is the only continuous family relationship that endures from childhood to old age. . . . Siblings provide companionship and emotional support, needed material resources, and guidance in old age. . . . Reminiscences about family experiences validate the older person's memories and feelings about these events and help them to have positive feelings about their family life. A number of studies have shown that all siblings feel a greater sense of closeness in the later years, reducing feelings of conflict and envy and deepening their approval and acceptance of one another.[12]

Adult siblings can have much fun sharing common childhood memories.

Extended Family

Aunts, uncles, and cousins can be important members of our world when we are children. Family and holiday dinners are something special. I still remember fondly our extended family dinners at a local restaurant each Sunday, sitting around one long table. Holiday dinners at the homes of various aunts and uncles were also special and memorable. As we grow older, these individuals can continue to be a source of family continuity and pride, adding much to our lives.

Cousins, particularly those within our age range, can become almost sibling-like as we grow older. They broaden our family circle and serving as a repository of childhood memories. In childhood, aunts and uncles, with whom we have a good rapport, can serve to increase our quality of life and raise our self-esteem with their praise and acceptance. As we age, there are less people left in these categories. Keeping in contact with those who remain can give you a sense of family and allow you to remember the good times that your relatives had shared. Cousin clubs and yearly family reunions can be a lot of fun and give you a feeling of inclusion. I am fortunate to have an aunt, age ninety-two, who is my last older relative on both sides of the family. I try to call her at least once a month, and visit her on occasion. She calls us at times. Each communication or visit always ends with the words, "I love you." It is nice, even as a retired senior citizen, to hear this expression.

CHILDREN

What is the role of your adult children in your retirement? After having spent years putting your heart and soul into their development, worrying about them and trying to fulfill all of their needs, your expectation may be that they will be there for you in a major way and repay your dedication. I suggest that you lower your expectations. They have their own world full of friends and household tasks. They may be working full time. They probably have their own children now with all the associated time restraints and responsibilities. Children grow up emotionally at different speeds. They may be mature behaviorally, and thus be able to take care of their own world responsibilities, such as going to work and paying their bills. Some children, particularly women, sometimes do not mature emotionally until around forty. At best, hope that they will be supportive of your decisions, keep in contact, and be available at times of health or other crisis. Hopefully, they will show that they are interested in you and care about you.

Your retirement may be difficult for your grown children. They may have feelings about your selling "their" childhood home. They may have thought that it would be there forever as a place of protection in the storm. "How dare you sell my childhood manse?" It may force them for the first time to acknowledge that time has passed and that they are older. They may have to face the fact that mom and dad have gotten older. Walking behind my mother one day, I suddenly was aware that she was walking slower and was somewhat stooped. I realized for the first time consciously that she was getting older. I remember the first time that my daughter said, "Dad! When did you get so old?" They may have to face their and your mortality.

It may be a time to share important information about your wishes for the future. Share with them your living will and basic financial information. Tell them where you keep your will and other important papers. Be sure that they understand that although you appreciate their input and opinions, that the final decision is yours. There is no one rule as to how these two generations should relate at this time of life. What you really want from your children at this point in your journey is their presence, their care, and their support. I would suspect that you also want acceptance and approval, honesty and trust, and hope, respect, and dignity, but most of all love and affection.

GRANDCHILDREN

Grandchildren are a precious gift given to retirees. When asked about their grandchildren, an older person tends to beam with pride. Without even realizing it, they add so much to our lives. I will never forget when my five-year-old grandson would run up to me when I entered the house, shouting, "Grandpa, Grandpa" and wrap his arms around me in a tight bear hug. I will never fail to remember the joy I felt when I received his first e-mail when he went away to college many miles away. How proud I was when I went to my granddaughter's first dance recital. It works both ways. Grandparents are special people to their grandchildren. They offer acceptance, support, and praise. Grandparents tend to make a fuss over and indulge their grandchildren. Who would not enjoy getting so much attention and being sprinkled with unconditional love? Spend more quality time with your grandchildren. You will all benefit.

When doing therapy, I always ask about the significant people that helped raise my patients. Talking about parents often engenders various emotions. However, when ask about their grandparents, patients invariably glow with positive feelings. A grandparent can help maintain family stability by preserving traditions and values. They provide a sense of family continuity and a perspective on an earlier era. Interaction between grandparents and grandchildren provides a sense of psychological immortality and biological continuation with the future. Not having to deal with parental responsibilities and being more relaxed and confident in their new stage of life, senior citizens may be able to enjoy and interact with their grandchildren more authentically than they did with their own children. [13]

When doing research for this book, both on the Internet and in the public library, I was surprised to find that most works on retirement dealt only with financial planning. Although finances are an important issue in retirement, the Brinks truck never follows the hearse. As people age, their focus shifts from finances to finding meaning in their lives and trying to figure out what is really important to them. A balanced approach to retirement planning also requires attention to emotional and physical health issues and a social network. As I have shown, relationships, including those with family and friends, become more important in retirement. Interaction with other people has the power to sustain and add joy and pleasure to life as one ages. They are the ones that will give life meaning. Remember what author and inspirational speaker, Leo Buscaglia, said, "Too often [in life], we underestimate the power of touch, a smile, a kind word, a listening ear, an honest compliment, or the smallest act of caring, all of which have the potential to turn a life around." [14] People, not money, are the only ones that have the ability to give these things and truly fulfill emotional needs.

Physical changes are inevitable as one grows older. In the next chapter, I will look at some of these more common possible bodily disorders that can influence our emotional state and color the senior world.

4

PHYSICAL CHANGES

It is not a prerequisite of retirement and getting older to become feeble of mind and body. In spite of slowing down a bit and being a little forgetful, most people age comfortably and in good health. For the active retiree with a positive attitude, this time of life can be a time to develop a new lifestyle full of new interests, activities, and relationships. Many enjoy doing things that they had put off while they were working; however, though this idyllic picture of life in retirement is shared by many, it is not universal. As with many things in life, physical health in retirement, during our mature years, is variable on a gradient between good and bad.

For some, retirement can be a time of increasing illness and a decline of physical and mental ability. Wendy Lustbader generalizes in her book, *Life Gets Better: The Unexpected Pleasures of Growing Older*, when she tells us that "life gets better as we get older on all levels except the physical."[1] She has a point. Therefore, this chapter will focus on common health problems that can occur during this period of life, in the hope that it can increase your awareness of what is possible. I recommend that you see your own physician for accurate diagnosis and an individualized treatment plan. This section will also suggest various preventive measures and other actions that can help you deal with these common medical problems, if they occur. It will also comment on dealing with the challenges of living with a chronic illness.

Earlier in life, I always toasted success, friendship, or happiness. However, since turning sixty-five years old, and particularly since retirement, I only toast to good health. I live in a fifty-five and older community where a "Viewing" or a "Shiva Call" can be a common occurrence. Many of my friends have chronic illnesses, such as diabetes and Chronic Obstructive Pulmonary Disease (COPD). Some have had cancer of various organs. Others have cardiac diseases that have required bypass surgery or a pacemaker. Living among this age group makes you acutely aware of the importance of the issue of health and wellness. In spite of these health issues, my friends and neighbors remain active and engaged in life.

Here are some common medical and emotional problems affecting those over fifty-five years old:

- Arthritis
- Balance Problems
- Breathing Problems
- Diabetes
- Memory Loss / Dementia / Alzheimer's Disease
- Hypertension
- Leg Pain
- Obesity
- Sensory Problems (hearing, taste, and vision)
- Sexual Issues (impotence or dyspareunia)
- Mental Health
- Depression
- Anxiety
- Substance Abuse

ARTHRITIS

Arthritis is an umbrella term used for a group of one hundred medical conditions that affect the joints. They include connective tissue diseases such as rheumatoid arthritis, scleroderma, and systemic lupus erythmatosis. Osteoarthritis (OA) is the most common form of arthritis, affecting 27 million people in the United States. It is also the most prevalent in people over sixty years old. Osteoarthritis is also called degenerative joint disease (DJD) or "wear and tear disease." Arthritis related symptoms include joint aches and pain with movement; stiffness, most noticeable when you get up in the morning, or during damp, cold weather. Inflammation (swelling and redness), warmth and tenderness, and damage to the joint cartilage (tissue that covers the ends of the bone and cushions the joints) can occur. A grinding sound can sometimes be heard when a joint is put through a full range of motion.

You are more prone to OA as you get older, if you are obese, have previous joint injury, weak thigh muscles, or overuse the joint. There is also a genetic vulnerability. There is no cure for osteoarthritis. However, an early evaluation can both prevent damage and disability as well as make optimal treatment easier. Maintaining a healthy weight can take pressure off of the joint. Staying physically active is also helpful. The pain will diminish with movement and warmth. There are medications to help relieve pain, when needed. Your physician may recommend physical therapy or occupational therapy to help improve strength and function. When pain is severe and frequent or movement and daily activities become difficult, surgery may be considered.[2]

BALANCE PROBLEMS

Nine percent of adults over age sixty-five have problems with balance or being able to maintain their body's position while moving or standing still. One of the main causes of balance problems is a disturbance of the inner ear that makes people feel unsteady. They may also experience vertigo or the feeling that they or the things around them are moving, spinning, or floating. Balance problems can cause falls and related injuries, such as hip fractures. According to the Centers for Disease Control and Prevention, more than one-third of those over age sixty-five fall each year.[3]

BREATHING PROBLEMS

Shortness of breath or dyspnea can be a symptom indicating problems with the lungs, with the airways leading to the lungs, or problems with the heart. Here, I will only discuss asthma, congestive heart failure, and COPD, a sampling of the many causes of difficulty breathing. Asthma, also called bronchial asthma or exercise-induced asthma, is an inflammatory disorder of the airways, which causes attacks of wheezing, short-ness of breath, chest tightness, and coughing. Triggers include aller-gens, changes in weather, chemicals, exercise, respiratory infections, strong emotions, and tobacco smoke.[4]

COPD includes emphysema and chronic bronchitis. It affects 12 million people in the United States. It causes inflamed bronchial tubes, increased mucus production and results in the stiffening of air sacs in the lung. Symptoms include shortness of breath that worsens with activ-ity, coughing, wheezing, and tightness in the chest. COPD is treated with inhaled medications. Acute exacerbations are treated with antibio-tics and steroids. Severe cases require oxygen use. Evaluation for lung reduction or lung transplant surgery is possible.[5]

Shortness of breath can also be caused by various heart or cardiac problems including congestive heart failure (CHF). Low cardiac output of blood elevates lung capillary pressures and stimulates lung receptors, which increases fluid in the lung and causes shortness of breath. The shortness of breath can be worse with exercise or by lying flat. CHF can also show "air hunger" or an increased drive to breath as well as swell-ing of the ankles and lower extremities.[6]

DIABETES

Diabetes mellitus is a life threatening disease that affects 33 million people in the Americas. It is caused by a complex interaction of genetics and environmental factors that leads to high blood sugar. Two broad categories are called type 1 and type 2. Type-1 diabetes is the result of complete or near-total insulin deficiency. It is treated by diet, exercise, weight control, and insulin replacement. Diabetes mellitus can lead to end-stage renal disease, skin infections, lower extremity amputations, and blurred vision or blindness. It can also affect the nerves of the feet and lower extremities causing pain in those areas.[7] It also puts a person at increased risk for blockage of a blood vessel which can lead to a myocardial infarction (heart attack) or stroke.

Type-2 diabetes is the most common form of diabetes. It is also called adult onset diabetes or non-insulin-dependent diabetes mellitus (NIDDM). Genetics and obesity contribute to its onset. In type-2 di-abetes, insulin is produced, but the pancreas is "lazy" and produces less insulin secretion, or the body is resistant and does not respond as well to the effect of insulin. The symptoms that can alert you to possible low insulin production or high blood sugar include increased thirst, increased urination, and appetite. There can also be weight loss, weakness, and fatigue. It is often a difficult disease to treat. One of the factors is that diabetics often are self-destructive and have difficulty maintaining a healthy, sugar-free diet and lifestyle.

MEMORY LOSS / DEMENTIA / ALZHEIMER'S DISEASE

Memory loss is a common occurrence as people get older. One-in-four people over sixty-five experience this problem.[8] People begin to lose brain cells in their twenties, and their bodies begin to make less of the chemicals that their brain cells need to work efficiently. As time goes by, these changes can begin to affect memory. In recent years, my friends and I joke that it now "takes the elevator a little longer to reach the top floor," as we search for a word, our keys, or our glasses, which are safely perched on top of our heads.

Recent or short term memory deals with things that happened moments ago, such as information from recent activities or what one ate for breakfast. Remote memory includes things that happened in the past. Many things other than aging can cause memory problems. These include being overwhelmed because you have too much to balance, depression, other medical illnesses, dementia, side effects of drugs, strokes, a head injury, and alcoholism.[9]

When I first started in the field of psychiatry, many years ago, memory loss issues were divided into two classes. They included organic brain syndrome (OBS), either acute or chronic, due to impairment of brain tissue function with impairment of orientation (time, place, and person), memory (particularly impaired immediate recall), intellectual functions, judgment, and diminished affect. The second main diagnosis was Alzheimer's disease, which was considered a more rapidly progressive deficit usually occurring between sixty and ninety years of age. It was felt to be more common in women and showed brain atrophy with senile plaques upon autopsy.

Times have changed. Now diagnosis all these disorders as dementia of the Alzheimer's type, with early (before age sixty-five) or late onset.

Dementia is a brain disorder, which is defined by a negative change in intellectual ability. This can include memory impairment (impaired ability to learn new information or to recall previously learned information), and at least one or more of the following: language disturbance, impaired ability to carry out motor (physical) activities despite intact motor function, failure to recognize or identify objects despite intact sensory (vision, hearing, touch, and smell) function, and disturbance in executive functioning (planning, organizing, sequencing, and abstracting). The cognitive deficits cause significant impairment in social or occupational functioning and represent a significant decline from a previous level of functioning, making it difficult for the person to carry out daily activities.[10]

HIV/AIDS

You may be surprised to learn that 11 to 15 percent of US AIDS cases occur in seniors over age fifty. Between 1991 and 1996, AIDS in adults over fifty rose more than twice as fast as in younger adults. Older people are unlikely to use condoms and have weakened immune systems. HIV symptoms such as fatigue, weight loss, dementia, skin rashes, and swollen lymph nodes are similar to symptoms that can accompany getting older. Stereotypes suggest that older people do not have sex or use drugs and hence keep this problem largely unrecognized and not well-represented in research, clinical drug studies, and prevention programs.[11]

HYPERTENSION

Sixty million people have hypertension or high blood pressure. It has been called the "silent disease" because, initially, there are no symptoms. It is present when your blood pressure is above 140/90 mm hg. Hypertension can contribute to emotional feelings of anger, irritation, and anxiety. A few people show symptoms of headache (a tight band around your head), tiredness, dizziness, or nosebleed. Treatment is important. Untreated, it can lead to coronary heart disease, congestive heart failure, stroke, and kidney damage. Factors that increase the risk of having high blood pressure include family history, being female over age fifty, being African American, smoking, heavy alcohol consumption, obesity, increased dietary salt intake, and stress. [12]

LEG PAIN

Leg pain is not just a symptom of getting older. It could be related to a serious medical problem. Potential causes include arthritis, arteriosclerosis, atherosclerosis, peripheral arterial disease, thrombophlebitis, and restless leg syndrome. See your physician if you are experiencing leg pain particularly if it happens when you are exercising and goes away when you stop, This is called Intermittent Claudication and can lead to decreased circulation to the extremity. [13]

OBESITY

Obesity is a major problem in the United States today. It can increase your chances of dying from hypertension, type-2 diabetes, coronary heart disease, stroke, gallbladder disease, osteoarthritis, sleep apnea, respiratory problems, dyslipidemia, and endometrial, breast, prostrate, and colon cancers. [14] A sedentary lifestyle and an unhealthy diet can cause the retiree to become overweight and even obese. Exercise is important to avoid the problem. Since obesity can be a cause of many common health problems, it is imperative that you visit your physician if you find yourself becoming overweight. It is also important to follow your physician's advice. [15]

SENSORY PROBLEMS

Imagine that you are sitting at a restaurant with your wife, enjoying the taste and aroma of a glass of Shiraz, having a nice conversation and listening to the background music. The waitress puts your entree on the white tablecloth holding the hot plate with a cloth. You immediately are impressed by the presentation of the dish. You can still hear the sizzle of the steak and smell the wonderful garlic potatoes and the thin, green asparagus. Can you imagine what it would be like if each time your partner spoke, you had to say "what, what," because your hearing was diminished. What a loss it would be if you couldn't smell the wonderful aromas of the wine and food or see clearly your beautiful surroundings. Perhaps this picture is exaggerated; however, often one's sense of smell, sight, and hearing start to diminish as one ages.

The sense of smell determines the flavor and palate pleasing nature of food and drink and serves as a monitor of inhaled chemicals. More than half of the population over age sixty has problems with the sense of smell. A sampling of possible causes include allergic rhinitis, nasal polyps and tumors, drugs/toxins, x-ray therapy, alcoholism, cigarette smoke, and diabetes mellitus. Hearing loss is one of the most common sensory disorders in human beings. It can emerge at any age. Nearly 10 percent of the adult population has some hearing loss. One-third of people over age sixty-five have a hearing loss requiring a hearing aid. Some hearing loss is genetic, some is noise induced, and other hearing loss is due to drugs, infection, or trauma.[16]

Glaucoma and cataracts are two vision problems that are common in those over age sixty-five. Glaucoma occurs when there is a buildup of fluid in the eyeball. Normally fluid circulates and nourishes your eye keeping it healthy. It then empties through a drain in the front of your eye. Glaucoma blocks the drain; fluid builds up and increases pressure in the eye. The increased pressure causes nerve damage and subsequent loss of vision. This pressure can be measured by your eye doctor. Cataracts are another visual problem that can occur in this age group. Sixty percent of people over sixty have this issue. This condition involves a clouding of the lens portion of the eye which can cause visual changes. Cataracts can be easily diagnosed during a routine eye examination and can be corrected by your eye doctor by replacing the damaged lens with a new lens during cataract eye surgery.[17]

SEXUAL ISSUES (IMPOTENCE OR DYSPAREUNIA)

Retired older people do have sex. Reduced anxiety and a decrease in external pressure can increase the pleasure. There may be some modification of sexual responsiveness with age. Many men will achieve erection more slowly and may be more easily distracted requiring a more peaceful sexual environment. They may have some degree of impotence requiring the use of erectile dysfunction medication, if they are in good physical health and not taking nitroglycerin.

You may remember actor Jack Nicholson's panic, in the 2003 romantic comedy movie with Diane Keaton, *Something's Got to Give*, when he discovered, while being wheeled down the hospital hallway on a gurney that he had taken medication for erectile dysfunction and the doctors had started him on an intravenous drip of nitroglycerin, because they thought that he was having a heart attack and had not taken any other medications. Male erectile dysfunction can be related to fatigue, blood vessel and hormonal disorders, alcohol and drug abuse, nutritional deficiencies, antihypertensive medication, and diabetes mellitus.

More foreplay may be necessary to stimulate arousal in both men and women. Women will have a decrease in the number of orgasmic contractions. They may develop atrophic vaginitis causing dyspareunia (pain upon intercourse) and requiring hormonal replacement or extra lubrication. However, physical closeness is important in a relationship. I, therefore, recommend to my patients that regardless of the degree of sexual activity that is still possible in the life of an aging couple that they "cuddle" and hug and see what happens. Despite the outcome, the closeness is healthy. Everyone has a need for love.

MENTAL HEALTH

Anxiety is the most common mental health problem affecting 40 million people in the United States. It is second only to depression over the course of a lifetime. Both diseases have a genetic vulnerability and run in families. They overlap with and complicate one half of all psychiatric and medical conditions. Chapters 5 and 6 of this book elaborate on these syndromes, including their common symptoms, and review information relevant to retirement and aging. They are included in this chapter for completeness.

Surprisingly, substance abuse and dependency, can be an issue as people grow older and retire (see chapter 7 for additional information). Seniors can self-medicate using legal and illegal drugs and alcohol. There are 9 million alcoholics in the United States. One million of them are women. This public health problem is one of our nation's most serious hazards. Alcoholism is a disease involving body, mind, and spirit. Those who work in the field of substance abuse rehabilitation see alcoholism as a symptom of something that is happening inside or outside the person; it is often a sign that a person is trying to cope with life problems, and is often behavior reflecting psychological stress.

Life can change in a flash. One minute you feel that you are healthy and okay but the next instant you are diagnosed with a chronic physical illness. At first you will be fearful and wonder if you will ever be the same. You may have feelings of sadness and loss. Dark thoughts swirl around in your head. Will I die? Will I be able to do all the old things that I loved? Will I be a burden to my family? Most people who have chronic illnesses will eventually find that the quality of their life will be different, but not necessarily terrible. Hopefully, you will have the courage to look closely at your doubts and fears and refuse to be intimidated by the negative mindset. The end result depends on acceptance and on the attitude that you choose.[18]

No one can control all of the above health issues. There are genetic and environmental issues that play a part in their onset; however, there is much that you can do to optimize your status. Exercise, diet, and nutrition are important variables. Dietary supplements and vitamins can also be helpful. It was the purpose of this chapter only to raise your awareness of these conditions and not to go into prevention and treatment. Go for your yearly physical examination and keep your follow-up visits with the specialists that are following any chronic conditions. Get your influenza and pneumonia vaccinations. Do what you can to reduce stress. Get help early, as soon as you see signs of a problem. As I often say when I say goodbye to people, "Take care of yourself. Stay well."

The next part of this book looks at the common mental health problems that can occur as people age. These include anxiety, depression, drug dependency, sexual issues, Alzheimer's disease, and elder abuse.

II

Common Mental Health Problems as We Age

5

STRESS AND ANXIETY

Anxiety is a universal feeling that all have experienced at one time or another. This symptom is particularly common for those over age sixty-five as they deal with change, loss, and life adjustment. Retirement and aging are not always fun. The social, physical, cultural, and personal stressors accompanying this stage of life can cause increased stress and feelings of nervousness. All people are a complex of challenges and tensions. No one is immune to the emotional difficulties of living. At these times, we can feel helpless, scared, and angry. Everyone has felt the emotional symptoms of anxiety such as apprehension, worry, and irritability. All have experienced the physical aspects of anxiety such as heart palpitations, hyperventilation, sweating, and butterflies in the stomach.

In certain situations, anxiety can be positive and can be considered "normal." It can serve as a biological warning system during times of potential danger or threat. It is the rapid beating of your heart as you await important news such as the results of your medical blood tests or x-ray report. It is the tension that you experience prior to giving a presentation or speaking in public. It is the nervousness that you may feel before meeting a new person or moving to a new location. It is the worry that an older spouse feels when their husband or wife is seriously physically sick, hospitalized, or is undergoing surgery.

If these feelings of anxiety become free-floating and increase in frequency and intensity, it may have shifted into the "abnormal range." In the abnormal range, anxiety is nonadaptive, more severe and interferes with functioning. Anxiety may affect twice as many older adults as depression. Anxiety can show itself in various diagnostic formats. As noted, it can be a normal reaction to acute stress as a response to fearful experiences.. If the symptoms differ somewhat in intensity and interfere with functioning, then they are referred to as an acute stress reaction. Next on the continuum is an adjustment reaction with anxiety features. Here the anxiety symptoms last more than thirty days. Further down the continuum is generalized anxiety disorder (GAD). Here, the person has been nervous all of their life, but find that their anxiety is escalating due to current difficult events. GAD may be genetic in origin and affects 7 percent of seniors.[1] Some of these conditions overlap and represent a combination of categories. None are a form of hypochondria or a sign of weakness. If your anxiety is troublesome, interfering with your life and happiness, see your physician to see where you stand on the continuum.

Living with stress can produce emotional symptoms of anxiety, including feelings of restlessness, irritability, tension, and worry and feeling panicky. Anxiety can make one believe that they are losing control or going crazy, that something terrible is going to happen or that they are going to die. If you are experiencing these symptoms, remember that your mind does not speak to you directly in clear-cut words. These feelings are the mind's way of communicating to that you are feeling anxious. If the anxiety is caused by stress, it will dissipate when the stressful situation is over. With the various anxiety disorders, such as generalized anxiety disorder, panic disorder, social phobia, and obsessive compulsive disorder, anxiety is more pervasive and longer lasting.

Physical complaints such as headaches and muscular aches and pains or a fast heartbeat are common symptoms of stress and anxiety. Some may experience dizziness or lightheadedness, shortness of breath, hyperventilation, or a lump in their throat. Some ruminate and cannot turn off their thinking causing them to sleep poorly. Anxiety can cause you to experience dry mouth, indigestion, nausea and vomiting, butterflies in your stomach, or diarrhea. It can make you feel tired and weak. It can cause skin disorders or make you sweat or experience chills. It can cause numbness or a tingling sensation.

When you are anxious, you may experience a constant urge to urinate or urinate more frequently than normal. Difficulty in concentration or your mind going blank can at times be contributed to anxiety.

Stress can also contribute to physical illness. Hypertension, asthma, migraine headaches, heart disease, allergies, and ulcer disease often have an emotional component linked to stress. Chronic sleep loss can contribute to high blood pressure and lower our immune response. Your physician will have to differentiate whether your complaints are physical, emotional, or a combination of both.

As was shown in chapter 2, living with stress can produce behavioral disturbances such as overeating, smoking, drug and alcohol abuse, or gambling. Marital and relationship problems, outbursts of temper, and overreactions to minor issues can occur. The stress of loss can lead to sadness and depression and may show itself through symptoms of withdrawal, poor appetite, reduced energy, loss of interest and motivation, decreased libido, crying spells, and sleep disturbance. In the extreme, some wish they were dead or have suicidal thoughts.

Where does this anxiety come from? Psychoanalysis sees anxiety as a signal that certain unacceptable impulses (sexual or aggressive feelings) are trying to escape the unconscious and are trying to break into consciousness. This mental pain serves as a signal to mobilize other defense mechanisms to try to keep this material out of consciousness.[2]

A more contemporary view focuses on the biological causes of anxiety. This approach involves looking at three hormones, or neurotransmitters, that cause a nerve impulse to move from one nerve cell to another. The hormones are gamma-aminobutyric acid (GABA), serotonin, and norepinephrine. GABA acts as an internally produced tranquilizer that decreases anxiety. Serotonin and norepinephrine also play a role in anxiety regulation. Anxiety is an over-stimulated state that originates in the brain.

What can we do to deal with stress? How do we quell our anxiety and that feeling of impending doom? How do we chase away the negativity and the fear that something terrible will happen? I do have a few suggestions that may help calm your shattered nerves and put the situation in perspective. There are three basic alternatives to any stress situation. One can do something to change the situation; one can get out of it; or one can change so that they can live more comfortably with the state of affairs. Sometimes, it is only the third alternative that we may be able to control. The following are several specific ways to do this and reduce stress:

- *Refocus*: Concentrate on the here and now. Don't get lost in the past. Distract yourself. Throw away those negative feelings. Do not take everything so seriously. Lighten up; smile, laugh and enjoy the moment. Give yourself permission to relax and have fun. Don't let anxiety interfere with your enjoyment of life in the present. Do not watch the stock market each day. Even if you are retiring tomorrow, you will not be taking out all your savings in one day. Do not focus just on negative news reports. Look at and appreciate the beauty of nature. Listen to uplifting music. See a happy or comedic movie. Go to a musical stage show.

- *Express your feelings*: One of the worst things that you can do is to hold it all in and mope. Harold was a pro at using this unsuccessful coping method. Suppressing negative feelings can contribute to anxiety. This practice can eventually cause emotional or physical problems. You are not alone. Talk out your problems and share your feelings with someone that you trust. The support of your friends and family is crucial. You will find many people who can commiserate and understand. As we get older, we realize that in so many ways, we are all alike. It is easier to go through a tough time with others whom are also walking in the same direction. Ask for reassurance and even physical comfort if you need it. A hug goes a long way.

- *Exercise*: One of the best ways to deal with stress and anxiety is exercise and physical movement. Activity, whether it is a brisk walk or an hour at the gym, is one of the best stress busters. It is a way to work off your feelings of frustration and excess aggressive energy. Many seniors still play golf and tennis or swim. A friend of mine was delighted when, while vacationing in Florida, he learned to play "Pickle Ball," which is played on a half tennis court and therefore requires less exertion than using a full tennis court. Exercise can also be helpful by allowing muscles to relax and providing an escape from the anxious worrier's tendency to think, think, and think. Even if you are limited physically, you can easily learn relaxation techniques.

- *See your physician* before you start a new exercise program to check on your physical limits.

- *Take a problem-solving approach*: Take action. This is one of the best ways to stop the cycle of anxiety and worry. Take charge of your life. Ask for what you want. People cannot read your mind. Check out your assumptions. Take charge of your financial life. Talk to your accountant and your financial advisor about financial worries. Talk to a mentor who can give you a new point of view or make suggestions about how to solve current problems. Rather than feeling overwhelmed by health or other worries, get the information that you need to put things in perspective, place you on a more positive road, and allow you to feel more in control.

- *Avoid avoidance*: Many people when they are under stress or feeling anxious handle it by limiting their activity and not taking risks. Staying in bed, hiding under the covers, will not solve your problems. One of the best ways to take action and reduce your anxiety is to avoid avoidance. Say yes rather than no when someone asks you to do something with them. I used to instruct some of my patients, who had a tendency to say no to everything, to put a post-it on their refrigerator door or even in their wallet or on their pocketbook saying the word "Yes." Even if you anticipate failure, make that phone call, try that new activity, and reach out to the world. In spite of your negative assumptions, you may find that these actions actually reduce your feelings of anxiety and work out better than you anticipated.

If your stress escalates and if the anxiety symptoms continue, you may be dealing with a more complex psychiatric problem. Chronic anxiety can be demoralizing, limit your life, and interfere with your enjoyment. Its clinical manifestations have social, medical, and economic consequences. The anxiety disorders are real biological conditions and true medical illnesses that can be helped by a physician, psychiatrist, or other mental health worker. Treatment options include education and reassurance, psychotherapy, cognitive behavioral therapy, pharmacology, relaxation / meditation / biofeedback, exercise, and diet. Religious affiliation and spirituality are helpful to many. See chapters 14 and 15 for more information on the treatment of anxiety, stress, and the other emotional and behavioral issues often encountered during retirement and aging.

Anxiety is often undiagnosed in the elderly. Physicians and caregivers sometimes think that this condition is rare in older people or that it is a normal part of aging. The truth of the matter is that anxiety is possible throughout the life cycle. Senior citizens suffer from anxiety more often than depression. They are prone to life stressors such as illness, disability, widowhood, financial distress, and social isolation. All these things can precipitate feelings of anxiety. However, the diagnosis can be hard to make in this age group due to overlapping or comorbid physical or emotional symptoms or concomitant medical conditions or treatment modalities that can produce anxiety.

In *Ten Steps to Relieve Anxiety*, I wrote about anxiety in the eldery, saying:

> They are more prone to vague bodily symptoms and they often complain of fatigue, insomnia, aches and pains and bowel symptoms. Sleep problems particularly can signify anxiety in the elderly and overlapping symptoms such as depression, dementia and substance abuse can mask and/or signify anxiety. Primary medical problems such as irritable bowel syndrome, asthma/COPD, diabetes, and thyroid disease can manifest anxiety. Hyperthyroidism, hypertension and cardiac arrhythmias can also cause anxiety. Medications such as steroids, inhalers and theophylline can trigger anxiety-like symptoms.[3]

Based on what I have seen over the course of my many years in psychiatric practice, I feel that the four most common precipitators of anxiety in retirement and as we age are isolation, physical problems, chronic illness, and financial worries. These are the things that my older patients were concerned about most. Although I have touched on some aspects of these topics elsewhere in this book, I feel that some repetition of these important subjects including some added information is warranted in this chapter and may be helpful to you.

Isolation: My divorced and widowed patients tell me, "No matter how many friends that I have, when I close the door of my house or apartment, I am alone." They say it as if loneliness has taken a piece of their soul and left them empty, afraid, and isolated. Some older singles have a small and constantly shrinking pool of people to draw from which makes them feel increasingly socially sequestered. Many of their friends and relatives have passed away. Some have moved out of town to be with their children. One woman complained, "Almost daily, the ambulance comes to my complex and transports someone to the hospital. Sometimes, they do not return." This is one of the down sides of being elderly. If not dealt with, isolation and loneliness can lead to anxiety and depression.

One of the major themes of this book has been to stay active and engaged in the world. I always encouraged my patients to take an active rather than a passive approach to life. With this in mind, I usually told them, "If you feel lonely, pick up the phone, call someone and say hello. You don't have to tell them that you feel lonely." We would then discuss other ways that they could fill in the gaps of time when they were normally by themselves. Perhaps, they can schedule an evening card game, play bingo, or meet a friend for dinner and a movie on occasion. When they are alone, perhaps they would enjoy keeping themselves busy by cooking or baking, reading and playing games on the computer, or even solitaire. They could take up a hobby such as painting, knitting, or crocheting.

Although it is true that the best way to handle the losses and changes of retirement and aging is to be proactive, take a problem-solving approach, and find creative ways to solve your problems. These approaches will not solve everything. Life is not perfect. No one can be active all the time. Everyone will have, and even needs, down time to relax and reconstitute. Hopefully, when you are alone, you can learn to feel content and not lonely. If all the above suggestions fail, I may have chosen in therapy to ask you if perhaps your feelings of discomfort in being alone have an underlying meaning. Often that bubbles up feelings that are harder to avoid thinking about when you do not have people or other distractions around you. Perhaps you still feel angry that your husband died and left you with a lot of responsibility. Maybe, your feelings today remind you of your childhood when you felt alone and unloved.

Physical changes and chronic illness: When I was younger, I used to toast to good luck, success, and friendship. However, now that I am older, my friends and I toast only to good health. With age, the body begins to deteriorate and health issues become very important parts of life. Health can determine one's future path and destiny. As you age, physical health becomes part of cocktail conversation. When older people meet socially, they compare physical complaints, their cholesterol numbers, and their surgeries with their friends. There is value in sharing. It allows people to realize that they are not alone and it allows them to ventilate some of their worries and fears.

The gradual loss of physical abilities can cause you to feel helpless, frightened, and anxious. The loss of independence caused by physical decline can precipitate feelings of anxiety and sadness. You may resent having to be dependent on others. My wife is also a physician. She once had a hundred-and-four-year-old women as her patient who greatly valued her independence. The women was frail and had started to suffer from falls. She denied these physical changes. She wanted to remain in, and die in, her own home. Her guardian, concerned about her welfare, insisted that she move to an assisted living facility. This was not a good match for a woman who valued her independence and being in control. The patient stopped taking her pills. She died several days later in her sleep.

Life can change in a flash. Suddenly being diagnosed with a chronic physical illness can turn your world upside down. It can also cause you to feel frightened, worried, and angry. It is a challenge to negotiate for anyone, regardless of prior abilities or training. Initially, there is fear of the unknown. Suddenly filled with anxiety, you wonder, "Will I ever be the same again? Will I be able to do the things that I value and live a 'normal life?' Will I be able to fulfill my goals and dreams? Will I suffer or die?" You may be overwhelmed with feelings of sadness and loss.

How you handle these feelings and changes depends on your attitude and life approach. It may take you some time to digest these emotions. However, as we have seen elsewhere in this book, a positive attitude and proactive approach is best. After a while, your friends may no longer be able to be empathic; they may become tired of listening to you complain or really not know what to say. There are support groups that you can attend for various medical conditions such as heart disease ("the Zipper Club"), Addison's disease, cancer, lung disease, and dementia and Alzheimer's disease.

Financial worries: Financial concerns are one of the main worries that seniors have. Nonfiction books dealing with retirement and aging tend to focus on money and financial planning. Although it is an important topic, this book has not focused on the financial aspect of retirement and aging. I have limited myself to my area of expertise, as a physician/psychiatrist. With this perspective, I have dealt mainly with the emotional, physical, and spiritual aspects of being older and no longer working full time. However, all seniors are concerned about their finances in retirement. It is an important subject and can cause the aging retiree much emotional distress. Therefore, I decided to mention it here. If you want more information, there are many good books out there on the subject.

Having your financial house in order is of primary importance or else it will compound the emotional turmoil of aging. The recent recession, having taken a heavy toll on retirement savings, is causing many on the threshold of retirement to recalculate their plans. A 2009 Pew Research Center project on social and demographic trends showed that 68 percent of working adults, between ages fifty-seven and sixty-four, may delay their retirement and 16 percent never expect to stop working.[4]

All seniors wonder, "Can I afford to retire? Will I outlive my money? Will I be a burden on my children?" It is wise, before your retire, to review your finances. Estimate your monthly income from all sources, including any pensions, Social Security, 401(k) and IRA/Sep IRA plans, and other savings and investments. Add up your estimated monthly expenses. If your expenses are greater than your income, you may have to work for a few more years.[5] Professional advice is also obtainable. Talk to your accountant or financial advisor and see what they suggest. Senior organizations can offer advice. Having a definite plan will help quell your anxiety and allow you to feel more in control of your life.

Reduced income may require an adjustment in lifestyle and a need for outside assistance. There are helpful solutions. Part-time work may save the day. Although federal and state help is available, many older people feel ashamed or are too proud to apply to the Department of Public Assistance (DPA) for food stamps or other financial or medical support. Neighborhood resources are available. Food banks offer free food. Meals on Wheels can deliver food to shut-ins. Senior centers often offer a hot lunch at minimal cost. Religious organizations frequently have resources that can help.

The physical, mental, social, and economic losses that we experience as we retire and age makes depression and grief the second most common emotion that we may experience. Let's look at these issues in the next chapter and see what we can learn.

6

DEPRESSION AND GRIEF

Depression is often a reaction to loss and change. It can be experienced as we retire and start to age and these challenges increase. The possibility for social, economic, and physical losses run rampant during the senior years. Feelings of sadness can result from an older person not feeling needed or capable anymore. The last stage of life may not always conform to poet Robert Browning's line, "Grow old along with me! The best is yet to be." Unhappiness can be an element of the retirement years and the aging process. However, it need not be a time of frustration, pain, and helplessness. Most people fall within the middle range.

During the first several months after you leave work, sadness and grief may manifest until you are able to make peace with this change and formulate a new way of life. As time goes by, additional losses may occur in the form of forgetfulness or impairment in mental ability. Changes in health, strength, and physical ability; changes in sexual ability; a reduced income; and changes in prestige, status, and respect can also be losses that can lead to depression. The death of family members and friends creates additional interpersonal losses.

It may take a few months to a year after a spouse dies to fully overcome your grief. The death of a spouse is the one life event that ranks the highest on the social readjustment rating scale. Devastating at any age, it is particularly challenging for the aging or retired person. They will have to deal with the normal cycle of grief. However, they may also find that at this time of life, they have less resilience in dealing with their spiritual and emotional needs as well as the complex legal and financial decisions and transactions that may be needed. They may also have more difficulty planning for a new future without their spouse. (This topic will be explored in more detail in chapter 8.)

If the mourning process is persistent or exaggerated, you may be experiencing clinical depression. A professional medical or psychiatric evaluation followed by appropriate treatment could be helpful. See your doctor for an opinion. When a person is feeling upset and discouraged, it may be beneficial for them to talk over their concerns with a knowledgeable person, such as a rabbi, pastor or priest, physician, or mental health professional. The situation is not hopeless. Depression in the elderly is a treatable and correctable condition. Identifying and managing depression and other senior mental health issues as quickly as possible will improve your quality of life.

GRIEF

All of the losses, noted above, that are common as we age have the ability to precipitate feelings of sadness and depression. The gloom can also be precipitated by feelings of failure, discouragement, or disillusionment, particularly if your life does not live up to your expectations. As noted, these feeling states can be transitory or become prolonged as grief blends into clinical depression. The dictionary defines grief as mental distress caused by affliction, loss, or remorse. It defines depression as a deep dejection of spirit.[1] The difference between the two seems to be that depression takes on a longer time factor and degree of intensity indicating sadness greater and more prolonged than that warranted objectively.

Freudian, psychoanalytic theory suggests that both grief and depression can occur in response to loss of an emotionally significant person or personal ability or attribute. Freudians think that grieving turns into depression when the bereaved feels ambivalent about the loss. Thus, in broad strokes, if they feel both love and anger, negative and positive, toward the absent person or situation their period of mourning may be prolonged.

For instance if a parent, family member, or significant other passes away, you may grieve for several months and then perhaps have an anniversary reaction in that you may feel sad on their birth date, your anniversary, and at family holidays. Otherwise you are able to move on with your memories of the parent or significant individual after a reasonable period of time. However, if you loved the person but also carried with you a large amount of anger toward them, your period of sorrow will probably last a lot longer and be harder to deal with. Freudians further theorize that unresolved losses from early in life could result in more difficulty dealing with loss as an adult.[2]

The classic work of psychiatrist, author, and pioneer of bereavement and hospice care, Elisabeth Kübler-Ross, in her 1969 book *On Death and Dying*, provides a framework for understanding the dynamics of the grieving process. Her five stages of grief can be experienced due to death of a significant other, dealing with a chronic illness or deformity, or after another significant loss. The stages are:

- *Denial*: A conscious or unconscious refusal to accept that the loss has taken place.
- *Anger*: Negative feelings toward self or others at the loss or the unfairness of it.
- *Bargaining*: People beg their "higher power" to undo the loss or negotiate a compromise.
- *Depression*: Here people confront the inevitability and reality of the loss and their helplessness to change it. They may also blame themselves for having caused or contributed to the loss.
- *Acceptance*: Person achieves some emotional detachment and objectivity. They have processed their initial grief emotions, are able to accept that the loss has occurred and cannot be undone, and are once again able to plan for their futures and re-engage in daily life.

Dr. Kübler-Ross stresses that acceptance is coming to terms with the situation rather than resignation or hopelessness. At this point the grieved will return to their prior level of functioning and resume their normal personal, social, and work interactions.[3] The timing of these stages vary according to many factors including the person's life situation, prior personality characteristics, and their support system. Not all people will experience all of these stages, nor will they always occur in this exact order.

Dr. Kübler-Ross's ideas have been subject to debate and criticism by some because it is felt that they are not based on scientific research. Death means different things to different people. The five stages of grief were originally developed as a model for helping dying patients cope with death and bereavement. The concept is now also used in a general sense to help people deal with personal trauma, loss, change, and other life challenges.

DEPRESSION

A true clinical depression (major depressive disorder)[4] requires that an individual feels sad almost every day for at least two weeks and have multiple symptoms including at least five of the ones noted below. The feelings interfere with everyday functioning and are not due to a physical disorder or drug or alcohol abuse or dependency. It is not just about being upset for twenty-four to forty-eight hours because things did not go well in your life on Tuesday. Typical symptoms may include:

- Feeling sad or empty
- Loss or increase of appetite / weight loss or gain
- Tearfulness
- Difficulty in sleep pattern
- Decreased energy, feeling slowed down
- Restlessness, irritability
- Feelings of helplessness and hopelessness
- Feelings of guilt / worthlessness
- Difficulty in concentration and making decisions
- Diminished self-esteem and feelings of worthlessness
- Loss of sexual interest
- Persistent physical complaints that do not respond to treatment
- Recurrent thoughts of death or suicide

Suicide

Suicide is the most serious consequence of depression. The highest suicide rate in the United States is among the elderly.[5] It should be taken seriously. Although people in our country over the age of sixty-five only make up 13 percent of the population, they account for 18 percent of all suicides.[6] The suicide rate is higher among men. White men over age eighty-five have the highest suicide rate in the nation—nearly six times that of the general population. Predictors include older age, male gender, widowed or divorced status, isolation, alcohol or drug abuse, and debilitating illness.[7] All of these factors make it easy to see why depression is a common affliction affecting those ages sixty-five and older and why it should be looked for and taken seriously.

Do not be afraid to ask about suicide directly, if you feel that someone is contemplating killing themselves. As I often tell my patients, if you say something, they may feel that someone is now helping them hold up a heavy log or burden. Talking about it will not cause a person to commit suicide. If anything, it may show them that someone cares, break down their isolation, and relieve some emotional pain. A patient's threatening suicide is a warning sign that should never be ignored.

A Confusing Diagnostic Picture

Although depression is one of the most common psychiatric reactions in the geriatric population, statistics of depression in the elderly vary and are confusing, perhaps due to the fact that it is often not diagnosed for multiple reasons. A correct diagnosis must take into account the body and the brain. Physicians and psychiatrists must address the biological, psychological and social dimensions of the illness. It is glossed over or misdiagnosed due to masked depression and the myth that unhappiness is a normal part of aging. Even some physicians assume that feeling sad is a natural reaction to be expected in the elderly, and dismiss depression as being age appropriate.

But depression is not just a normal consequence of aging. In fact, the Centers for Disease Control (CDC) says that "the majority of older adults are *not* depressed. Some estimates of major depression in older people living in the community range from less than 1 percent to about 5 percent but rise to 13.3 percent in those who require home healthcare and to 11.5 percent in older hospital patients."[8] The incidence can be as high as 25 percent for those in nursing homes.

Another issue that causes variation in statistics is the fact that senior citizens are prone to "masked depression." They may offer multiple vague nonspecific bodily complaints in several parts of their body that may eclipse a depressed mood. Other "depressive equivalents" common in older people include headache, chronic pain, gastrointestinal upsets (constipation, nausea), and decreased energy and drive. Other barometers of depression in the elderly include sleep disturbances or an internal feeling of nervousness or restlessness. Pessimism, loneliness, and hopelessness, as well as apathy with subtle fears of failure can be silent indications of underlying depression. [9]

There is even a condition called "pseudodementia," where the patient offers complaints of diminished memory, concentration, and thinking mimicking dementia. However, when the depression is treated, these symptoms go away. As many as one-third of patients diagnosed as demented may be suffering from depression. [10] Taking all of these factors into consideration, it is not surprising to find that, "Seven million Americans over the age of sixty-five suffer from depression." [11]

Depression is often loosely defined. It is a term applied to everything from transitory unhappiness to incapacitating suicidal despair. [12] However, because of the high incidence of depression in the elderly, people should be sensitive to this continuum and not just assume that feeling sad is a natural reaction to be expected in the senior citizen. Therefore, you can see why physicians, mental health workers, and others frequently interacting with people age sixty-five and older need to remember to consider depression as a possible diagnosis in the older person and not be fooled or distracted by other physical or emotional presenting complaints. Without careful medical evaluation, the wrong diagnosis might be made and even harmful treatment provided delaying helpful management.

Psychological Causes of Depression

As I mentioned above, Sigmund Freud felt that both grief and depression can occur in response to loss of an emotionally significant person or personal ability or attribute. Having been trained in psychoanalytically oriented psychotherapy and having done therapy with patients for forty-three years, I wholeheartedly agree that loss and repressed anger are significant harbingers of depression.

Another psychological theory of depression is based on cognitive theory that maintains that depression is a result of our distorted thought processes (cognitive distortion). This approach was proposed by Aaron

T. Beck, the father of Cognitive Behavioral Therapy (CBT), in the 1960s. He maintains that it is our thoughts, not external things like people, situations, and events, that cause our behaviors. Instead, three major distortions, or patterns of thinking, including a negative view of self, a negative view of the world, and a negative view of the future, are associated with depression. By identifying and then challenging our inaccurate thinking, we can learn to think and act in a healthier, more positive, and constructive manner.[13]

Biological Causes of Depression

A more modern view of the causes of depression is based on neurobiology. It advocates that people with depression have a chemical imbalance in their brain. The neurotransmitter hypothesis of depression, originally proposed in 1965, maintains that depression is a result of a deficiency of various hormones such as serotonin, norepinephrine, glutamate, gamma-aminobutyric acid (GABA), endorphins, and perhaps dopamine. Antidepressant medications increase neurotransmitters (hormones) in the brain.[14]

There is probably not one single cause of any mood disorder. It is likely that multiple factors including genetics, abnormalities in brain function, and environmental issues lead to these disorders. Many unanswered questions remain. Statistics have demonstrated that a biological vulnerability toward depression runs in families and that a propensity toward mood disorders is inherited and genetic. The brain can also be damaged by head injury, tumor, strokes, or various medical diseases, resulting in depression.[15]

Medical Causes of Depression

Older people are prone to physical illness and often take multiple medications. Both of these issues can be associated with depression in the elderly. There are various medical diseases and physical problems that can cause symptoms of depression. They include endocrine disorders such as thyroid disease, parathyroid disease, diabetes, and menopause; malignant diseases such as pancreatic carcinoma, brain tumor, or lymphoma; central nervous system disorders such as Parkinson's disease, multiple sclerosis, or stroke; nutritional deficiencies such as low levels of vitamin B-12, iron or vitamin C; infections such as influenza, hepatitis, and viral pneumonia; collagen-vascular diseases such as rheumatoid arthritis, systemic lupus erythematosus, and giant cell arteritis; gastrointestinal diseases such as cirrhosis, inflammatory bowel disease, and celiac disease. Other medical disorders that can be associated with depression include sleep apnea, alcoholism, congestive heart failure, and sensory deprivation, hypoxia (low blood oxygen), and heavy metal intoxication. This is only a sampling. There are a number of other medical diseases associated with depression. You can see why it is so important that older people receive a full diagnostic medical workup, including a physical examination, appropriate laboratory tests and an electrocardiogram as part of preventive care to rule out these conditions.

Medications Associated with Depression

Medications also share a relationship with depression. Some of the drugs associated with depression include antihypertensive drugs such as clonidine, hydralazine, and propranolol hydrochloride; cardiac drugs such as digitalis, propranolol, and lidocaine; hormones such as estrogen and progesterone; antineoplastic drugs such as vincristine sulfate and vinblastine sulfate; the anti-Parkinson drugs, levodopa and amantadine hydrochloride; psychotropic drugs such as benzodiazepines, chlorpromazine, and other aliphatic phenothiazines. Other drugs that may cause symptoms of depression include corticosteroids, cimetidine, timolol maleate, cycloserine, and alcohol, sedatives, and stimulants.[16]

You can see why a review of all of the patient's medications is an important part of any initial medical or psychiatric evaluation. There are several things that can be done if a depression is treated but shows no improvement. These include being sure that the patient is being compliant in taking the medication, increasing the dose of the medication, or switching to another form of treatment. However, one of the important things to remember is to look for an underlying, undiagnosed, medical cause. These steps will help your physician better formulate a treatment plan that meets your individual needs. (See chapter 14 and chapter 15 for additional information on the psychiatric treatment options for depression.)

At the beginning of this book, our composite couple, Vivienne and Harold, was feeling angry about their new circumstances. Harold and

Vivienne were sliding slowly into a clinical "major depression." Harold worked in his garden feeling sad and unhappy. He had trouble sleeping. He had vague physical pains, "depressive equivalents," and complained about an increased frequency of his arthritic pain. Equally unhappy about the changes in her life, Vivienne tried to use her usual household routine to cover up her unhappiness. Perhaps, she felt, "As long as I get it all done perfectly, I will feel better." Could her method have been an example of denial and bargaining?

Both felt worried, helpless, and hopeless. They both felt stuck. With poor communication skills and limited flexibility in their coping skills, they saw no way out of their dilemma. They were fortunate that their friends provided a lifeline for them, which prevented them from going over the cliff of despair. I am hopeful that the information noted above will help reduce any stigma about depression. It is not your fault. It is not a character flaw. It is a biological, medical illness that can be treated. I am also hopeful that the information in this book, including the coping skills in section V, help you take charge of your life, as you retire and age, improve your mood and light the road ahead taking you to a more fruitful existence and improving the quality of your life. Good luck.

The next chapter looks at drug and alcohol abuse in the elderly. You may be shocked to learn that this is a growing problem in this age group.

7

DRUG AND ALCOHOL ABUSE

You may be surprised to find a chapter on drug and alcohol abuse and addiction in a book on retirement and aging. However, substance use is an important topic to be aware of in this age group. Substance abuse among the elderly has been called one of the fastest growing health problems in this country. Substance addiction among those sixty years old and older currently affect 17 percent of the elderly population in the United States.[1]

Senior citizens are more vulnerable to addiction due to various physical, psychological, and social factors. Seniors can self-medicate using legal and illegal drugs and alcohol. Older people taking many medications prescribed by more than one doctor are at risk for prescription drug abuse. Issues of medication compliance may contribute to this problem. Older people often make mistakes with their medications. Forgetfulness may cause them to take extra doses.

Financial problems may cause the elderly to choose which medications to refill. Often they choose the ones that give the most bang for the buck. Senior citizens may become dependent on drugs prescribed to deal with joint pain, sleeping problems, or injuries from falls. The "fix it" philosophy states that if one pain pill helped two will be better. Emotional issues, such as sadness over losing loved ones or being far from family may also increase the risk of drug dependence. Substances may stay in older bodies longer, because a decrease in renal function with age causes decreased clearance of drugs. Aging can alter the reaction of individual neurons causing alteration of central nervous system and cardiovascular and respiratory function due to less sensitivity of the target organ.

ALCOHOL ABUSE AND ADDICTION

Alcohol abuse by senior citizens is an increasing problem and one that is often undiagnosed. Four out of five people of retirement age who seek substance abuse treatment do so because of alcohol problems, not drug abuse. Older drinkers are more sensitive to the effects of alcohol due to a slower metabolism and a reduction in body water available to dilute alcohol.

"Alcohol abuse statistics [also] tell us that a total of 23 million Americans suffer from substance abuse addiction, and 18 million is alcohol related. Almost three times as many men as women are problem drinkers."[2] This public health problem is one of our nation's most serious hazards. Those who work in the field of substance abuse rehabilitation see alcoholism as a symptom of something that is happening inside or outside the person. It is often behavior reflecting psychological stress. Alcoholism is a disease involving body, mind, and spirit. It is often a sign that the person is trying to cope with the problems of life.

It is easy to fall into a pattern of substance abuse, particularly with the popular media image that there is a pill for every need. When the substance becomes disruptive in their life, a person has moved up the ladder and become a substance abuser. They are now using the drug for some other purpose than it was intended. When tolerance develops or a withdrawal syndrome appears, and the substance itself has taken over the person, he or she graduates to becoming an addict (having a pattern of pathological use). Help is available. However one of the main roadblocks is the person's own denial.[3]

I have had two professional experiences that taught me a lot about the addictive personality and the substance abuse culture. Although the treatment populations with which I worked were not totally geriatric, but varied from age eighteen to the aging alcoholic, much of the education that I obtained could be transposed to an older group. Both instances immersed me totally in a hospital treatment program. The first was the original drug treatment program at Haverford State Hospital, in Haverford, Pennsylvania. The second was an alcoholic treatment unit in a psychiatric facility then call "Fairmount Farm," in Philadelphia, Pennsylvania. It is now called the Charter Fairmount Institute.

The then-superintendent of Haverford State Hospital, Jack Kremens, MD, in spite of much Philadelphia Main Line community resistance, felt that an inpatient drug treatment program was needed in the Delaware County area. I had just finished my fellowship in psychiatry and had little experience in the field, but Kremens asked me to be the medical director of this new unit. I attended a two-week course in drug education and addiction treatment at the Eastern Pennsylvania Psychiatric Institute, assembled a staff, and we were off and running. It was a lot to take on.

Not every mental health worker is comfortable working with every type of patient. Staff training involved sorting out those men and women whose "counter transference"[4] issues interfered with patient treatment because their partly unconscious feelings and attitudes interfered with their understanding and therapeutic handling of the individual that they were trying to help. An example would be someone who "over identified" (saw themselves in the patient) with the lonely, depressed, or fearful drug addict. This idea of "counter transference" can be transposed to working with any age group population, including those over age sixty-five.

Some cannot work with the elderly because they feel that older people (parents, grandparents, and elderly people in general) should be obeyed and feared. They may also feel threatened by the authority of the older individual and therefore have difficulty setting necessary therapeutic limits. As I tell my patients who are caregivers for an elderly parent, "There will be times that you the child will have to become the parent and make the executive decisions."

Some mental health workers cannot work with addicts until the worker is free of any hostility that they may have toward addictive individuals whom they may see as dependent and weak. They must shed outworn prejudices. The same feelings may occur when they work with the elderly, whom they may see as dependent and helpless. If anything, the older person is trying their best to be independent and not be a burden on others. Most addicts are not truthful about the reason they are seeking help. They may say that they want help; however, the real reason that they are there is because of legal action, to reduce their habit so that it would be cheaper to support, because they have been a nuisance to others at work or at home, or because they have no place to go. The older person may also fabricate the reality of their situation in an effort to maintain feelings of control.

It is easy to see why some older people fall into the trap of addiction. Imagine yourself alone in a small apartment sitting most of the day in a recliner with little stimulation aside from the sound of the television. The phone seldom rings and there are not many people left in your world who you can call. The alcohol or drug abuser or dependent older person is usually suffering from the "Three L's," loneliness, loss, and lack of love. The doctor-patient bond is a strong therapeutic tool. Talking to an accepting and understanding therapist may help fulfill some of these needs. Time in therapy is often spent reestablishing the elder's self-esteem and decreasing their feelings of helplessness as well as trying to get them to reengage with the world outside.

One of the main points that I learned on the alcohol unit at Fairmount Farm was that alcohol and feelings of depression go hand in hand. I try to explain to patients that although alcohol has the ability, initially, to relax you, that chemically it is a depressant. If you are already depressed, in the long run, drinking will only get you more depressed emotionally. I had never before seen people of various ages, including the elderly, so clinically depressed, except, perhaps, for bipolar depressed patients, when they stopped drinking and entered inpatient treatment. Regardless of their outward façade or the feelings they expressed, older addicted individuals are harboring feelings of depression that need attention.

THE VOID

Another concept that is relevant to the field of abuse and addiction is that of the "void." This is the emotional deficit caused by the lack of nurturing, support, and other wounds that people experience while growing up. Psychiatrist, Viktor Frankl, in his discussion of logo-therapy, says that addiction is due to "the existential vacuum," a feeling of emptiness and meaninglessness.[5] Patients often are aware that something is missing but may experience only vague feelings of emptiness and unhappiness. Regardless of later world experience, residual issues of this feeling cluster remain as the addict or other affected individual grows older. However, neither drugs nor alcohol, or other negative acting out, can fill the internal void left by the lack of childhood nurturing.

The void at times is also described as the individual not having a subjective inner feeling that life has meaning or purpose. It deals with the fundamental issues of truth and values. It takes on more of a spiritual framework. The philosophy of Alcoholics Anonymous sees addiction as a spiritual problem; step twelve of its twelve steps speaks of having a spiritual awakening. A *Current Psychiatry* journal article uses a vignette about a Mr. W. to make this point. Mr. W. is quoted as saying,

> I believe that every time I drink I am on a spiritual search. . . . I have this emptiness inside of me and alcohol would temporarily fill the enormous hole in my insides. Just for a short period of time, I would feel at peace and connected to others, and maybe even with God. . . . Every time I relapse it's because I'm going through a spiritual withdrawal. Booze filled the void inside of me and now the void is back again. . . . I'm just empty inside and when I can't stand it any longer, I drink again.[6]

What Mr. W. and other substance abusers have to learn is that nothing can completely fill this hole, particularly if the childhood deficit is extreme. The void must be accepted. The patient must learn to accept that they have this defect and then, in spite of it, reach out to the world to find things that interest and satisfy them in some way. Passively sitting back and waiting for someone to save you will not work. Substance abuse is not a helpful way of coping with the stress of life. An active, problem-solving approach may certainly be more helpful and pay more dividends.

A therapist or willing spouse or partner can be helpful in filing some of these prior unfulfilled needs. In a *Philadelphia Inquirer* article, columnist, Darrell Sifford, interviewed Philadelphia therapist, Herbert Cohen, about this issue. Cohen said, "if deficiencies were so extreme, you're never going to fill up for what you have missed. But, you can get some (and) begin to fill in some of the cracks in your foundation . . . and begin to identify yourself not as incomplete and insufficient but as incomplete and getting better, getting what you need to be healthy."[7] This problem can affect people of various ages and socioeconomic status.

In another *Philadelphia Inquirer* column, staff writer Ashley Fox interviewed Eagle football team owner, Jeffrey Lurie, born in 1951, about his own personal void. Lurie lost his father to cancer at age nine. Four months later, his maternal grandfather died unexpectedly. In this short period of time, he lost the two most significant male figures in his life. The article maintains that "his father's death was a big blow in his life . . . it has so much to do with who he is today." The event shaped his outlook and adult behavior.

> It is why he's the upbeat, live-for-the-moment man he is today, why he embraces adventure and encourages free thought. . . . He is a self-proclaimed risk taker. . . . He escaped his sadness by submerging himself in sports . . . the loss of his father is a loss Lurie will never get over. . . . [T]here is one thing Lurie longs for, one thing neither his wealth nor his fame can provide. He is chasing a void he can never fill. Jeffrey Lurie just wants his dad. [8]

I first heard of "the void" at Haverford State Hospital while working with a depressed male adolescent, who had a history of drug addiction, and subsequently committed suicide several years later. He told me in a moment of insightful truthfulness that he realized that he took drugs in an effort to fill the void left inside of him because his parents had not given enough of themselves to him emotionally.

This is particularly relevant to the older adult living alone. I had an elderly patient, who had been raised by two busy parents, and had been given the role of taking care of a younger sibling. She grew up feeling lonely and sad. She tried to overcome her feelings of anxiety, dependency, and helplessness by being efficient, competent, and independent. This worked while her husband was alive. He let her run the house and take care of their three children. She did well, but was constantly depressed. As a widow, she found herself alone in a large house with nothing to do but watch television and wait for the mail. Her children called and visited weekly. They encouraged her to visit neighbors and get out more. For some time nothing changed.

While doing therapy with her, for depression, I suggested that she participate in a senior citizen program at a local mental health clinic that served lunch. She refused stating that she did not want to be with "old people." After several months of my suggesting this activity and explaining that her isolation was counterproductive, she finally allowed me to arrange for her to register for the program. At first she would only go once a week, and would only allow her daughter to drop her off and pick her up from the center. Within three months, she was going daily and even let their bus pick her up and take her home. Do not give up. There are answers. Things can be found to help seniors reconnect to the outside world and start to feel better. The void can be addressed. Positive rather than negative coping mechanisms and activities can be suggested to reduce the emptiness. Volunteerism is also helpful as it gets you to deal with others and their problems rather than just think about yourself.

One of the most frustrating aspects that a family member, friend, or therapist has to deal with is an addicted persons' tendency to relapse. On the drug unit at Haverford State Hospital, we worked hard to push our patients forward by letting them see that support was available and that they had the ability and intelligence to better their lives. However, some of their personality traits, negative coping mechanisms, and lack of true motivation to change, created a situation where they seemed to do well, but six months later were once again readmitted to the unit. We called this the revolving door syndrome.

There was a large rate of recidivism in addiction treatment programs. This tendency to relapse is something that you will see even when dealing with an elderly relative who has been abused or become addicted to drugs or alcohol unless the underlying problem causing the psychological stress is discovered and addressed. Listen to what they are saying as well as what they are not saying. Try to see what basic needs are not being fulfilled. These can include such needs such as acceptance and approval, intimacy or being close to others, honesty or trust, hope, respect and dignity, freedom from pain, and of course, love, affection, and tenderness.

It is helpful when dealing with addicted individuals to see substance abuse or addiction as a symptom, and not a sign of weakness or moral decay. It is a means of adapting. It may be the only mechanism the person has available at the moment to cope with life's problems. It is a behavior reflecting some sort of psychological stress. It is an attempt to meet, deal with, or master some form of personal imbalance, conflict, or excitation. A person can use substances to handle stress by avoiding pain and trying to satisfy the pleasure principle. For some, it is a kind of last grasping toward something to forestall the horrible feeling of self-

disintegration or disorganization that spells the doom of total helplessness or being out of control of their environment. It is helpful to deal
with the whole person rather than just concentrate on the individual
substance involved. As when dealing with patients in general, it is helpful to try to understand the person in their totality.

Previously, this book dealt with specific treatment modalities to deal
with alcohol and substance abuse. The above material concentrates
more on attitude issues and the person's complete gestalt. These are
helpful modalities to allow you to establish a therapeutic bond between
yourself and the afflicted individual. With the younger alcoholic or drug
abuser or addict, your efforts may not pay dividends right away. They
may be dealing with chronic problems. They are masters at manipula-
tion and "getting over." They may have a different agenda than that
which they are sharing with you.

Older people also may be carrying with them residual psychological
problems or a void. However, the retired aging individual's drug or
alcohol use may be a more recent problem that they have enlisted to
deal with a new and acute difficult life situation. They may just be using
the substance to deal with an unhappy life, where they feel out of
control and have no clue as to what steps to take to improve their
situation. Usually, although they may be resistant at first, they are
thankful for your care and intervention. They appreciate someone taking an interest in them and often give you genuine positive feedback
and gratitude.

The next chapter will examine how retiring and getting older can
affect your marital and sexual life.

8

MARITAL AND SEXUAL ISSUES
LATER IN LIFE

Marriage is a complex relationship requiring love, compromise, perspective, and laughter to blossom and survive. When two people first meet and there is an initial attraction or "chemistry," the association may continue. Initially, wearing rose-colored glasses, each person projects their early wishes onto the beloved, just as the person in analysis or psychotherapy does with the analyst or therapist. After about three months, the honeymoon is over and people begin to see other, less pleasing aspects of others' personalities. If these traits do not make you bolt and you still feel positive about the person, the relationship will continue. In *Passages*, Gail Sheehy discusses the myth of the all-purpose marriage as the automatic fulfiller of all dependencies and needs. She cautions that love develops gradually and encourages acceptance of individual differences in a relationship.[1]

Middle age can be a time of agonizing reappraisal of a martial relationship, with divorce a frequent result. Common areas of marital conflict involve unfulfilled needs based on unrealistic expectations, cultural differences, outside stress, communication difficulties, and unresolved childhood problems. Retirement often brings some of these same issues to the fore. Therapists usually try to go with the positives in a relationship. They want to see if the relationship is still viable. In marital therapy, I give both partners a chance to express why they feel upset. After they vent their anger, I am hopeful that they will look at the positive reasons that they married in the first place and see that most of these qualities are still there. Using these good memories as a foundation, they can start to build the relationship again. Then, I spend time trying to get the individuals to examine their needs and see if they can fulfill them in the relationship. If after a time, having considered both the negative and positive aspects of the relationship, it becomes obvious that the love is gone and they cannot fulfill each other's needs, it is all right to separate.

MARITAL SATISFACTION

A good adjustment in retirement requires having a secure income, good health, and meaningful activities. For those married retirees, high marital satisfaction is also important.[2] Enjoying a good marital relationship is one of the key elements for a successful retirement. The stress of retirement can put strain on a marriage. It can inflame old problems, bring back old insecurities, and cause role confusion. John E. Nelson and Richard N. Bolles in their book, *What Color Is Your Parachute? For Retirement*, call marriage during retirement "marriage on steroids." "It [marriage] becomes a bigger version of itself. Whatever a marriage is like before retirement, left to its own devices, it tends to become more that way in retirement. A marriage that's harmonious and loving can tend to become more harmonious and loving. A marriage that's discordant and intolerant can tend to become more discordant and intolerant."[3]

A closer look at Harold and Vivienne's marriage certainly shows this to be true. Although there was an initial attraction, they had married in their early twenties because they felt that that was what was expected of them. Then, they concentrated on what they felt they should be doing. Vivienne concentrated on her housework, and having and caring for their two children. When the children were older, she went back to teaching a third-grade elementary school class. Harold focused on work and bringing home a paycheck. Although they did go out socially at times and often attended family functions, they did not talk much and their bond was thin. In therapy, if a patient says, "I *should* be doing this or that," I always answer "according to whom." They both did what they thought they should be doing. In retirement, they did not have much personal or couple equity to bring to the table to pay dividends. Their marital history was one of isolation, poor communication, and unfulfilled needs. Harold and Vivienne's situation illustrates the point that you cannot assume that once you retire your marriage will automatically be happier.

If Harold and Vivienne came to me for marital therapy, I would assume that by showing up, they each had an interest in staying married and improving their marital situation. I would point this out to them and then try my best to rekindle in them the initial spark that brought them together in the first place. To get them talking, I would ask them each to tell me three things that they liked about the other person and three things that they disliked. I would ask them each to comment on what the other person said. Then, I would ask them to tell me a few of the things that they enjoyed and liked about the other, both now and when they first met. I might ask them to look through a scrapbook of pictures taken when they first got married. These exercises hopefully will allow more positive feelings to reemerge and lead the way for reconciliation. Later, I would ask them to communicate their expectations of what they thought would happen to their relationship during retirement and try to build a more realistic consensus.

TIME AND SPACE

In retirement, relationships between spouses become a larger part of people's lives. Issues of time and space are a problem that both partners have to resolve.[4] Vivienne and Harold illustrate the problem of time and space in retirement. Prior to retirement, Harold had his work space and his home space. At work he spent time with others. Vivienne had her house space, her work space, and spent time with her girlfriends outside the house. In retirement, time is expanded as both partners mostly spend time interacting with each other. Space is compressed as both partners occupy the same home space. You can now see why Vivienne felt that Harold was intruding on her home. On the other hand, I would suspect that Harold resented the way that Vivienne relegated him to his small garden space.

COMMUNICATION

Communication is important in marriage. Mel Schwartz got it right in his January 13, 2014, blog entitled "Silence: A Relationship Killer." He maintains that "couples that are struggling in their relationships often succumb to the default mode of silence. [This] speaks to the absence of verbal and emotional intimacy. . . . Not only does it sabotage the lifeline of a healthy coupling, it chokes your expressive needs. . . . Problematic feelings that go unexpressed tend to percolate and boil over . . . [and] result in substantial resentment." He further maintains that the partners may be using silence "to control the other's reactions and behaviors. . . . At other times silence is used to punish. . . . [Silence leaves] no opportunity for resolution, let alone growth." He further explains, "Besides creating an obvious roadblock to the health of the relationship, silence can lead to despair and depression . . . expressing of one's voice is life affirming."[5]

Good communication, during which you express your dreams, expectations, needs, and desires, is an important prerequisite in preparing for retirement for married couples. Kerri Anne Renzulli calls this having "The Talk." She suggests that you and your spouse independently make a list of what you want and then sit down together and share the information with an emphasis on what will make you both happy in retirement. Talk about your finances and see if you can afford some of these ideas. Express your concerns and worries. She says that it is helpful if you try to understand "the back story"—why your spouse wants to do certain things. Then stress your similarities and go to the middle ground. Try to work your initial plan around these common issues.[6]

INTIMACY AND SEX

Intimacy and sex are important in marriage, even in retirement. Sex is also a form of communication, fulfilling our needs to be loved and cared for. Sex is a normal and healthy part of life for most adults, at any age. Years ago, when I was in medical school, a professor of mine, a gynecologist, wrote an article called, "Sex after Sixty Is Nifty."[7] My classmates, mostly in their twenties, and I thought this very funny and had difficulty imaging "elderly people" having sex. However, it is a fallacy that senior citizens are nonsexual. "Desexualizing people as soon as they qualify for Social Security is a popular tendency. However, sexual activity and interest, as well as the need for affection and companionship certainly continue long after age sixty-five."[8]

Betsy Crane, a professor of human sexuality at Widener University, was interviewed in the *Philadelphia Inquirer*. The article was called, "Sex after 50, or 75? But Of Course." Professor Crane maintains, "Sex is good for your health. It lowers blood pressure, elevates mood, boosts immunity, burns calories and helps you sleep better."[9] Sexuality has even become a hot button issue in nursing homes. For some it is difficult to reconcile these two images. This awareness has brought about uncomfortable debatable issues involving talking points of patient autonomy, their decision-making capacity, privacy, regulatory issues, concern for patient safety, dignity, and the obligation of the staff to protect residents from harm, including freedom from abuse or exploitation.[10]

Harold and Vivienne were very attracted to each other when they first met. Throughout their life, intimacy and sex had been an integral part of their time together. As they aged, there was some change in their sexual responsiveness. Sexual intercourse became more painful for Vivienne, and she achieved less orgasms. Harold was less able to achieve a full erection and worried about performance failure. He was more easily distracted and the environment had to be perfect for him to get aroused. Physical fatigue at times slowed them both down. However although they had less sexual encounters as the years went by, they still considered themselves sexually active. A sterile lubricant for Vivienne and "a little blue pill" for Harold proved helpful. As they continued to age, sex took longer but became more tender, more loving, and in some ways better than it had been when they were young and full of passion. However, feelings of anger supersede any feelings of sex or affection. This was the case when Harold initially retired.

As you have seen, if they came for therapy, I would try to deal with their expectations of retirement and try to reduce their negative feelings. I would point out to them that in spite of their anger, they seemed to love each other. As the anger diminished, I would encourage them to start making an effort again to be more affectionate during the day and to initiate some physical contact when they get into bed at night, even if it was just holding each other. If they became aroused and they had sex, so be it. However, if not they would still have enjoyed some physical contact with each other, which was pleasurable and helpful and would fulfill their needs for affection and companionship.

No matter how old they are, all people need and appreciate being loved.

THE CAREGIVER ROLE

The last issue that you may need to face in marriage in retirement is the caregiver role. With age can come infirmity. Frequently, at least one partner will need some type of care due to a physical or emotional illness. Our society values and promotes independence. The loss of independence is not an easy adjustment for either partner. Once again, it may require changing roles in the relationship. The injured party, who was used to being independent, may resent having to lean on their spouse or significant other. They may be irritable and resentful, causing them to be uncooperative and antagonistic. Do not feel guilty about any negative feelings that this may arouse in you as the caregiver. Resentment, angry feelings, and even an occasional death wish do not mean that you are a bad person or that you hate your spouse or partner.

There is no one "right way" to care for an ill spouse or partner. However, it does help if you take on the role voluntarily, rather than through a sense of obligation, guilt, or even love. Remember to take care of yourself and know your limits. It is okay if you ask for help from other family members such as your grown children. Friends, neighbors, and even community resources can often offer relief, allowing you some much needed rest. I always tell patients that even though they may wish to continue to keep their ill spouse at home, if the situation starts to require professional level care, it may be time to think of an assisted living facility or nursing home. It is helpful to plan ahead of time, just in case. Put you name on the waiting list. Often, a bed may not be available when you really need it. You can always say no if admissions calls and you are not ready to make the change.

WIDOWHOOD AND BEREAVEMENT

Loss and death are part of life, particularly during retirement. Widowhood brings about many changes in finances, physical and emotional health, and social support. Becoming widowed in later life usually means a significant decline in income. Recently widowed persons report more health problems than those who are married. They also show symptoms of depression, such as sadness, tearfulness, insomnia, appetite changes, and weight loss. Usually as time passes, these feelings subside, they adjust, and the negative effects of the loss decrease. Immediately after a spouse's death, emotional support from other widowed persons is helpful. There are groups available where you can share your fears and hopes and get support in figuring out how to go forward. As time goes on, the widowed are more apt to turn to their children, friends, and other relatives for support.[11]

From what I have seen professionally, bereavement diminishes after about three months. However, there can be mild depression with feelings of sadness that remain for a year after the death of a spouse. It takes that long to go through the first series of birthdays and holidays without your spouse. In doing therapy, I noticed two recurrent patterns of prolonged depression and emotional problems. Women came to therapy because they had a prolonged depression with continued tearfulness. In therapy, I usually discovered that under the tears and sadness were feelings of anger and feelings of abandonment that their partner had left them to take care of life's responsibilities and problems on their own. Regardless of their intelligence or ability, they feel helpless and resent the fact that their spouse had taken care of everything and now they have the world on their shoulders. Men, on the other hand, come to therapy after the loss of a partner because they feel helpless taking over some of their wife's tasks, such as cooking, household work, and making social engagements.

Jan Fawcett, MD, editor of the journal *Psychiatric Annals*, gives his solution to these problems in an editorial entitled "Bereavement and the Four Noble Truths." Here, he says,

> Life is replete with losses . . . we suffer and grieve . . . [to deal with these feelings], the Four Noble Truths of Buddhism tell us: giving up our attachment to relationships, to our own egos, our own thoughts, and to material possessions, is the path toward happiness. . . . Learn-

ing to deal with loss is one way we can come to appreciate what life and consciousness offers. Given the truth, how can we maximize our appreciation and enjoyment of life? By learning compassion, being helpful to others, by promoting our own creativity and that of others, and learning to live in the beauty of the present, free from our ego and material gain. This is our best response to the fact of life that there is death and loss.[12]

These are some of the themes that psychiatrists try to share with people in bereavement therapy.

DATING IN THE NEW MILLENNIUM

If you are patient, you can love again after the loss of a partner. Remarriage is less likely as a person ages. However, dating after divorce or widowhood can be helpful in providing intimacy, companionship, and reducing loneliness.[13] The rules of the dating game are different this time around. Women seem to be more aggressive in making contact with men than they were earlier in their life. They no longer wait for the men to be asked out. Widowers often laugh and tell each other, "beware of the casseroles." They tell stories of eligible women calling them or ringing their doorbell, several months after their wife died, offering them a casserole or other food to eat for dinner. Some consenting older adults no longer marry because they do not want to lose their social security benefits, like having their own place—which guarantees them their own space when they need it—and because they do not want to jeopardize their will and the bequeaths that they have made to their children.

In that we are living longer, it is not unusual today to meet couples who are on their second and even third marriage or relationship since divorce or the death of their initial spouse. My wife and I meet them frequently when we go away on vacation. I remember an eighty-five-year-old woman, who came to me for therapy due to depression following the death of her third husband, one year ago. After coming for several therapy sessions, she admitted, "Dr. Zal, I know what I have to do. But, I'm too tired and old to go through it again." What she meant was that she knew how to attract a man and find a new companion but did not have the emotional or physical strength to go through the process again.

Today, some unmarried but committed older couples see each other several times a week, travel together on vacation, visit with their children together, and attend functions together, but still maintain their individual homes. Widows and widowers now use social media and online dating services. According to Terri Akman, in her *Philadelphia Inquirer* article entitled, "Online Dating, Turns Out, Isn't Only for the Young," on January 22, 2014, "senior couples are part of a fast-growing trend of mature adults . . . searching for companionship online. According to AARP's 'love and relationship ambassador,' Pepper Schwartz, about half of this population has tried online dating, up from about 10 percent ten years ago." Online dating services such as ourtime.com, seniorfriendfinder.com, youngatheart.com, and silver-singles.com, focus on attracting older adults. More conventional sights such as ChristianMingle and JDate have seen an increase of elderly registrants.[14]

I recently attended a religious service. An older woman came in with her certified nursing assistant (CNA) and sat in front of me. She looked unhappy and weak. She had used a walker to help her balance. She needed help getting into her seat. After about ten minutes, an older man came and sat next to the woman. They spoke briefly and quietly with their faces close together. The interchange seemed intimate and loving. Her whole countenance changed. She brightened up and seemed more alive. At first, I was surprised at this tender interaction. Then I realized the obvious. People need and appreciate love, affection, and tenderness at every age. Everyone needs comforting and nurturing at times. It is nice to know that someone cares.

Changes in memory and thinking can serve as a roadblock to a successful retirement and happy and content aging. The next chapter will tell you about dementia and Alzheimer's disease.

9

DEMENTIA AND ALZHEIMER'S DISEASE

Harold was upset. Lately, he had noticed that he was having trouble finding the right word, remembering a name, or where he recently put items, such as his car keys and cell phone. He was concerned that this was the beginning of the end. He had read the *New York Times* best-selling book, *Still Alice* by Lisa Genova. He was worried and scared that he was suffering from Alzheimer's disease and would soon be a dependent person, unable to remember his wife's name. Memory loss, particularly of immediate recall, is one of the most common psychological effects of aging. This does not mean that we are developing Alzheimer's disease. However, difficulty in remembering recent events can be frustrating to you and those around you.

A friend of mine, who constantly could not find her glasses solved the problem by keeping a pair in every room of her house. Giggling one day, she told us that one time, she found her glasses in the freezer. She had gone to take something out, put them down and forgot what she had done. My friends and I laugh and say that it now takes the elevator a little longer to reach the top. However, we are not really pleased about this change.

Organic brain disorders describe a group of illnesses, caused by structural damage or destruction in the brain. Many years ago, when I initially did my psychiatric training, brain disorders were divided into organic brain syndrome, which progressed slowly, and Alzheimer's disease, which was more serious and could progress rapidly. Today, medical professionals speak of diseases of the Alzheimer's type to include both types of disorders. What they all share in common is a loss of mental abilities.

At one end of the spectrum is *dementia*, which means loss of mental powers, including thinking, reasoning, and remembering, due to impairment of brain tissue function. It can interfere with a person's functioning. The term comes from the Latin meaning "away the mind."[1] These changes include symptoms of impaired orientation (time, place, or person) and memory, particularly of immediate recall. There can also be changes in intellectual functioning, including problems in performing simple calculations, recalling simple items of general information, comprehending, and retaining and reacting to questions and commands. Patients with dementia may also show emotional lability, shallowness of affect (emotional tone), and impairment of judgment.

Acute or reversible brain syndrome, a subset of dementia, which will not be elaborated on here, can be reversed by treating the causative condition. It can be produced by drug intoxication or side effects, hyperthyroidism, Parkinson's disease, pernicious anemia, sleep disturbance, paresis (partial paralysis caused by muscular weakness due to nerve damage), subdural hematoma, benign brain tumor, stroke, hydrocephalus, insulin shock, and tumor of islet cells of the pancreas.

Alzheimer's disease was first described by German psychiatrist, Alois Alzheimer, in 1907. Alzheimer's disease is a chronic, irreversible, progressive deterioration of brain cells, which accounts for 40 to 60 percent of dementias. At this time, it cannot be cured or prevented. The Alzheimer's Association estimates that 5.2 million Americans over age sixty-five have Alzheimer's disease in 2014. The number of cases increases every year, as the population grows older. Up to 16 million will have the disease by 2050.[2]

Alzheimer's has been called the most expensive disease in America. However, the greatest cost of the disease is not financial, but personal. Those who experience this more progressive disease will have to deal with significant changes in memory, loss of orientation (time, place, and person), mood, and behavior, as well as being unable to accomplish the basic activities of daily living. It thus steals your independence and dignity. The person's decline can be rapid. Primary degenerative dementia of the Alzheimer's type is inherited. At this time there is no way to prevent or cure this disease.[3] (Chapter 15 discusses some drugs that profess to slow down the progression.)

A PORTRAIT OF AN ALZHEIMER'S PATIENT

What does an Alzheimer's patient look like? There is not just one picture that will do justice to the disease and its manifestations. Patients do not progress at the same rate. Each brain unravels in its own way and in its own time span. At one end of the spectrum is the forgetful individual, who knows emotionally that something is not right. In the middle range is the individual who is forgetful and more irritable than usual, but can confabulate to fill in the blanks. (Confabulation is the unconscious filling in gaps in one's memory by fabrication that one accepts as facts. There is no conscious attempt to deceive.) If people question their change in behavior, they might just say that they are tired or not feeling well. At the other end of the spectrum is the individual with vacant eyes, sitting on the living room couch in the middle of the night, fully clothed, confused, childlike, and helpless, not realizing where they are or how they got there.

Multi-infarct dementia is a subset of irreversible dementia associated with high blood pressure that will not be elaborated on here. It is caused by small strokes that gradually cause a loss of brain tissue due to insufficient circulation to the affected areas of the brain.

CAUSATION

The cause of Alzheimer's disease is an unresolved medical mystery. Research on this disease has confounded researchers due to its numerous facets. During the first decade, no symptoms show themselves. When symptoms do show themselves, they are not always specific to the disease. Patients do not progress at the same rate. By the time the person regresses further, the brain has already suffered severe damage and therefore treatment has come too late. In the past, there was no way to be sure that a person had Alzheimer's until they died and a pathologist could search for characteristic clumps of beta-amyloid plaques (a protein) and neurofibrillary tangles of tau protein in the brain at autopsy.

There are three main changes in the brain during the course of Alzheimer's disease. They include plaques and tangles of protein fibers that get worse over time, and loss of connections between neurons (nerve cells). Over time the nerve cells lose their ability to communicate with each other and eventually die. As this happens, affected areas of the brain shrink. The damage can spread to the part of the brain called the hippocampus, which is important in forming memories.[4] Other causative possibilities that have been considered include aluminum in the brain, inappropriate levels of the brain enzyme choline acetyltransferase, or a slow acting virus.

Things are changing and improving. It is likely that the causes include genetic, environmental, and lifestyle factors. There is interest in looking at the association between cognitive decline and vascular and metabolic conditions such as heart disease, stroke, high blood pressure, diabetes, and obesity. Researchers now have brain imaging techniques (PET scan-positron emission tomography) that allow them to watch changes in the brain "biomarkers," abnormal levels of the proteins, amyloid and tau, while people are alive, even before they have symptoms. Scientists can now see in a petri dish (a shallow circular transparent glass or plastic dish with a flat lid used to culture microorganisms or in other research) how the disease develops. This is a huge advance over animal models that can allow us to see what goes wrong with cells in the brain. This knowledge can help develop drugs that interfere with or stop the nerve-damaging disease.[5]

There are now tests that can show changes in memory and thinking ability. These improvements make it possible to test drugs and other possible treatments. Scientific trial approaches have varied, which has slowed down successful research comparison. The International Conference on Clinical Trials for Alzheimer's disease, met in Philadelphia, Pennsylvania, in 2014. "One of the group's big initiatives, the Collaboration for Alzheimer's Prevention (CAP), has worked to share some study-design elements among multiple early trials. This should make results easier to compare and build upon." A speaker at the conference said that he was hopeful that there will be "effective disease-slowing agents" within ten years, showing that researchers believe progress is being made.[6]

The Cleveland Clinic Florida's TOMORROW study is part of a long-term, nationwide clinical trial designed to test the efficiency of the FDA-approved type-2 diabetes drug, Actos (pioglitazone), to delay Alzheimer's disease in otherwise healthy subjects. Most clinical trials for Alzheimer's focus on people who already have memory impairment.

The TOMORROW study will also focus on whether a new genetic biomarker, TOMM40, is an additional indicator of a patient's elevated risk of developing the disease. The hope is that the anti-inflammatory properties of pioglitazone can protect the brains of those who may be at higher risk for developing Alzheimer's from actually getting the disease. The study is scheduled to last for five years.[7]

One roadblock to making progress in the battle against Alzheimer's is the fact that the approval process for developing new medications or treatment options are long and tedious. A clinical trial to prove the drug's efficacy requires three years. A prevention trial could take about three additional years. In that Alzheimer's is a disease of older people, even with successful results the medicines are often given too late to do much good. Therefore, there is no incentive for a pharmaceutical company to invest the resources and time needed for this procedure. It has been suggested that drug companies be given an incentive, such as market exclusivity, to make discovery of dementia drugs a priority.[8]

Wouldn't it be nice to have a simple blood test for Alzheimer's disease like we have for cholesterol? However, such a test may do more harm than good for a malady like Alzheimer's disease, for which no cause or effective treatments have been discovered. On the plus side, such a test would allow us to start treatment earlier and institute lifestyle changes such as a heart-healthy diet, physical activity, and social and cognitive stimulation which can help preserve cognitive function and can help slow the likelihood of developing dementia. Early detection would allow people to make informed decisions about their care before the symptoms of Alzheimer's get in the way.

On the negative side, a positive test result may be very upsetting emotionally, causing depression, anxiety, and withdrawal. People may catastrophize and feel a sense of doom. Some may feel stigmatized or ashamed. In general, people don't want to talk about Alzheimer's, much as years ago they didn't want to talk about cancer. Stigma also interferes with obtaining research funding. The stress that this knowledge can bring may even worsen the symptoms of memory loss and confusion. There may be false positives on a percentage of the tests. Such results could turn a person's life upside down for no reason. A test for the disease has been developed. The observed blood changes are believed to result from the breakdown of brain cell membranes in people prone to develop Alzheimer's. However, the test is in preliminary stages of development; results must be confirmed by other independent research teams.[9]

While on vacation recently in a warm-climate state, I decided to call a high school friend who had moved to the state early in his professional career. His wife called me back and said that Paul would be glad to talk to me and then put him on the phone. He seemed glad to hear from me. However, three sentences into our conversation, he announced, "I have Alzheimer's." My heart went out to him and his family. Many of my friends have chronic physical problems which they live with. But, Alzheimer's? Even being a psychiatrist, I was at a loss for words. I encouraged him to stay active and engaged. He seemed to smile at the other end of the phone and said that he knew that and was trying.

We talked and reminisced for a while, with his wife at times prompting him with needed words that he could not remember. He proudly told me about a talented grandson. I promised to e-mail him and keep in touch. For a while after we hung up, I felt sad for this vibrant and intelligent physician, who had helped so many during his professional career. It didn't seem fair that such a smart man could be losing pieces of his intellect and independence as the circuitry of his brain malfunctioned. I also became acutely aware of my own age and where I was in the life cycle. I hoped the best for him and his family.

CAREGIVERS

My next thought was about the amount of emotional support that Paul and his family would need as the disease progressed. Their lives would never be the same. The stress on him and his family could be overwhelming. Alzheimer's has large effects on the person who has it, but also on their family, which has to go through it as well. Most books written by caregivers on the subject only deal with the affirmative and do not focus on the whole story. They only focus on devotion and love, or present beautiful memorials to the patient, making use of such statements as "He was always there for me. Now I want to give back and be there for him." Such lily-white, altruistic situations do exist in reality, but they are rare. Most caregivers are in the middle range, somewhere between abandonment and full commitment to minute by minute care.

Recently, my wife and I went on a cruise. I happened to sit next to a woman and her husband in the lounge. He was quiet and passive, staring straight ahead, his face showing no emotion. Occasionally, she spoke to him in a soft, loving voice and he responded with a small smile. We struck up a conversation and she told me that he had Alzheimer's disease. She introduced us, but he looked past me as if I were transparent. Each time that I saw them on the ship, I was gratified to see that, in spite of his disorder, they were eating together, walking together, and sitting in the theater watching the entertainment. She was trying to keep them both active and engaged in the world. Although I am sure she had much work to do behind the scenes, she was at least making an effort not to be isolated and was taking a partial vacation.

Few articles or books deal with the other, negative, side of the coin. How frustrating it must be to deal with a disease that has no solution. How upsetting to watch someone you love deteriorate mentally to the point that they cannot take care of their own activities of daily living, such as bathing, shaving, dressing, and eventually even going to the bathroom themselves. How difficult it must be to keep your cool when the patient lashes out in anger or otherwise acts irrationally. As the patient becomes a stranger, being a caregiver to someone with Alzheimer's can be physically exhausting and emotionally devastating. Here are some things that you can do to make your job as a caregiver just a little bit easier:

1. *Educate yourself about the disease*: Doctors sometimes tend to avoid giving an Alzheimer's diagnosis, preferring to rule out other conditions first. It is helpful to educate yourself about the disease, so you can gain a perspective, ask intelligent questions, and understand what you are being told. Knowledge is power and will help you handle the situation and symptoms as they arise. The Alzheimer's Association in Chicago, Illinois, and the Alzheimer's Disease Education and Referral Center, in Silver Springs, Maryland, can be helpful. Your local library may also have useful resources.

2. *Do it voluntary*: Being a caregiver to an Alzheimer's patient is not for everyone. It may involve unpleasant tasks such as helping with toileting to difficult situations such as handling violent outbursts. Take on the role only if you want to and not because you feel you

have to out of obligation, guilt, or even love. There is no one right way to do this job. However, you are more apt to be successful if it is a voluntary choice. This will give you a greater sense of control and prevent you from feeling trapped. If the job is too overwhelming or more than you can emotionally and physically handle, reach out and see what other resources are available.

3. *Know your limits and take care of yourself*: Some of the signs that you are under stress include feelings of depression, not sleeping, feeling overwhelmed, losing weight, drinking too much, using pills to get through the day, drinking too much coffee, or are more irritable or angry than usual. If you are going to help someone in need, particularly in a difficult situation, you must take care of yourself. Avoid isolation. Exercise can work off aggressive energy. Staying physically active provides physical and emotional benefits. Take time off. Know your limits and seek additional help if you need it.[10] Don't feel guilty about taking care of yourself. This is not being selfish; it is self-preservation and will help you be a better caregiver.

4. *Share your feelings (including anger) and don't feel guilty*: A male patient of mine, who was an only child, felt that it was his duty to take care of his aging mother with Alzheimer's disease in her own home. She had contractures of her limbs and could be uncooperative, thrashing around and yelling when he tried to toilet her, feed her, or get her out of bed. He felt overwhelmed and angry. He couldn't understand why she was not more cooperative. After all, he was just trying to help her. However, he didn't voice his unhappiness and confusion or ask others to help. He just endured. Ten years later, when he was in therapy with me for anxiety, he mentioned in passing that he still felt guilty that he was so angry at his mother's behavior and lack of cooperativeness. I tried to give him a perspective and reduce his feelings of guilt. In this difficult situation, feelings of resentment, anger, and even an occasional death wish do not mean that you are a bad person or hate your relative. These are just signs of stress. After our talk, he admitted that he had no idea that his mother's behavior and his emotional response were normal under those circumstances.

5. *Develop a strong support network*: You don't have to be a pillar of strength and do it all alone. You can share your situation and your

feelings. Keep in touch with supportive friends. Don't neglect others in your family. They need you and can often be prompted to be of help to you and allow you to vent. They can also be called on to help with your duties. Talk to a professional such as a mental health worker, social worker, or religious leader, who may be able to give perspective to your situation. Participate in a support group. The Alzheimer's Association has chapters in many cities and a nationwide network of family support groups.

Harold mentioned his concerns about his occasional simple momentary lapses of memory to his friends at the bowling league and was comforted to learn that they had had similar experiences. He also visited his family physician, who checked him for possible reversible causes of his symptoms and reassured him that he did not have early onset Alzheimer's like *Still Alice*. This is a rare form of the disease that occurs in people ages thirty to sixty. The doctor felt that he had the garden variety of dementia common to those over age sixty-five. What Harold was experiencing is often called having "senior moments." This progresses very slowly and does not develop into late-onset Alzheimer's disease, where the symptoms are much more severe and happen more frequently. The severe decline in mental capacity caused by Alzheimer's disease is not a normal sign of aging. Harold left his doctor's office smiling and feeling much relieved that his symptoms did not mean that he had the terrifying, dreaded Alzheimer's disease. Another crisis of retirement and aging averted.

Abuse and neglect of older people is more common than most people want to admit. The next chapter examines this sad and horrifying behavior.

10

ELDER ABUSE

Physical and emotional abuse are inexcusable and abhorrent at any age. However, when the victim is a defenseless senior citizen, they are situations of extreme cruelty beyond belief. Although statistics are incomplete, they indicate that over 1 million older people in the United States have been subjected to some type of elder abuse.[1] The Centers for Disease Control and Prevention define elder abuse as "any abuse and neglect of persons, age sixty and older, by a caregiver or other person in a relationship involving an expectation of trust."[2] The Administration of Aging (AOA) adds that it refers "to any knowing, intentional, or negligent act by a caregiver or any other person that causes harm or serious risk of harm to a vulnerable adult."[3] The State of California, Office of the Attorney General calls it "one of the most disturbing and rapidly growing areas of crime in the new millennium."[4]

TYPES OF ELDER ABUSE

Elder abuse comes in many forms. They include at least seven inappropriate and potentially harmful behaviors:

1. *Physical abuse*: The purposeful infliction of pain or injury by scratching, slapping, bruising, hitting, restraining (including physical or chemical restraint or inappropriate use of psychotropic

medication), burning, or biting. This type would also include threatening a senior citizen with a knife, gun, or other objects.

2. *Sexual abuse*: This includes any sexual contact which is against the persons will, including intentional touching of the genitalia, groin, breast, mouth, anus, inner thigh, or buttocks. Rape or other sexual acts can occur. Sexual abuse can also involve forcing the elderly to look at pornographic material.

3. *Psychological or emotional abuse*: Threatening nonverbal or verbal acts that cause mental pain through humiliation, threats, intimidation, isolation, or fear is a form of abuse. It can also include controlling behavior that prohibits the individual's access to amenities such as telephone or transportation as well as minimizing a person's needs or damaging or destroying property.

4. *Neglect*: Failure of a caregiver to provide food, shelter, health-related services, or protection from harm. It can also include failure to provide personal hygiene or clothing.

5. *Abandonment*: The desertion of a vulnerable senior citizen by a caregiver or someone who has taken responsibility for their care.

6. *Self-neglect*: Behavior by an older person that threatens or compromises his or her health or safety. Both elder abuse and self-neglect can diminish physical and mental health, decrease your quality of life, and threaten longevity.

7. *Financial or material exploitation*: The improper use of an older person's resources (funds, property, or other assets), without their consent, for someone else's benefit. It also includes changing a person's will or the improper use of guardianship or power of attorney.

WARNING SIGNS OF ELDER ABUSE

Many suffer in silence. Often they are unable to, or may be too afraid to, share their problems out of fear or poor communication ability. Therefore, it is important to learn the warning signs and symptoms of elder abuse. Elder abuse can occur in any setting, in the assisted living facility, the long-term care facility, domiciliary care home, nursing home or even the older person's family home. The first clue that there may be a problem would be changes in the senior's personality or behavior. Warning signs include: bruises or broken bones; malnourishment or dehydration; bedsores and unattended medical needs; excessive weight loss; scratches, lacerations, or pinch marks; they are unkempt, smelly, or dirty; their clothing or undergarment are torn or bloody; strained or tense relationships; isolation; caregiver will not allow you to see the person without he or she being present; the older person talks about signing over their home to a relative. These warning signs are not proof of abuse but certainly should alert you to keep a watchful eye and investigate the situation further.

RISK FACTORS FOR ELDER ABUSE: PSYCHOLOGICAL PROFILES

Marcie had been a beautiful blond haired, blue eyed, baby when Erma and Sid adopted her. She was two months of age. They were forty. During her childhood, they were a happy little family unit. I still remember her, at age nine, resplendent in a gold satin dress with a bell skirt, throwing white rose petals out of a small white basket with bows at the top, as she walked down the aisle, when she served as a flower girl at a relative's wedding. In adolescence, everything started to go wrong. She became resentful that she was adopted, her school grades plummeted, and she started running wild. At age sixteen, she began abusing heroin. She soon was addicted and stealing to maintain her habit. Erma and Sid tried everything from rehabilitation to tough love. Nothing worked. When Marcie was thirty years old, they decided to sell their house, in New Jersey and move to Albuquerque, New Mexico, hoping that a change of venue would help the situation.

In 1996, my wife and I visited them in their new apartment. We were shocked at what we saw. The atmosphere was tense. The rooms contained minimal furniture. The kitchen cabinets were empty and the refrigerator was almost bare. Erma and Sid were stick thin and malnourished. They both had pressure marks on their arms. Sid told us that at age seventy-three, he still was working part time, doing piece work at a local factory. Marcie was acting peculiar and kept asking us to come out into the back alley to see something behind the apartment. We had a sense that she wanted to rob us. We suspected that she had sold most of her parent's belongings and was controlling their lives through intimidation. We took Sid and Erma out to lunch. They were famished and acted as if they had not eaten in some time. We bought them some groceries and dropped them back at their apartment with much sadness in our hearts at what we had seen. On the way out of town, we called protective services. Erma and Sid are both deceased now. I often wonder what happened to Marcie.

Taking care of an older person can be stressful. Many factors can come together to increase the layperson caregiver's, and even the professional health care worker's, frustration level that can push them over the line into the land of abuse. There are several theories to try to explain this phenomenon. First are issues that involve the caregiver. Risk factors for elder abuse increase drastically when adult children are living with the senior citizen. This is particularly true if the abuser is dependent on the victim for housing, financial assistance, or other form of support. It is often true that these abusers need funding due to personal problems, inability to maintain employment due to dysfunctional personality characteristics, alcohol or drug abuse, or mental illness.[5] Some believe that violence and abuse are learned problem-solving behaviors transmitted from one generation to the next. If you were abused, you are more apt to be an abuser.

Children taking care of their older parents, who have not resolved old issues and do not realize that their parent is not the same person that they were thirty years ago, may have difficulty dealing with the older person standing before them. Old baggage may get in the way of being able to take care of a parent effectively. Unrealistic expectations of the parents and themselves may also get in the way of success in the caregiver role. Taking care of mom or dad may cause you to face your own mortality. You may experience sorrow and loss as you see these strong figures of your childhood becoming more needy and vulnerable. Additional risk factors among lay caregivers include: "Inability to cope with stress (lack of resilience); lack of support from other potential caregivers; the caregiver's perception that taking care of the elder is burdensome and without psychological reward."[6]

Second are the issues that involve the personal characteristics of the parent or patient. As people age, their personality traits harden. A person who tended to be pessimistic and irritable may become more so. A content, pleasant person will usually continue to behave in that fashion. Aging is not always a pleasant process. As a body ages, aches and pains become part of everyday life. Chronic illness for some can add new limitations and discomfort. Anxieties and fears can add to the turmoil. Losses can cause feelings of grief and depression. Other facts that increase the risk for abuse include: "The intensity of an elderly person's illness or dementia; social isolation; the elder's role, at an earlier time, as an abusive parent or spouse; a history of domestic violence in the home; the elder's own tendency toward verbal or physical aggression."[7]

Even professional caregivers in independent living facilities, assisted living facilities, and nursing homes can experience stress levels that can lead to elder abuse, if they lack training, have too many responsibilities, work under poor conditions, or are unsuited by personality. Certified nursing assistants (CNAs), who provide care-taking services in an older person's own home, often have limited education or training and will require supervision. Remember to check their references carefully. Older people can be cranky, unhappy, irritable, and demanding. However, they can also be grateful for your attention and kindness. They can share the story of their lives and offer much unconditional love and positive attention. Life is short. Try to keep things in perspective. Ask for help if you cannot do it all yourself. Be kind to one another.

PREVENTION

There are three things that you can do to prevent elder abuse. You can listen to seniors and their caregivers. You can intervene when you suspect elder abuse. You can educate others about how to recognize and report elder abuse.[8]

If you are taking care of an older person it is also helpful to avoid stress and burnout. The following are some of the things that you can do to combat caregiver burnout and help prevent yourself from becoming abusive:

1. *Do it voluntarily*: Take on the role of caregiver because you want to and not because you feel you have to out of obligation, guilt, or even love. Doing so will give you a greater sense of control, prevent you from feeling trapped and help you be a caregiver in a way that best fits your own situation. You are allowed to write your own job description.

2. *Have realistic expectations*: Don't try to be a super caregiver. Please remember that there is no one "right way" to provide care for an elderly parent, relative, or friend. There are no magic solutions. Try for a balance between the ideal and reality. You can provide for the needs of your aging parents but cannot solve all of their problems or make them young again. You are not responsible for their happiness. You do not always have to do something. Sometimes just listening is enough. Have reasonable expectations about your behavior. Don't expect yourself to always be cheerful. Feeling irritable is often part of the caregiver persona.

3. *Resolve old feelings*: To work with the elderly, you have to be free of old baggage. You have to have resolved your feelings about them as well as about growing older yourself. If you still feel that old people should be obeyed and feared, then you will have difficulty. You will also be ineffective if you are threatened by old age or over identify with their feelings of loneliness, depression, or fearfulness. The older person in front of you may not be the same as the parents you remember. You may be frustrated if you expect to start where you left off many years ago. They may no longer have the capacity to resolve old issues or interact in the way you expect. You may have to get to know a very different person.

4. *Ask for help*: It is not uncommon for one family member to take primary care of a parent. Sometimes other family members do not volunteer because they know that you will do it. Ask your brothers and sisters for help with chores and in providing care. Ask them to share in the cost of caring for your parent. Try to be assertive rather than aggressive and demanding. Make use of support systems. Neighbors, friends, and other parties in the community can be called on to help. This will allow you to take a break, even if only for a couple of hours. Homemaker services, transportation resources, and meal delivery services are available. Counselors, social services, and support groups can offer advice, information, and assistance. Find an adult day care center. Seek a support group or counseling if you are experiencing the signs or symptoms of mental health problems. Call an elder abuse hotline.

5. *Be good to yourself*: Don't neglect the quality of your life. Your emotional and physical health is also important. Stay healthy and

get medical care for yourself when necessary. Don't isolate your-self. Take time for yourself. Make use of as many techniques as you can to relax and rest. Exercise to work off aggressive energy. Leave time for relaxation between work and home. Lighten the situation with laughter. You may need some privacy and time for yourself. A long weekend away or other time off can do wonders. Some nursing homes will allow respite care where they take care of your relative for a short period of time so that you can go on vacation.

6. *Don't neglect the others in your household*: This includes your spouse and any children living at home. No matter how hard you try the emotional equilibrium in your family relationships will change once you become a caregiver. This can lead to conflicts and misunderstandings. Being a caregiver can also affect the bal-ance of your marriage as new responsibilities leave you less time to interact with your spouse. Schedule time to be together. Fa-tigue can start to erode your sexual desire. Frustration and irrita-bility can land on those you love most. You will have to continue to work on these important relationships. Don't expect your spouse to feel exactly the same way as you do. Good communica-tion will help and can also increase the emotional bond between you.

7. *Communicate openly*: Good communication between all family members in the household is one of the most important aspects of coping successfully with caring for an elderly person, particu-larly if they are in your house. A family meeting can be helpful in resolving problems and making plans. The key to god communi-cation is nonjudgmental, active listening where you accept each other's feelings. Keep communication open and honest with your parents also. Tell them how you feel and include them in any decision-making process.

8. *Try not to feel guilty*: Caregivers are already carrying a heavy burden. They do not need to be further weighed down with guilt. Don't feel guilty about your negative feelings. Resentment, angry feelings, and even an occasional death wish do not mean that you are a bad person or hate your parent. Such thoughts only mean that you are under stress. Sometimes you may promise or want to do more than is possible. This is human. You may feel that you

are in a no-win situation torn between your life and the life of your parent. Don't feel guilty about taking care of your own needs. This is not being selfish. It is self-preservation.

Mary was taking care of her mother in her home in her last stages of life. It was a difficult and demanding situation. Her mother was demented, incontinent of urine and feces, was diabetic, and was extremely aggressive and irritable. Her care was beyond Mary's ability as a layperson; however, she felt that she wanted to do it—had to do it. She was constantly frustrated and could not understand why her mother could not be more cooperative. Even now, ten years after her mother's death, she felt guilty about her feelings of anger and frustration and felt that he should have done a better job. This information came up in her therapy with me. I explained that she was being too hard on herself and that she had a right to have asked for help and moved her mother to a nursing home. I also explained that although a person wants to stay in their own home and die there, if their care requires more than your ability can provide, than it is time for professional help and perhaps placement in a facility. She wondered out loud why no one had ever told her this before. I had her read the book, *The 36-Hour Day*, by Nancy L. Mace and Peter V. Rabins.[9] It helped her put her mother's care situation in perspective and relieved some of her guilt.

9. *Plan ahead*: Constructive worry is helpful. Plan what to do if things go wrong. Investigate nursing homes or other institutional placements before a crisis occurs. You can always say no when your name comes up on the waiting list. Don't avoid discussing such issues as health insurance, finances, wills, burial arrangements, and views on life support or living wills.[10]

WHAT CAN YOU DO IF YOU SUSPECT ABUSE?

If you suspect that an older person is being abused, emotionally or physically, tell someone. If in doubt, err on the side of caution. The reporting person is protected from both criminal and civil liability. The laws governing elder abuse vary from state to state. On the federal level, two laws have been passed to deal with this problem. The federal Older Americans Act (OAA) was passed in 1965. The Vulnerable Elder Rights

Protection Program came into being in 1992.[11] The National Center on Elder Abuse is an organization formed to prevent abuse against senior citizens. Physicians and medical professionals, clergy, all employees of health care facilities, and any individuals who assume responsibility for the care of an older person are legally mandated to report known or suspected abuse.

Agencies to call to report abuse vary by state. In California, if the incident occurred in a long-term care facility, contact the local long-term care ombudsman, the local law enforcement agency, or the Bureau of Medi-Cal Fraud and Elder Abuse. If it occurred anywhere other than in a facility, report it to the local county Adult Protective Services agency or to the local law enforcement agency.

In 1988, Pennsylvania passed the Older Adults Protective Services Act.[12] The Pennsylvania Department of Aging's Bureau for Advocacy, Protection and Education, Consumer Protection Division is responsible for services that protect older Pennsylvanians against fraud, abuse, neglect, exploitation, and abandonment through this act. The Office of the Attorney General is authorized to take formal legal action against persons and organizations who engage in unfair and deceptive conduct in the advertisement or sale of goods or services within the Commonwealth of Pennsylvania. Pennsylvania also has a statewide elder abuse hotline.[13]

Emotional problems and challenges can occur throughout the life cycle. The next part of this book will look at mental health in the final phase of life.

III

Mental Health in the Final Phase of Life

11

PSYCHOLOGICAL CAREGIVER CHALLENGES

To the young, parents seem invincible and omnipotent, strong and capable, able to solve all problems and make everything better. Adolescence and young adulthood quickly pop the bubble of this fantasy. In middle age, children start to see their parents as real people with good and bad points. Hopefully, children realize that their parents love them and did the best that they could. Then a strange thing happens. Children suddenly realize that their parents are getting older and have become very different people.

It is not easy watching your parents' age. It is difficult seeing them go downhill mentally and physically. It is hard seeing them deal with disability or chronic illness. It is frightening to see them in a hospital bed. It is sad to visit them in a long-term care facility or nursing home. It is alarming to see them in a wheelchair or using a cane to walk. It is beyond belief to watch them die. These repositories of unconditional love, which were always there "just in case" you needed them for support, are gone and you are floating free without a safety net in the atmosphere of life.

In time, during this last stage of their life, the emotional and physical dependence of your aging parents, spouse, or partner will increase. You may face enormous pressures as you become their major support system and do your best to care for them. You will gradually experience a subtle shift in the balance of power which may leave you feeling trapped, frustrated, and fatigued. This difficult situation may cause you to be moody and irritable. It may leave you overwhelmed, unable to cope, feeling anxious, worried, angry and depressed, or guilty.

Caregivers often sacrifice their own needs in taking care of the other person. If they do not get help, the overall quality of the care that they are trying to give will erode. Let us look at the various emotions that you may feel as a caregiver of the elderly and see what you can do to help yourself and subsequently your older charge.

OVERWHELMED, WORRIED, AND ANXIOUS

Problem

Since my mother had a heart attack, I'm always nervous. She is seventy-five years old. Every time that the phone rings, I jump. Mom lives by herself. I worry that she is not eating or taking her medication properly. I am worried that someone will call to tell me that she fell or is being rushed to the hospital by ambulance. I envision her lying on the kitchen floor, dying, and there is no one there to help her.

Solution

There is no perfect resolution to this problem, particularly if you have generalized anxiety disorder, which is a lifelong condition. However, try to put things in perspective and try not to catastrophize. Ask yourself, "What is the worst thing that can happen?" The unknown is often harder to handle than the reality of the situation. Ask yourself why you are so worried. Perhaps you are afraid of what the neighbors will think and that they will blame you for what happens to mom. For some, individual, group, or family counseling may be helpful. Investigate services offered by your spiritual community. Your church or synagogue may be able to offer emotional support, spiritual guidance, and volunteer assistance. Look into other community resources. There are agencies that will deliver meals to your house. Once the fog of worry has cleared, perhaps you will want to make some real changes. Maybe an emergency call button that she can wear around her neck or on her wrist that attaches to a monitor via the telephone, a seven-day pill box, or having a neighbor look in on mom daily would help relieve your concerns. Perhaps you need to visit her more often. Maybe it is time to discuss a possible move to an assisted living facility.

PHYSICALLY TIRED AND EMOTIONALLY DRAINED

Problem

Since caring for Dad, who has dementia at age eighty-two, I am always fatigued and worn out emotionally and physically. He is often up all night and I feel that I have to be up with him to watch him to be sure that he is safe and doesn't run out of the house. All he does is sit on the couch and stare until the morning. I feel so responsible for everything that happens to him. The physical demands of helping him with his personal hygiene and toileting wear me out. I am constantly running, trying to take care of my family and Dad. I am exhausted. When he is in a more lucid period, he puts me down and criticizes everything that I do. He did the same thing when I was a kid. I'm working so hard, and yet I feel so unappreciated.

Solution

It sounds as if you need some rest and need to start asking for help. In a family, there is usually one person who is the designated caregiver. You probably do a great job and they are happy to pass you the baton. However, it is all right if you ask your brothers and sisters to help out or do occasional chores or take on certain responsibilities. If you are concerned about your dad wandering at night, put a double lock on the front door to prevent him running out into the street. Schedule time to be with the other members of your household. Good communication will help and can also increase the emotional bond between you. Have reasonable expectations. Know your limits and do not compromise them out of love or guilt.

Schedule some time off for yourself for rest and relaxation. Take care of yourself and try not to neglect the quality of your life. Be sure to take breaks and try to get sleep, exercise, and pay attention to your own nutrition. Learn to delegate and ask for help. Taking care of an elderly adult takes place in the context of a long, complex relationship history.

Putting some physical distance between you and your charge, occasionally, may allow you time to reconstitute and see things clearer. Remember, you are now Mrs. Jones, an adult and not Marylou, a dependent child.

IMPATIENT AND IRRITABLE

Problem

Since mom broke her hip a year ago, when she was seventy-eight, and has been staying with us, I feel constantly under strain. I am irritable and moody. I argue more with my wife, kids, and co-workers. I am drinking more after work and find that I cannot fall asleep without taking a pill. I have lost weight and have multiple aches and pains. Everyone asks me what is wrong. I just answer, "Nothing, nothing. Everything is fine. Leave me alone. I'm just doing what I have to do." Can you believe it; my family is frustrated with me? They tell me to just "man up" and stop complaining about my physical symptoms.

Solution

The first key to caregiver success is to do it voluntarily. Do not take on this job out of obligation, guilt, or even love. You may want to look at your motivations for taking on this role. Good communication skills may help your situation. In doing therapy, I often made use of the ideas of transactional analysis, a school of psychotherapy developed by Eric Berne.[1] Berne felt that we all have a set of feelings, thoughts, and behavior patterns related to a child, adult, and parent ego state. We communicate in these states at various times in relationships and can elicit child, adult, or parental responses from others. Berne talks about how we relate to people in various "transactions," including that of parent to child and more effectively as adult to adult. I hope that you will start communicating adult to adult. Irritability can merge into feelings of anger and depression.

ANGRY AND DEPRESSED

Problem

Some people have a difficult time using the word anger to express their negative feelings. They can say that they are upset, annoyed, or frustrated, but they seem to feel that saying the words "I am angry" is taboo. Typical issues dealt with in psychoanalysis involve sexual (love) and aggressive (anger) impulses. Emotional maturity can be defined as the ability to accept someone's anger and love as well as being able to tell someone that you love them or are angry at them. They unconsciously may try to prevent these dangerous emotions from coming to the surface by producing and experiencing feelings of anxiety and guilt. If the aggressive feelings are held inside too long, they can morph into feelings of sadness and even clinical depression. They can express themselves physically through the bowel and precipitate irritable bowel syndrome. These people may compensate by being nice, good, and perfect, and always doing everything precisely. It is understandable that a caregiver of an elder person may feel frustrated and angry at times. They may resent having to be a caregiver and feel trapped. They may be angry with other family members for not lending a hand and angry with the older person for not being more cooperative, and instead being irritable and stubborn.

Solution

Allowing these dangerous feelings to come to the surface and be expressed in the safe environment of therapy can be a helpful first step. Psychiatrists say that anger is a normal feeling. You can be angry at a person's behavior and still love them. These two emotions are not incompatible. In a child's unconscious, the word angry is equivalent to wishing someone dead. Sometimes, people carry this false idea into adulthood where they are concerned that if they displease the parent figure, the person will go away and not be there to support them. It is helpful to explain to the caregiver that their charge's behaviors are symptoms of their dementia or other illness. They are not acting up to purposely defy you. Psychiatrists suggest positive ways that the caregiver can work off their frustration and blow off steam. These include such things as exercise, including swimming and walking, asking for help, and taking a break by putting the patient into respite care and taking a weekend mini-vacation with their spouse.

ISOLATED AND FINDING NO TIME TO TAKE CARE OF YOUR NEEDS

Focusing only on someone else's needs can leave you feeling isolated and empty. Feelings of inadequacy coupled with strong dependency needs may cause the caregiver to overcompensate, do more than they have to, and fail to ask for help. Balance is the magic word that best describes how to lead a content and fulfilled life. A work-life balance is important. Ignoring your own needs for rest, substance, and companionship will not help you do a better job. If anything, it will diminish your success. To do a good job as a caregiver, it is important to pay attention to the quality of your life and take time for yourself. This is not selfishness. It is self-preservation. Even strong people need support at times. Asking for help does not make you weak. The following vignette illustrating a period of time in Arlene's life, will illustrate some of these points.

Problem

Arlene's father entered a nursing home nine months ago at the age of eighty-four. He had mild memory loss, was not motived to be active, and was not reliable in taking his medications on his own. He had a heart condition and a tendency to lose his balance and fall.

Arlene was a people pleaser. In spite of holding a full-time job, and having a husband and teenage son, she was at the facility at least three times a week. She took home her father's laundry, and made sure that he got to his many doctor appointments and had his blood tests. She checked that he ate and pushed him out of bed to socialize with the other residents. She constantly felt pressured by the limited amount of time that she had. In spite of having a brother and a sister, she was the designated caregiver. She demanded a high level of performance from herself, which left her with no time to relax, unwind, or take care of her own needs. She felt alone and isolated and was starting to feel depressed. Under her aggressive, controlling facade was a scared little girl with low self-esteem.

Solution

In therapy, she revealed that her mother was a workaholic, who was seldom home, was hard to please, and often made her feel guilty. Arlene felt that if she could do things more perfectly, she could gain her mother's love. She said that her father, although seldom home, was calm, not strict, and took good care of the rest of her family. He made her feel safe and was always there for his children. Months later, she started to realize that some of her caregiving behavior with her father was due to her need to keep him alive and thus maintain her protector. Arlene had grown up trying to please people so that they wouldn't leave her. That way people would be there to protect her so that she wouldn't feel bad or guilty. Gradually, she was able to ask her siblings to help out, feel better about herself and be more proactive about asking her husband to spend time with her and fulfill her needs. She gave herself permission to relax, spent more time with her friends, and started taking care of herself.

FEELING GUILTY

Problem

Dad has diabetes and emphysema. No matter how much I talk to him about maintaining his diet, he continues eating whatever he wants. He loves sweets. He does not always take his medication. He seems self-destructive. I feel guilty. I should be able to do more for him. Perhaps, if I tried harder he would be more compliant with his diet and medication. I feel badly that sometimes he makes me so angry that I wish he would die already. I promised that I would visit him twice a week. Sometimes, I am only able to get there once a week. I have responsibilities with my children and husband. I have errands to run, shopping to do, laundry to finish, and dinners to cook. I have thought about paying someone to stay with him a few hours a day. The person could put out his pills and monitor his diet. However, I feel guilty about doing this, and wonder if they will give him the right kind of help. At this time of my life, I thought that I would have a little more time for myself and my own needs. Then Dad began to age and become even more difficult to care for.

Solution

Guilt is a powerful emotion. It can make you feel badly and give you a negative outlook. Give yourself credit for your concern and caring and what you are doing for your father. Promising or wanting to do more than is possible is just being human. Hiring someone to be with your dad a few hours a day may be helpful and relieve your time pressures. It is a viable option that needs to be considered. You may feel that you are in a no-win situation, torn between your life and the life of your parent. Do not feel guilty about taking care of your own needs and your family's needs. Do not feel guilty about your feelings of resentment, anger, and even an occasional death wish. They do not mean that you are a bad person or hate your parent. You seem to be a good person, who cares about her father and is trying to be helpful. You are doing more than you think. Although he doesn't seem to be following your advice, I am sure that he knows that you care about him and love him. That counts for a lot.

FINANCIALLY FRUSTRATED AND DRAINED

Problem

My wife developed breast cancer several months ago when she was sixty-six. Initially we were both in shock and mired in disbelief. We were sure that the doctor had made a mistake. We were using denial to help us cope with this frightening news. A second opinion confirmed the diagnosis. Subsequently, she had a mastectomy. At surgery, they found that the cancer had spread to her lymph nodes. The doctor gave her radiation and started her on chemotherapy. It was hard, but we got through it. We are trying to take a problem-solving approach. We have each other and try to be supportive. Some days, I feel depressed and know that it is time to go out for my walk. However, the main issue now is our finances. We both worked. I retired six months ago at sixty-eight. She had retired at sixty-two. We have some money put away, but we are on a fixed income. Medications are expensive. All the trips to the doctor and the hospital have increased our transportation expenses. We order in food more, too, which has increased our food expenses. We had to hire cleaning help. We had a retirement financial plan. I worry what will happen to it now and how we will get by in the future.

Solution

Providing care for a person with a chronic illness can be costly. It is particularly troublesome if you are on a fixed income. It sounds like your fear is based on the unknown. You sound angry that you both have been placed in this situation. Your negative feelings are getting in the way of your developing acceptance and finding new practical solutions. As you said, you had a plan. It is now time to sit down and redo it in light of your new situation. Professional help, in the form of your accountant, bank, or financial advisor may be helpful. Try not to take money out of your Sep-IRA, 401(k), pension plan, or other retirement funds to pay for daily expenses. When you know the reality of your new financial situation, you may feel less anxious and more in control. Talk to your wife about your concerns. Together, you can decide what items you will have to give up and which you can still afford. Share your expectations and your ideas. Together you can plan your financial future.

THE REWARDS OF CAREGIVING

Taking care of an aging parent or relative is not all bad. It has some positive aspects. In fact, "caregivers report approximately three times more positive than negative emotions related to caregiving. Ninety-six percent report feeling 'loving,' 90 percent report feeling appreciated, and 84 percent report feeling proud."[2] Caregivers may gradually experience closeness with their charge if they take the opportunity to have meaningful discussions, resolve old issues, and express forgiveness and love. Laughter and joy are still possible. Caregiving can be a life-enriching experience and provide spiritual growth. The caregiver may learn new medical and personal care skills, how to deal with people, community resources, legal and financial planning, and time management. They may increase their problem solving and communication skills. All of these abilities can be useful in the future, can help improve their self-esteem, allow them to feel more in control, and engender emotional growth.

As a person ages and nears the end of their life, they will have to deal with various emotional decisions as they face important legal and ethical dilemmas. The next chapter will cover some of these potentially problematic issues.

12

EMOTIONAL DECISIONS AT THE END OF LIFE

As we have seen retirement and aging brings with it many emotional and physical challenges, which can affect our relationships and cause stress, anxiety, and feelings of depression. Just as we think we have it all together and are finally adjusting to our new lifestyle, we find that it is time to make other decisions about the end of life. These decisions involve housing as well as legal and ethical dilemmas that can be emotionally tinged and difficult to embrace, sometimes involving feelings of frustration and guilt. They can include making a will, signing a power of attorney, making a medical living will, and dealing with guardianship. You may consider buying cemetery plots or even prepay burial arrangements. If your spouse or partner becomes ill, you may even be placed in the caregiver role. You may have to learn about independent living facilities, assisted living, and nursing homes. You may be required to deal with the intricacies of palliative care and hospice care.

LIVING ARRANGEMENTS

Housing and living arrangements can present major concerns and complex decisions, sometimes filled with unrealistic expectations. Many people believe that if they work hard and are good parents that they will be taken care of in their old age. It does not always work out that way. The answer to the question "where shall we live" presents major choices that run the gamut from downsizing to a smaller house or a fifty-five and older community or even nursing home placement. It may involve moving to a different state closer to your children or other family members or a different climate near friends.

Some may value continuing to live in their own home or perhaps downsizing to a smaller place. This option maintains independence and familiarity and diminishes the disorientation often predicated by change. Some may need the supportive environment of an independent living facility or assisted living, where they are free to come and go on their own but have the advantage of having their meals prepared for them and being in a community with other older people for companionship. Continuing-care communities, which include independent living, assisted living, and nursing home care in one location, offer the advantage of a step down program that allows movement from on stage to another as the need arises.

My aunt was grateful to be in such a community. When my uncle developed Alzheimer's disease and had to enter a nursing home, she was able to just walk across the driveway from her independent living apartment to visit and help feed him each day. This arrangement allowed her to feel independent, useful, and involved in his care. She liked being able to spend time with her sweetheart of over sixty-five years. Although his memory was poor and he slept a lot, he still smiled when he heard her voice. Some may require round the clock care available in a skilled nursing facility or memory care facility (Alzheimer's care facility).

These are big decisions for families to make. In some cases, children must take charge and make the decision as they see their parents progressing downhill but continuing to deny that they need additional support or professional help. Everyone would like to stay in their own home forever. However, when the problems get bigger than what children can handle, it is time to turn the situation over to the professionals. For many, it brings to the fore the fact that they are in the last stage of their life, how much time has gone by, and makes them acutely aware of their own mortality. Children may also be affected by this decision, as they face their own mortality and also realize that they may not always have their parents to fall back on. Many feel guilty because they feel if they really loved their parent, they would take care of them in their own home. Some will loudly proclaim, "How dare you sell my childhood maze?" Even grandchildren may grieve stating, "We won't be able to go the grandma and grandpa's house anymore."

Decisions will have to be based on your finances, your personality and interests, and the proximity of supportive relatives, friends, and other important people in your life. Deciding where you want to live as you retire and age is an ongoing process due to shifting priorities and needs based on your physical and mental status at the time. There are no easy or perfect solutions. Compromise may be required. It is important to plan ahead. Facilities may not have an opening just when you want it. Do not wait until a crisis to precipitate a search for solutions. To reiterate, it is best to place your name on a waiting list, thus avoiding the stress for placement in an emergency situation.

Each move will require adaptation and change, often taking its emotional toll. Feelings of anxiety, vulnerability, confusion, anger, embarrassment, and shame may surface as you gradually deal with the loss of independence. The names assigned to senior housing options vary geographically. For simplicity here, I have decided to divide them into three possibilities based on the degree of professional help needed for activities of daily living and medical care:

1. Independent living
2. Assisted living
3. Nursing home placement

INDEPENDENT LIVING OR "AGING IN PLACE"

Although many older people voice their desire to die in their own bed, the decision to remain in your own home has to be based on the reality of your physical and emotional status as well as the reality of your available support network. Is your physical health good enough to perform basic functions of daily living, such as cooking, bathing, and getting around safely? How connected are you to your community? Does the community offer services such as food stores, a pharmacy, doctors, and a hospital? Are there any family members who live close by and can check on you?

Your independence can be maintained and companionship guaranteed by downsizing to a fifty-five and older community with a bedroom on the first floor. Another option is to move to an apartment building that caters to the elderly and offers some amenities and opportunities for socialization. Some prefer to move in with a relative if the physical plan and family dynamics allow it. Moving in with one of your children can bring to the fore unresolved conflicts. In-home care, paid for directly or by a long-term care policy, making use of a personal care attendant, or certified nursing assistant (CNA) can help push off an unwanted move.[1]

Moving from your big house can be emotionally trying. Memories. Memories. Memories. Packing your worldly belongings after twenty-five to thirty-five years in the same location can be difficult physically and mentally. Each possession, the size-six white ice skates, the little ball and bat, and the art plate that your son gave you for your twenty-fifth anniversary, has its own set of memories. Each item takes time to wrap as we reminisce. We haggle for the best price. Even this act is emotional charged. The real-estate agent doesn't seem to understand all the sweat and blood that went into this house and why you are insistent that it get a good price. For her it is only a property. For you, it was your home. As you pack, you are also acutely aware of how much less energy that you have than you had years ago when you first moved into this house. You know that it is time to move.

ASSISTED LIVING COMMUNITIES

As your need for help with personal care increases beyond your ability or the ability of your family caregiver, but before you need the round-the-clock medical care or supervision of a nursing home, a move to assisted living may be right for you. Here you can receive help with some of the activities of daily living, such as dressing, eating, and bathing. Most communities offer housekeeping and meals. There will be someone there to remind you to take your medicine. Your social and recreational needs can be taken care of in the community. Religious services are usually available. Boarding homes and domiciliary care are other options in this category. Religious groups often offer senior housing.

NURSING HOME PLACEMENT

If your medical problems become more complex and you require twenty-four-hour medical care and supervision, a skilled nursing home facility would be a good choice. Memory care (Alzheimer's care) facilities also fit in this category. Such accommodations provide more structure and security than is possible in a home setting. Here you can receive nursing, rehabilitative (physical, speech, and occupational therapy), and social services. A physician supervises each resident's care. Specialists can come in to consult. A good nursing home can supply stimulation through exercise therapy, entertainment, and recreation. Residents can potentially make new friends. Volunteers and community resources can augment their programs. Visitors are very important in maintaining the patient's morale and emotional well-being. Therefore, try to choose a home that will facilitate visitation by relatives and friends.

At the other extreme, nursing homes can be ill-smelling warehouses in which the older person is dehumanized, may lose his or her sense of autonomy, and can be at the mercy of overworked, irritable, and intolerant personnel. Some are manned by agency nurses, who may only be working a shift or two and really do not get to know the patients. Choose your facility with care. An ombudsman is available through the state or local office of aging if you experience problems. Flyers are usually posted on their bulletin boards.[2]

In my experience, having done nursing home psychiatric consults for many years, most skilled nursing facilities lean to the left of center and require more staffing per patient. Some are clean and attentive to their charges. Some are noisy, due to agitated and combative patients that require much staff attention. Some patients wander and need constant redirection. Some buildings do smell. It is sad to see a dayroom full of patients in wheelchairs, often half asleep, clustered in semicircles, with one small television playing in the corner. It is hard to pass a room where a resident is calling out in pain or see a patient who constantly maintains that her relatives will soon return her to her own home, when the chart notes clearly show that her home has been sold and that this is a permanent placement. Many sit in their room in the dark. How depressing. The first thing that I would do upon entering a room was to open the blinds and let the sun shine in.

From what I have seen, nursing home residents, like other older people, are responsive to attention and grateful for kindness. I remember well, being called in to see a supposedly agitated woman in her eighties who was suffering from dementia. I was told that she was confused and could not communicate except by being resistant to care and combative. I spent some time in her room just talking to her kindly as if she was able to hold a normal conversation. Two days later when I again visited the home, the nurse said to me, "What did you do to Mrs. Smith? She has been an angel." All that I had done was talk to her as a human being. Even if a patient is confused, I believe that they are able to absorb the affective tone of your voice and thus obtain some emotional sustenance.

Movement to any of the above options can be emotional for another reason. Some elderly people do not see it as a new beginning, but rather view it as the last stop before death—the beginning of the end. Some may verbalize their anger, "I took care of my spouse, parent or in-law and now there is no one to take care of me." Hopefully, you will see these housing changes as a new beginning; a place where you can meet different people and learn new hobbies; a place where you can get the medical care, rehabilitation, and supervision that is needed; a place where your family can feel secure about your safety and not worry that you are alone and in danger of falling or harming yourself accidently by wandering outside.

Even after housing choices have been made and you have adjusted to your new environment, there are still other decisions, involving legal and ethical issues, that you will have to make as a senior citizen that can be very emotional and trying and sometimes confusing. I have included the following to make you aware of the possibilities. For more detailed information and clarification, consult your attorney, physician, or other advisors. These options include:

1. Making a will
2. Signing a power of attorney
3. Choosing a medical healthcare agent
4. Making a living will
5. Do not resuscitate decisions (DNR)
6. Dealing with guardianship

MAKING A WILL

A will is a document that advises how you want all of your worldly assets dispersed. It is often helpful to make a copy for each of your children as well as keeping a copy for your executor. To make a will, a person must be competent or be able to make their own decisions. This means that the person knows, at the moment, without prompting, that they are doing so, the names and their relationship to the people who will receive their property, and the nature and extent of the property.[3] Therefore, it often includes the words, "Being of sound mind."

An attorney can be used to write a will or you can get a template off of the Internet. By making a will before your memory fails, you are disabled, or no longer legally competent, guarantees that your property is distributed the way that you want, rather than as mandated by a court or by state law. It is also helpful to plan ahead and discuss with your spouse, significant other, and children your desires and the location of important papers such as wills, deeds, stock certificates, cemetery lot deeds, and other legal papers.

SIGN A POWER OF ATTORNEY

A limited power of attorney gives a spouse, child, or other person legal authority to manage your affairs and act in your behalf. It can give broad powers to cover all of your property or it may be limited to specific duties such as paying bills or selling real estate property. Any power of attorney documents must be completed while you are still competent and are void if you become mentally incapacitated.

A durable power of attorney authorizes someone else to act on your behalf once you are incapacitated and no longer able to competently make your own decisions. This document may also include a provision that the appointed person be allowed to make major health care decisions as per your living will or to request that no heroic measures be used to postpone death. Every state and the District of Columbia has adopted general durable power of attorney statues.

CHOOSING A MEDICAL HEALTHCARE AGENT

If you become unconscious, confused, or otherwise mentally incapacitated you may want to have someone of your choice designated to make medical decisions for you. If you did not include such a person in your durable power of attorney, you will have an opportunity to appoint such a person in your medical record when you are admitted to the hospital.

MAKING A LIVING WILL

A living will is a written document that specifies the circumstances under which a person will permit the cessation of extraordinary treatment to prolong life, and would allow death in accordance with the natural progression of their disease . . . they may indicate that in the event of a terminal illness . . . no life-sustaining measures [be] used merely to postpone the moment of death. Not every state recognizes the legality of the living will. [4]

Items addressed in a living will include whether a person wants antibiotics, blood products, cardiac compressions, pulmonary support such as a ventilator, dialysis, artificial feedings, or an electoeletroencethalgraph (EEG) to determine brain function in the event of a stroke.

DO NOT RESUSCITATE DECISIONS (DNR)

A DNR or "no code" decision is a request that no extraordinary measures, such as ventilation or emergency cardiopulmonary resuscitation, be initiated if a patient stops breathing or their heart stops. A DNR form allows you to check off the specific modalities that you will or will not allow. If all modalities are to be avoided, only passive comfort medical care would be allowed. Advanced directives, such as a durable power of attorney or a living will need to be taken into account if they exist.

GUARDIANSHIP

Guardianship is a legal procedure where a judge decides, based on medical reports or expert testimony, if a person is legally competent. If the judge rules that the person is not competent, the judge may then appoint a legal guardian to act for the person in both financial matters and medical decisions.

A *guardianship of property* petition (conservatorship) is filed by a lawyer in court when a person is unable to manage their affairs, and does not have or is unwilling to sign a power of attorney. After a hearing, a judge decides whether the person is legally competent and may appoint a legal guardianship to act for the person in financial matters only. The guardian must file financial reports periodically with the court. This procedure is helpful when a couple owns a home jointly and the well spouse wishes to sell the house.

The same procedure is followed to obtain a *guardianship of the person* to have someone make medical decisions for an individual, such as ordering needed medical care or sending the person to the hospital.

PALLIATIVE AND HOSPICE CARE

The goal of palliative care is to improve the quality of life for the patient and their family who are dealing with problems associated with life limiting illnesses. It provides them with relief of symptoms, pain, and the stress of life limiting illness. It may also include day-to-day care, medications, and bereavement counseling. It can be provided along with curative treatments. . . . The goal of end of life care is to live a full life in spite of the length of the journey of one's life. The holistic approach of osteopathic medicine and its manipulative skills can be helpful here in reducing pain, optimizing body dysfunction, and improving the patient's quality of life.[5]

Hospice care, based on a holistic vision of life, dates back to the eleventh century, when religious orders in Europe opened special homes for the dying that focused on offering spiritual comfort to the terminally ill. In 1967, British nurse-turned-physician, Dame Cicely Saunders founded the first modern hospice in a London suburb. In 1974, the first American hospice was established in Bradford, Connecticut. Hospice provides spiritual, emotional, and palliative care to the dying and spiritual and emotional care to the bereaved family. Hospice helps the family say a meaningful goodbye to a loved one. In addition to spiritual and professional support for the patient and their family, insurance companies may cover expenses for hospice, such as oxygen equipment and therapy that might not be covered elsewhere.[6]

DEATH AND THE FINAL GOODBYE

Death is an abstract idea that is almost beyond comprehension. We all carry the illusion of immortality and usually try consciously not to think about death. Many of my patients are concerned about death, worry about it, avoid talking about it or use euphemisms or synonyms to describe it. I usually tell them, "Since we really do not know what death is, perhaps you are really just worried about the unknown." Admitting that death is part of our life cycle is a good way to begin the dialogue. According to T. A. Gonda, how people deal with dying is "shaped by previous experiences with death, as well as by cultural attitudes and beliefs. In essence, one tends to die as one has lived."[7] Similarly, Dr. Alice Zal says, "Just like there is an art of living, there is an art of dying. . . . Play death with dignity to a compassionate audience."[8]

The next section of this book will deal with psychiatric treatment options, including therapy and medication, that may be helpful for many of the emotional and mental health conditions noted previously.

IV

Psychiatric Treatment Options

13

CAN A PSYCHIATRIST HELP?

People are often afraid to come for evaluation, treatment, or therapy with a psychiatrist. They feel that psychiatrists can read their minds. They feel that they will be judged and put down. They feel that they will be told that they are bad, wrong, abnormal, or crazy. They feel that they will be shuttled off to a mental hospital. Many think that they will lose their jobs or the respect of their friends and family members if it is known that they are seeking psychiatric help. They feel that psychiatrists will discover some dark secret about which they feel guilty. A psychiatrist is not your parent, your rabbi or priest, or a court of law. You are not on trial in a psychiatrist's office. They cannot read your mind; however, if you let them, they can help in various ways. A psychiatrist is a physician who is a medical specialist, who diagnoses and treats people suffering from mental disorders. Nothing unusual or strange happens in psychotherapy: Psychiatrists and patients will simply talk to one another.

First, a psychiatrist will perform a psychiatric evaluation. This will include a medical and mental health history, including substance abuse. Knowledge of the patient's physical problems and current medications allows for recommendations for appropriate treatment, helps with the understanding of overlapping syndromes, and creates an opportunity to discuss physical disorders that can produce emotional symptoms. These medical facts will also guide medication choices and help psychiatrists better understand the side-effect profiles of medications. A family history of mental illness may be helpful in diagnosis of mental health issues that have a genetic propensity. Certain medications cannot be used if there is a history of drug or alcohol abuse or dependency. Senior citizens realize more than ever that there is a powerful mind-body connection through which emotional, mental, social, spiritual, and behavioral factors can directly affect health. The following are some of the other things that a psychiatrist can do.

1. *Make a diagnosis*: Initially, a psychiatrist must rule out other emotional disorders (this is called a differential diagnosis) and rule in other overlapping or "co-morbid" conditions. For instance, patients with a normal reaction to stress, major depression, personality disorders, or who are withdrawing from drugs can all come in the door complaining of anxiety. Generalized anxiety disorder patients may also suffer from other anxiety disorders such as obsessive compulsive disorder (OCD), social phobia, and panic disorder. Sometimes more than one disorder will have to be addressed in treatment. Being given a specific diagnosis can provide reassurance and even relief from anxiety to some patients. "You mean all I have is panic disorder? I thought that I was going crazy."

Harold's sigh of relief when he left his physician's office and had been told that he did not have Alzheimer's disease but rather was experiencing normal average "senior moments," common to those over age sixty-five, is an example of this phenomenon.

2. *Check for health issues that can cause psychological symptoms*: A psychiatrist initially needs to decide if your complaints are emotional or physical, or both. For instance, substance abuse, hyperthyroidism, hypertension, and cardiac arrhythmias can all cause anxiety symptoms. To differentiate this, psychiatrists need to know your health history, check all of your medications, question you about drug use or abuse, and look at your basic blood work. I usually ask patients to bring a complete blood count (CBC) and differential, comprehensive metabolic panel and thyroid profile at the initial evaluation. Psychiatrists often talk to family physicians or at times a specialist that patients have seen. Remember, a psychiatrist went to medical school prior to completing a three-year residency or fellowship in psychiatry and has the training to make a differential diagnosis and comment on health issues. Your psychiatrist may refer you back to your primary-care physician to rule out various possible physical causes of your emotional symptoms, if they suspect they are an issue affecting your mental health.

3. *Foster education, reassurance, and acceptance*: All three of these are important parts of the initial phase of therapy. Like Harold, you may have many fears and fantasies about what is wrong with you and what your symptoms mean. A clear understanding of your true diagnosis, the meaning of your symptoms, and an explanation of where they come from, hopefully will mitigate most of your fears that you have a serious physical illness, a brain tumor, or are going crazy or losing control. Once you understand the true nature of your mental health problem, you can be reassured that your symptoms are not a sign of weakness, childishness, or failure. Your mental health problem is not anyone's fault. You do not have to feel guilty or punish yourself. Starting to gain acceptance is also part of this initial process. You may find that your mental problem is a biological illness, that you have a genetic vulnerability which has been inherited. For many, individual psychotherapy can offer the reassurance that can give them a new perspective, change negative thought patterns, and quell apprehensions.

4. *Allow ventilation*: Everyone needs someone to listen to them at times. John Gray made a good point in his book, *Men Are from Mars, Women Are from Venus*,[1] about how men and women deal with stress differently. He says that men become quiet, go into their cave to mull it over and problem solve. Women on the other hand seek out someone that they can trust and talk in great detail about their problem. This premise is true; however, it is not just women who can benefit by talking about their problems. Because men tend to live emotionally isolated lives, it may take them a little longer to feel comfortable enough to share, but they also will feel better if they discuss their problems in a safe and accepting environment, such as the psychiatric consultation room.

Pent up feelings can influence your behavior, your attitude, and color your perspective. If held in, feelings will find another outlet to explode and have negative consequences, including physical illness. Negative feelings such as grudges and bitterness can crowd out positive feelings. This is particularly true of anger, guilt, resentment, and disappointment. They will not go away unless you release them. To truly grow and move forward, you have to stop suppressing emotions, get rid of old baggage, and make room for the new emotions. Talking to a psychiatrist offers a safe and optimal opportunity to do this. If one finds it difficult to discuss your feelings, perhaps writing them down in a diary or letter will help.

5. *Help you gain perspective*: A psychiatrist will encourage you to check out your assumptions. In life as in art and photography, perspective changes everything. Marcel Proust said, "The real voyage of discovery consists not in seeking new lands but in seeing with new eyes."[2] Psychiatrists may pose questions to you such as "what is the worst thing that could happen?" to reduce catastrophizing and get a clearer understanding of the reality of the situation. Through therapy, you may start to understand that people are not all good or bad. Things are not black and white; shades of gray need to become your favorite color. Life is full of trials and tribulations but it can also be fulfilling and good. You cannot choose your parents. Probably, they meant well and did the best that they could. Hopefully you are able to pick friends who are mostly to your liking. When a patient complains that someone at work or socially doesn't like them, I will often respond, "Do you like everyone? Therefore, why is it so important that everyone likes you?" I can sometimes see the light bulb go off in their eyes as they ponder this statement. Sometimes even late in life, as we meet new people in a new living situation or other venue, we have to be reminded of these essential truths.

6. *Facilitate dealing with feelings*: Sometimes patients feel emotions such as guilt, anger, or sadness, but do not know what they are or understand them. They avoid their feelings of discomfort by focusing on work or other distractions. In the words of one of my patients, "If I can identify what it is (that I am feeling), it sometimes takes the teeth out of it." Being able to identify and label your feelings will help you accept them, cope with them, and decide how you want to overcome them. All feelings are normal. However, how you deal with them defines you. There is a difference between sharing your feelings, for instance, to tell someone that you are angry about something that they did, and yelling at someone or calling them names. In therapy, psychiatrists will encourage you to let go of old anger, resentment, and inappropriate guilt. These feelings are self-defeating and self-destructive.

7. *Provide insight*: In psychoanalysis, insight is the subjective experiential knowledge of previously unconscious pathologic content and conflict. It can be energy-releasing.[3] In more common terms, it is the intellectual understanding of thoughts, feelings, and behavior. Perhaps,

when you were eleven years old, you were small and skinny. People bullied you and beat you up. You felt helpless and inadequate. Certain situations in life, such as dealing with retirement and the problems of aging, can cause you to feel small and bullied again, and default to old ineffective behaviors. Understand that momentary feelings of inadequacy are not indications that you are truly weak. You have more resources available to you than you did as a child and can perhaps handle your feelings differently than you did as a child. If you did not like it that your parents yelled at you, why are you yelling at your spouse? Perhaps you can work on reversing your behavior. If you are angry at your neighbor, who reminds you of your father and how he treated you, your psychiatrist may ask you to make a list of how your neighbor is different than your father. Some of his behaviors are probably the same as your difficult parent, but many will be different. This will help you differentiate the two people. Then you can look your neighbor in the eye and say to yourself, "you are not my father." Hopefully the whole dynamic will change between you.

8. *Give you some of what you need or are missing emotionally*: The doctor-patient relationship is a strong therapeutic tool. Once rapport and trust have been established, it can truly be a healing connection. Therapy can often give you the support, encouragement, and acceptance that you did not receive when you were young. It cannot make up totally for the things that you did not obtain in childhood. It cannot erase all of your bad memories. It cannot completely fill or reverse the void often left by earlier unfulfilled needs for love or nurturing. However, it can raise your self-esteem and allow you to feel more confident in your abilities. I often tell patients, who complain about the lack of support that they received in childhood, "You have been standing on your own two feet all these years in spite of the lack of that early support. Perhaps you are more capable than you think. Perhaps you do not need a safety net." If we can get you to feel better about yourself, it will go a long way toward balancing the deficit and allowing you to feel stronger and more in control of the present situation.

9. *Encourage better communication*: Your psychiatrist may be able to teach you how to be more tactful and frame things differently so that you can really be heard. They can share good communication skills, such as really listening to other people and not commenting before they have finished their statement. They can help you evaluate your assump-

tions, and give feedback on how you feel. The key to good communication is nonjudgmental active listening, where you accept each other's' feelings. Often in couples therapy psychiatrists find that there are problems with communication. She does not communicate what she really wants very well. He does not pick up on the signals very well. The couple keeps fighting about the same things. Perhaps they both just want more attention, affection, or nurturing; however, what they fight about is spending money or the house not being clean. Many of Vivienne and Harold's initial problems when they retired were due to this deficit.

10. *Foster acceptance and contentment*: Acceptance of yourself as human, despite your faults, is a great pathway to feeling better emotionally. Accept yourself as an imperfect human being with good and bad points. Focus on gratitude for what you do have. Shuck the anger, guilt, and negative feelings; they only use up energy that you can use more constructively. I tell my patients to evaluate themselves and their accomplishments: "look at all the people behind you not just the people in front of you that have achieved more."

People seek happiness. Many people enter therapy setting as their goal—"I want to be happy." This is not realistic. No one is happy every minute of every day. Instead, seek contentment. Physician and Indian yoga master, Swami Sivananda said it well when he proclaimed, "There is no end to craving. Hence contentment alone is the best way to happiness. Therefore, acquire contentment."[4] No one can do everything or fulfill every fantasy. Regardless of socioeconomic status or achievement level, contentment in life is a good goal for retirement and old age. If you can be at peace with yourself, the people in your life, your situation, and your choices, you will feel more content and more in control of your world. You will be better able to cope with the common adjustments that need to be made when entering retirement.

11. *Prescribe medication when needed*: During the course of my professional career, it has been established that psychiatric medications can be helpful in improving the course and often affecting the long-term outcome of mental illness. Used appropriately, medication can be a tremendous aid in reducing emotional pain. Remember, these are not "magic pills." Many people refuse medication because they are fearful of becoming addicted or giving up control. You are more apt to take your medication if you are an educated consumer. Ask as many ques-

tions as you like but listen to and consider your psychiatrist's professional advice. Medications sometimes have side effects. In my office, I will commonly compare the side-effect profiles of two or more medications that I am suggesting for the patient. I ask them which side effects, if they occur, they would be more comfortable tolerating. The choice to take psychiatric medication or not is yours. However, particularly with the more severe mental disorders such as panic disorder, schizophrenia, and bipolar disorder medication is definitely the right choice.

12. *Offer suggestions to improve your quality of life:* Often, the question, "What do you want to add to your life?" will open up a Pandora's box of possibilities and get you thinking proactively. Perhaps, you can try something that you always wanted to do but never had the time to explore. Perhaps, you always wanted to be an artist. Try taking an art class and see how you do. Perhaps you always wanted to play tennis. Try taking a lesson. The world offers so much; however, you have to reach out and find what appeals to you. No one knows everything; however, professionals usually have a great wealth of information in their field. Sometimes, because of their training and experience, psychiatrists can make suggestions about what you can do to broaden your horizons. They can suggest lifestyle changes such as exercise and diet. Your psychiatrist can also suggest other sources of information and tell you about community resources, including where you can get help in specialized situations, such as caring for the elderly or finding a local long-term care facility.

13. *Foster independence:* People often come to therapy wanting the physician to solve all of their problems and tell them step by step what they should do. This is not the psychiatrist's job. Their job is to foster emotional growth. They can accentuate the positive by choosing to comment on the line of reasoning that is more therapeutic or helpful. They can comment on what the patient has not said as well as what he has shared. Psychiatrists try to treat patients as adults, follow their lead, give them ideas to think about, and help them to reach their own decisions. Psychiatrists can be a professional friend, but not a personal friend. They can be your confidant. They can serve as someone to lean on and talk to at times of stress. It is not their job, however, to treat patients like children and make them dependent. If psychiatrists see their patients going in that direction, they will talk to them about it, and try to foster independence. I have found that as most patients improve,

move more out into the world and add people to their life, they tend to start canceling appointments and ask to come to therapy less.

The issue of independence often comes up when spouses retire. Husbands and wives, at first, will spend more time together. Shopping, socializing, visiting relatives, and vacations fill their new open time slots. However, in time, the new routine may become burdensome and unfulfilling. In therapy, I tell couples that it is important to have things that you do together and things that you do apart. This will give you more to talk about and enlarge your worldview. Independent activities with friends and other people also provide other individuals that can listen to your frustrations and commiserate with you. You will learn that you are not alone and probably have been having similar experiences dealing with health and interpersonal issues common during retirement and aging.

The subtitle of this book is "Coping with Change." Retirement and aging present various scenarios that may tax your emotional resources and require resilience on your part. Feelings of loss, loneliness, and grief may consume you and lead to depressive episodes. Your anxiety may increase. You may start to be concerned about your own mortality. You may experience feelings of guilt, anger, and frustration. You may wonder who you are now that you are no longer defined or identified by your employment. The stress of the new situation may cause you to act out negatively by overeating, drinking too much, or buying more things than you can really afford. You may experience relationship problems with your spouse or significant other. You may find yourself more irritable and emotionally labile with your friends and others. If these reactions are prolonged, perhaps, it is time to seek professional mental health help.

If you are troubled and having difficulty adjusting, when you retire and as you get older, and you feel that you need help, take a risk, and make an appointment with a psychiatrist. They will not embarrass, criticize, or diminish you. They are just going to talk with you. Give therapy a chance. If you just come and talk about yourself and your life, whatever has to come out will come to the surface. Psychiatrists can help you connect the dots. You may just find out that you are not alone and, perhaps, are more normal than you think.

The doctor-patient relationship is a strong therapeutic tool that can foster self-esteem and help you move in a positive direction. If anything, this experience may move you further down the road of emotional maturity, allow you to live life to its full potential, and be more content with yourself and your life. If you are suffering emotionally, during retirement and as you age, pick up the phone and make an appointment. This is the first step in a journey that can be most helpful. Sometimes even the strongest people need someone to talk to; someone who can offer support and light the way. Let a psychiatrist be your guide.

The next chapter offers information about the common therapeutic modalities that may be helpful to you as you retire and age.

14

THERAPY

There are numerous therapy choices available to address the common mental health problems often encountered during retirement and aging. They include individual psychotherapy, group psychotherapy, and cognitive-behavioral therapy (CBT). Couples therapy may be useful, too. At times, behavioral relaxation techniques, such as progressive muscle relaxation, deep breathing, meditation, mindfulness, or biofeedback may be an option. Lifestyle changes involving exercise and diet may be helpful. Eating healthy and exercising can reduce the occurrence of pathological conditions that disrupt the normal aging process. They can also promote active engagement in life. Spirituality and religion may offer support in this confusing and unpredictable world. Let us look at some of these options.

INDIVIDUAL PSYCHOTHERAPY

Individual psychotherapy is valuable and has the potential to help people with their mental health problems, especially for people entering retirement and starting to age. It can be a healing process. The doctor-patient relationship is a powerful force that can help engender trust, improve self-esteem, and improve the quality of patients' lives. In spite of new discoveries in pharmacology, the need for human contact remains constant, particularly to combat stress and neediness. Although medications can certainly be helpful, I firmly believe that it is people working with people on a sustained long-term basis that is equally or even more important in fostering emotional growth and maintaining improvement and recovery.

Sebastian Zimmerman, MD, emphasized the value of psychotherapy in a *Psychiatric Times* article. He said, "Psychotherapy can change the brain. The catalyst for change lies in the relationship between the client and the therapist." He further underlined his belief that "therapy has not only clinical—but also poetic and magical—moments."[1]

The initial phase in therapy involves education about the disorder to foster reassurance and acceptance. To establish a diagnosis, the psychiatrist will do a mental status examination. This examination is to the psychiatrist what auscultation and percussion and palpitation are to the family physician or the internal medicine specialist. It will test such variables as general appearance, manner, and attitude; consciousness and alertness; orientation to time, place, and person; memory, concentration, emotional tone, and mood; motor aspects of behavior; associations and stream of thought, thought life, and mental trends; and perception (illusions and hallucinations), fund of general information, judgment, and insight (self-knowledge).

Establishing rapport, transmitting empathetic concern, and establishing trust is the next order of business. Individual psychotherapy can then offer either insight or support, depending on your capacity for introspection. I find that a combined approach is helpful for most people. Psychotherapy in general teaches coping skills, helps boost self-esteem and self-confidence, and encourages a feeling of increased control. Therapy allows patients to talk and release feelings, place things in perspective and encourage active goal-directed behavior. The therapist tries to promote emotional growth, a more adult point of view and realistic expectations of people and situations.

If the patient is approaching retirement, the conversation in therapy may take on a different bent. Often confused and concerned about what will happen once they leave work, they are happy to talk about their anxieties. I will encourage them to plan ahead and define their new lifestyle. Doing this will help them feel more in control and less fearful.

BEGIN PLANNING EARLY

Time goes by so quickly. It's never too early to make a plan for retirement. As American educator, Arthur E. Morgan said, "preparation for old age should begin no later than one's teens. A life which is empty of purpose until sixty-five will not suddenly become filled upon retirement."[2] Retirement like other phases of life needs a plan to be successful. Otherwise, you will just go where the wind takes you, which may not be toward fulfillment or contentment. Achieving a successful retirement is a process that takes planning, time, and experimentation. Without some preparation financially, emotionally, and attitudinally, retirement can be a lonely unhappy phase of life.

If you prepare ahead of time and take charge of your life, you will reap more dividends. As American minister, teacher, and author Harry Emerson Fosdick so wisely said, "Don't simply retire from something; have something to retire to."[3] Planning ahead will help put things in perspective and give you a road map to follow as well as a safety net. As an unknown author once said, "It pays to plan ahead. It wasn't raining when Noah built the ark."[4] Planning ahead will not guarantee perfection or absolute success. However, it will allow you to have more impute about your future and feel more in control of your destiny.

TAKE AN ACTIVE APPROACH

For some, work and family is the only investment they have made in life. It is important to have parallel interests. Thinking about, developing, and practicing new interests, ahead of time, will help bridge the gap once you retire. Gail Sheeny in her book, *Passages*, talks about opening "new veins of energy," when she comments, "Secondary interests that have been tapped earlier in life can . . . blossom into a serious lifework. Each tap into a new vessel releases in the later years another reservoir of energy."[5] As I will elaborate in chapter 16, an active stance, rather than a passive attitude, will move you further along in a positive direction. People who have a self-assertive, problem-solving approach to life do best. Take risks. Get ready. Before you retire, try new things that are outside of your comfort zone.

Some of the things that you can do even before you retire include joining a weekly card game or a book club. Involving yourself in a new hobby or becoming more active in your church, synagogue, or other religious affiliation. Find things that you can do with your partner, as well as by yourself. Review the things that you wanted to do earlier in life that you could not accomplish due to work and family responsibilities. Some of these ideas can still bear fruit and revitalize you. This way you will have laid a foundation for your retirement before you stop working. According to a survey of recent retirees over half (57 percent) looked back and wished that they had done more retirement planning before they retired.[6] For a more stress free retirement, be ready by planning ahead and then continue to be proactive and take charge of your life.

If you look up "plan ahead" for retirement and aging on the Internet you come up with mostly financial planning advice on retirement Web sites, planner calendars, or journals. Financial planning for the future is important. However, it is only one piece of the retirement puzzle. Finding the magical financial retirement number is not the whole story. Many other variables are involved in being successful in this phase of life. Your health status will be a determining factor in your ability to explore new territory and add to your life. Having supportive family and friends also helps. Having an active lifestyle is paramount.

Your own personality traits will also play a factor. Do you see the glass as half empty or half full? Do you think mostly about yourself or do you reach out to help others? How needy are you? How well do you deal with change? How content have you been with your life up to this point? Your ability and availability to sustain relationships with friends and other significant others are also important variables. Your spiritual and religious background and beliefs also play a role. Retirement is a stage of life that involves the whole person: mind, body, and spirit.

DEFINE YOUR LIFESTYLE

This is one of the first things that you need to do. You need to decide what feels right to you and what will make you happy. Make a life plan and design a lifestyle that fits your needs. Figure out location, time utilization, and purpose.

Where do you want to live? Do you want to stay in your home? Do you want to move closer to your children? Do you want to sell your house and downsize to a smaller house or apartment? Is a fifty-five and older community right for you? Is a free-standing, single-level community right for you or do you prefer a community that allows you to move up to an assisted living or nursing facility if your needs change? There are many choices. Do you want to stay in your home state or move to a warmer climate? Would you prefer to move to a state that is more tax friendly, such as Delaware or Florida?

What do you want to do with your time in retirement? What do you want to do with the rest of your life? Consider what will make you happy. Retirement gives you a chance to re-invent yourself. Do you want to work part time to make it easier to maintain your current lifestyle? Is continuing education your thing? Do you want to train for a new career or learn a new skill? Do you want to help others by volunteering or mentoring? Do you want to travel? Do foreign lands appeal to you? Does going to Japan, China, or Australia excite you? Would you rather travel in the United States and see the Grand Canyon or other American landmarks? Do you want to live near a lake where you can participate in water sports? Do you want to live in the mountains where you can participate in winter sports? There are so many choices. Making a life plan for retirement is important.

Find a purpose in your new life. Think of things that you can do on an ongoing basis that will bring you happiness and contentment. Think of things that will keep your mind sharp and your spirits up. Adding structure to your life will make you feel more grounded and more in control. Do you want to babysit for your grandchildren once a week? Do you want to write a novel, take a course in painting, or learn to dance the tango? Do you want to study a foreign language, learn how to play an instrument, or join a book club? Do you want to play cards or mah jong once a week? Do you want to start a flower or vegetable garden that you can nurture? Consider walking with a neighbor on a daily basis. Get a pet that you can care for. Expand your social network by joining a new group or a community or religious organization. There are so many choices. It can make your head spin contemplating your new phase of life and its possibilities.

STAY CALM AND BE PATIENT

Even if you are not normally fretful, this process can engender stress and anxiety. Living with stress can produce symptoms of anxiety including feelings of restlessness, heart palpitations, and shortness of breath, nausea and vomiting, dizziness, irritability, difficulty in concentration, muscle tension, and sleep disturbance. It can escalate the cycle of fear. If your mind is saying that something terrible is going to happen, it may just be its way of telling you that you are feeling nervous or stressed. Change is often scary and difficult. Getting to the finish line may require some trial and error. Don't be discouraged. Try to maintain a positive attitude. Throw away negative thoughts. Don't catastrophize. Try to minimize worry. Prime Minister Winston Churchill said, "Let our advance worrying become advance thinking and planning."[7] Avoid avoidance. Try not to be overwhelmed by the apparent magnitude of the task. Take one step at a time. Find ways to work off your feelings of frustration and excess aggressive energy. Exercise works for many. Relaxation techniques can easily be learned.

Your whole plan doesn't have to be completed in one day. Keep a list of what you would like to add to your life when you retire. Weed out your ideas systematically and see which are best for you. Take your time. Time pressure can only add to your tension. Make sure that you save some time for yourself. Share your progress as well as your failures with others. If you are having trouble getting it together, ask for help. Talk to a specialist. There are professional retirement planning firms that may be helpful. A social worker or religious leader may be able to make some suggestions or offer ideas. Talk to your spouse or significant other. They may have some ideas that they can share.

What I wrote in *Ten Steps to Relieve Anxiety* also holds true:

> It is difficult to treat the elderly psychiatrically. . . . Their character traits are more solidified and harder to change. Insight interpretations about the past are less appropriate. They are often scared and avoidant and do not follow up on suggestions. . . . In spite of this, psychotherapy still has much to offer (as we age). Its supportive, nonjudgmental milieu can give (you) an opportunity to vent and release pent-up frustration and anger. It encourages relationships and decreases isolation. It reduces the stress of separation and fulfills some . . . emotional needs. It can diminish . . . guilt, . . . place things

in perspective, suggest alternatives and provide a degree of reality testing by acting not so much as the echo of conscience, but as the quiet voice of reason. It can foster optimism, reestablish self-confidence and encourage the development of new interests. It can help restore a sense of identity and direction.[8]

In this day and age, psychiatrists are often marginalized by insurance companies, who refer clients to psychologists for therapy and psychiatrists for medication management. I have always offered both individual psychotherapy and medication where appropriate to my patients. I think that there is value in someone seeing one person for all their therapeutic needs. I was thrilled to learn that the residency training programs in psychiatry, which for many years emphasized medication management, are again teaching psychotherapy.

GROUP PSYCHOTHERAPY

Group psychotherapy came on the scene in America in 1906, when J. H. Pratt, a Boston physician, held classes at home for tuberculosis patients.[9] Participation in group therapy can allow you to realize that you are not alone or "different." It can foster self-expression and ventilation. This process can improve communication as well as interpersonal relationship skills. It can help reduce feelings of guilt, anxiety, sadness, and anger. It can help improve self-esteem. It can be a supportive environment in which you can learn more about yourself and your disorder or problem. It is particularly helpful when the participants share a common bond such as the loss of a spouse or a chronic illness.

My own way of running a group is to teach good communication skills and use the psychoanalytic model to examine the needs of the individual members as they emerge in the group interaction. In leading group therapy, I found that the things that people speak about first, no matter how alarming or scintillating, are often material that they have already worked through and feel comfortable with. It will take a while for all people to feel relaxed and establish trust and share their "secrets." I remember one man who usually sat quietly during group sessions. One day, he stood up and angrily shared an incident in his life. At the end of the hour-and-a-half group session, as we were leaving, I told him "congratulations, you were wonderful tonight." His embarrassed response was "I wish I hadn't been so wonderful."

COGNITIVE-BEHAVIORAL THERAPY (CBT)

Cognitive-behavioral therapy is a form of psychotherapy that emphasizes the role of thinking in how people feel and what they do. The term "cognitive-behavioral therapy" is a very general term for a classification of therapies that share this over-all philosophy. They share the idea that *thoughts* cause feelings and behaviors, not external things, like people, situations, and events. They believe that people can change the way they think to feel and act better even if the situation does not change. The various approaches to cognitive-behavioral therapy, followed by the name of their founders, include rational emotive behavior therapy (Albert Ellis, PhD), rational behavior therapy (Maxie C. Maultsby Jr., MD), rational living therapy (Aldo Pucci, PsyD), cognitive therapy (Aaron Beck, MD), and dialectic behavior therapy (DBT), (Marsha Lineman, PhD). [10]

Patients often overestimate the likelihood of negative events and underestimate their ability to cope. Cognitive therapy corrects these distorted ways of thinking (cognitive distortion). I tended to take an eclectic approach in doing therapy. I would try to do everything that I could to help the patient. Although, I did not practice formal cognitive therapy, I would from time to time ask the patient such questions as "What is the worst thing that could happen?" to give them a perspective and stop them from catastrophizing. By helping you to become aware of inaccurate or negative thinking, cognitive therapy allows you to view challenging situations more clearly and respond to them in a more effective way.

BEHAVIORAL RELAXATION TECHNIQUES

The following techniques can be easily learned. They are helpful in relieving stress and can be used by any age group. They include:

- Progressive muscle relaxation (PMR). (Tense and relax muscles sequentially through various parts of the body. Taped instructions are available.)
- Deep breathing. (Lowers your heart rate and helps you relax.)
- Visualization or guided imagery. (A focused mental image of a desired positive outcome that can help you achieve a goal.)
- Meditation. (A way to empty your mind of thoughts in order to relax.)
- Yoga. (A series of poses for attaining bodily or mental control and relaxation. It can increase strength, flexibility, and balance.)
- Mindfulness. ("Focusing on the here and now." It helps you slow down by immersing yourself in the present moment.)
- Self-hypnosis. (Uses positive suggestion to induce relaxation.)
- Biofeedback. (Teaches you to relax tense muscles.)
- Massage therapy (Can relieve muscle tension, foster relaxation, and reduce stress.)

LIFESTYLE CHANGES

- Exercise. Physical activity is more important than ever as people age. It can help maintain a healthy weight, develop and maintain muscle mass, and increase strength and flexibility. It can help reduce the risk of diseases such as diabetes and osteoporosis. It can boost energy and improve mood. It is good for the mind, body, and soul (also see chapter 5).[11]
- Diet. A well-balanced diet with particular attention to important nutrients can help reduce the risk of heart disease, hypertension, stroke, type-2 diabetes, bone loss, some cancers, and anemia.[12] Limit your sodium intake to reduce hypertension. Keep yourself hydrated even if you are not thirsty. Foods rich in Omega 3 fatty acids, such as fish can reduce inflammation, which can cause heart disease, cancer, and arthritis. Calcium and Vitamin D are important to maintain bone health.[13]

To obtain more information on the topic of diet and nutrition in the elderly see the Web sites for the National Institute on Health (NIH Senior Health)[14] and RetiredBrains,[15]

- Sleep (see chapter 15).
- Take care of medical problems (see chapter 4).
- Expand your world (see chapter 18).
- Spirituality and religion (see chapter 19).

A positive adjustment to retirement and aging depends on good health, a secure income, meaningful activities, marital satisfaction, and supportive friends and community. Not everyone is lucky enough to have all of these variables. The therapies above can help you deal with change and loss and foster a successful adjustment to this new stage of life and its possible downside. The importance of relationships has been dealt with in chapter 3. Part V of this book will deal with important helpful coping skills such as staying active, maintaining a positive attitude, having a goal, and staying engaged and religious affiliation.

To be successful in this phase of life, you have to learn various skills and life lessons. These can be discussed in therapy. All the elements dealt with above were helpful to my older patients. Some have been illustrated by Harold and Vivienne's experiences. Choose the ones that you can relate to and feel will be useful to you. They are all not appropriate for every person. I hope that they will encourage you to take a proactive approach, to plan ahead, move forward successfully, and optimize your situation.

A psychiatrist is a physician, who is a professional, who has knowledge about all of the areas above. He or she can help you deal with your emotions and negative behaviors as you retire and age. He or she can help you deal with any roadblocks to growth that emanate from your childhood or prior negative experiences, help you plan ahead for life after retirement and help you be successful in your quest. I hope that this chapter has been able to give you a picture of various helpful therapies as well as topics that may be useful to cover later in life in talking to a therapist, mentor, religious counselor, or other helpful individual. The next chapter will look at another treatment option, psychiatric medication.

15

MEDICATION

When I finished my three-year fellowship in psychiatry in 1970 and entered private practice, there were a limited number of medications that I could offer to my patients to help their emotional suffering. There were the benzodiazepines, Librium (chlordiazepoxide), Serax (oxazepam), and Valium (diazepam) to treat anxiety and alcoholism. These products were called "minor tranquilizers." There was also phenobarbital to calm nerves. There were beta blockers such as Inderal (propranolol) to treat the physical symptoms of anxiety, including tremors and palpitations.

For psychoses, such as schizophrenia, there were the "major tranquilizers" including Thorazine (chlorpromazine), Stelezine (trifluoperazine), and Mellaril (thioridazine). These medications were also used in small does to treat anxiety. For manic depressive illness (bipolar disorder), I could prescribe Lithium carbonate, particularly for mania. For depression, I could offer the tricyclic antidepressants (TCAs) such as Elavil (amitriptyline), Tofranil (imipramine), Pamelor (nortriptyline), and Norpramine (desipramine). There were also the Monoamine oxidase inhibitors (MAOIs), such as Nardil (phenelzine) and Parnate (tranylcypromine).

Sleep problems were treated with Dalmane (flurazepam), Halcion (triazolam), and the antihistamine, Benadryl (diphenhydramine). There was much concern that Halcion and Dalmane could be abused and be addictive. There was little to offer for dementia or Alzheimer's disease, except for diet and vitamins, such as B-6, B-12, and folic acid. One of the biggest and most important changes during my long psychiatric career is the growth in the field of psychopharmacology and the benefits of psychiatric medication.

Because of this progress, today there are a much larger number of medications that psychiatrists can offer to retired and older patients to treat the conditions that are common to this age group, such as anxiety, depression, sleep disorders, and Alzheimer's disease. This chapter will examine some of them; however, remember that these medications are not "magic pills." Under no circumstances try them out by borrowing some from your spouse or friend. Understanding the possible side effects and advantages of each medicine will allow you to make a choice that is best for you. Discuss them with your physician before taking them and make a collaborative decision.

MEDICATION FOR ANXIETY

The field of anxiety changed drastically in 1980 with the advent of the tranquilizer, Xanax (alprazolam). At the same time, the *Diagnostic and Statistical Manual* (DSM-III) changed the category of anxiety from only "Anxiety Neurosis" and listed other disorders separately. Panic disorder, for instance, previously known colloquially as "high anxiety" was listed individually under the anxiety disorders that also listed such syndromes as obsessive-compulsive disorder, social anxiety disorder, and post-traumatic stress disorder, and generalized anxiety disorder. At this time, I wrote my first book, entitled *Panic Disorder: The Great Pretender*.[1] The subtitle underlined the fact that panic disorder can mimic many physical disorders and thus be difficult to diagnose.

Benzodiazepines are the most widely prescribed medications in the world. They include such anxiolytic or anti-anxiety products as Xanax (alprazolam), Librium (chlordiazepoxide), Tranxene (clorazepate), Valium (diazepam), Ativan (lorazepam), Serax (oxazepam), and Centrax (prazepam). They have some potential for abuse as well as physical and emotional dependency. The physician needs to take a good history, educate the patient, and set firm limits. I avoid prescribing them if there is a history of drug or alcohol abuse or dependency. The most common side effects are drowsiness and unsteady movements. They can cause depression when taken with alcohol, other psychotropic medications, anticonvulsants, antihistamines, or other depressant drugs.

Do not stop these medications abruptly. Withdrawal symptoms can occur. They include insomnia, dizziness, headaches, and lack of appetite, vertigo, ringing in the ears, blurred vision, and shakiness. Benzodiazepines selectively enhance GABA binding. In time, the body compensates for the presence of the anti-anxiety medication by lowering or ceasing production of the natural tranquilizer hormone GABA. If the benzodiazepines are tapered gradually, the body will resume its normal production of GABA and withdrawal symptoms will be minimized. Do not drive, use machinery, or do anything that requires mental alertness until you know how these medicines affect you. The medication can cause postural hypotension (drop in blood pressure). Therefore, do not sit up or stand up quickly, especially if you are an older person, to avoid possible dizzy or fainting spells.[2]

Buspar (Buspirone) is an alternative to the use of the benzodiazepines. It has minimal sedation, abuse potential or adverse interaction with alcohol or other central nervous system depressants. Therefore, I often use it to treat former alcoholics, drug abusers, or dependency-prone patients. Some patients tend to minimize their alcohol use. Tolerance and withdrawal symptoms are not an issue. Therefore, it can be stopped abruptly. However, symptoms return rapidly upon discontinuation. Side effects include dizziness, nausea, headaches, nervousness, and lightheadedness. These can be minimized by starting at a low dose and gradually increasing the dose over a seven-to-ten-day period. I often prescribe it twice a day, starting at 5 mg/day and increasing it gradually to 30–45 mg/day. Some people experience a "woozy feeling" in their head when they first take it. This can be avoided if the medication is taken with food.

MEDICATION FOR DEPRESSION

Prozac (fluoxetine), the first selective serotonin reuptake inhibitor (SSRI), brought to market in 1987, revolutionized the treatment of depression. The SSRIs are sometimes referred to as the second-generation antidepressants. They are the most commonly prescribed antidepressant at present. SSRIs help depression by affecting a naturally occurring chemical messenger in the brain called serotonin. This neurotransmitter or hormone is used to communicate between brain cells. SSRIs block the reabsorption (reuptake) of the neurotransmitter serotonin in the brain. The hormone is thus increased between nerve cells. This change helps brain cells send and receive chemical messages, which in turn boosts mood.[3]

The Food and Drug Administration (FDA) has approved the following SSRIs to treat depression. They include Celexa (citalopram), Lexapro (escitalopram), Prozac (fluoxetine), Paxil, Paxil CR, Pexeva (paroxetine), and Zoloft (sertraline). SSRIs also may be used to treat conditions other than depression, such as anxiety disorders. This particularly involves the more sedating SSRIs, such as Celexa and Zoloft. Eric J. Lenze, MD, principal investigator in two of the three randomized, placebo-controlled trials established the efficacy of SSRIs for later-life generalized anxiety disorder (GAD), including the largest study involving Lexapro (escitalopram). Bruce Jancin clearly states in an October 2014 article titled "Key Points in Managing Late-Life Anxiety" in the *Caring for the Ages* newspaper, that the SSRIs actually work to decrease anxiety symptoms in this age group.[4]

The first generation of antidepressants ((TCAs) work by inhibiting the reuptake of the hormones, norepinephrine and serotonin. The TCAs have anticholinergic, antihistaminergic, and cardiotoxic effects. These include dry mouth, urinary retention, blurred vision, constipation, and drowsiness (anticholinergic). Many of the antihistaminic side effects overlap with the anticholinergic side effects making them even more potent. The TCAs can also cause an increased or irregular heart beat (cardiotoxic).

Even though the second generation antidepressants, the SSRIs, have other side effects, they do not have the potential of causing the same side effects as the TCAs. You really have to choose which possible set of adverse effects that you are willing to tolerate. The side effects of the SSRIs include the following possibilities: nausea, nervousness, agitation or restlessness, dizziness, reduced sexual desire, or difficulty reaching orgasm or inability to maintain an erection (erectile dysfunction), drowsiness, insomnia, weight gain or loss, headache, dry mouth, vomiting, and diarrhea. Taking your medication with food may reduce the risk of nausea.

Wellbutrin (bupropion) is an antidepressant of the aminoketone class. It is chemically unrelated to the other known antidepressant agents. It is a relatively weak inhibitor of the absorption of norepinephrine and dopamine. It can cause dry mouth, headache, and insomnia. To avoid insomnia, take it in the morning. Do not use with alcohol for this combination may "increase the risk of uncommon side effects such as seizures, hallucinations, delusions, paranoia, mood and behavioral changes, depression, suicidal thoughts, anxiety, and panic attacks."[5] On the positive side, Wellbutrin has a low incidence of weight gain and sexual side effects. Since these are a possibility with the other antidepressants, it may serve as a good alternative, if these effects occur or if the patient does not want to tolerate taking a chance that they may occur. It was originally marketed as Zyban to help people stop smoking.

For completeness, I will also mention three newer antidepressants. They include the selective norepinephrine reuptake inhibitors (SNRI), Effexor, Effexor XR (venlafaxine), and Pristiq (desvenlafaxine); the noradrenergic and specific serotonergic antidepressant, Remeron (mirtazapine); and the selective norepinephrine reuptake inhibitor (tetracyclic), Ludiomil (maprotiline).

MEDICATION FOR SLEEP DISORDERS

Contrary to popular belief, older people do not require less sleep. Sleep patterns and circadian rhythms (biological clock) do change as one ages. The average adult spends approximately 20 percent in REM sleep. The elderly may spend only 15 percent in REM sleep and the rest of their sleep time in stage 1 of non-REM sleep. Consequently, they have less REM sleep and report frequent awakenings.

There are two basic theories of why we need sleep.

Restorative: Sleep enables the body and mind to rejuvenate, re-energize, and restore. During sleep, the brain performs vital housekeeping tasks, such as organizing long-term memory, integrating new information, and repairing and renewing tissue, nerve cells, and other biochemicals. Sleep allows the body to rest and the mind to sort out past, present, and future activities and feelings.

Adaptive: Sleep may have evolved as a protective adaptation—finding food in the daytime and hiding at night is easier. Nearly every animal sleeps to some degree. Thus, it only makes sense that predators sleep more than animals that are prey. For humans, the amount and quality of sleep achieved is directly proportional to the amount and quality of the next day's productivity.[6]

Hypnotics or sleep medications include ProSom (estazolam), Dalmane (flurazepam), Doral (quazepam), Restoril (temazepam), Halcion (triazolam), Lunesta (eszopiclone), Sonata (zaleplon), Ambien (zolpidem), Remeron (mirtazapine), and Rozerem (ramelteon). If you have a sleep disorder, please check with your physician before taking these medications to be sure that you understand how age-related physiologic changes can affect their use. You will also be wise to discuss the possible risk of adverse reactions.

Sleep aids can cause tolerance and dependency with long-term use. Therefore, I did not prescribe them gingerly. They should not be given to patients with a history of drug or alcohol abuse or dependency. If I did prescribe a hypnotic, I told my patients to take their sleep medication for several days, get a good night's sleep and then not take it again until they didn't sleep well for a night. As I said, I would hope that your physician gives serious thought and looks at the whole situation before prescribing medication for sleep. There are helpful alternatives to sleeping pills. As you saw in chapter 14 on therapy, there are various modalities such as cognitive-behavioral therapy (CBT) and relaxation therapy that may be useful to those with sleep problems. Your physician can also discuss good sleep hygiene with you, which may be helpful. Mindfulness meditation may also help older people sleep.[7]

MEDICATION FOR MEMORY LOSS, DEMENTIA, AND ALZHEIMER'S DISEASE

At this time there are no medications to cure dementia or Alzheimer's disease. However, there are several that purport to slow the progression of the disease. They are:

- Cholinesterase inhibitors Aricept (donepezil) approved for all stages;

- Exelon (rivastigmine) and Razadyne (galantamine) approved for mild to moderate disorders; and
- Cognex (tacrine). Cognex was the first cholinesterase inhibitor to be approved. It is no longer used due to serious potential for side effects.

The cholinesterase inhibitors prevent the breakdown of acetylcholine, a chemical messenger important for learning and memory. This supports communication among nerve cells by keeping acetylcholine levels high. They delay worsening of symptoms for six to twelve months, on average, for about half the people who take them. They are generally well tolerated. If side effects occur, they commonly include nausea, vomiting, loss of appetite, and increased frequency of bowel movements. Cholinesterase inhibitors can also help improve the patient's mood.

Memantine (Namenda) is approved for moderate to severe Alzheimer's disease. It is prescribed to improve memory, attention, reason, language, and the ability to perform simple tasks (higher cognitive functions). Memantine regulates the activity of glutamate, a different messenger chemical involved in learning and memory. It delays the worsening of symptoms for some people temporarily. It can cause side effects, including headaches, constipation, confusion, and dizziness.

Physicians sometimes prescribe both types of medications together. Some also prescribe high doses of vitamin E for cognitive changes of Alzheimer's disease. Vitamin E can interact with antioxidants and medications prescribed to lower cholesterol or prevent blood clots.[8]

In a monthly newspaper, *Caring for the Ages*, Michele G. Sullivan recently reported about a combination drug of dextromethorphan (a cough suppressant) and quinidine (used to treat heart rhythm disorders), called Nuedexta, which significantly reduced aggression and agitation in patients with Alzheimer's disease in a ten-week, phase-two trial of two hundred patients with moderate Alzheimer's. During this time measurement of caregiver distress also improved. This medication is already approved for pseudobulbar affect. The drug will have to go through a phase-three clinical trial before it can seek approval from the FDA to treat Alzheimer's disease.[9]

Age-related physical changes that affect the action of drugs within the body must be kept in mind when prescribing medications for the elderly, to avoid the risk of side effects, drug interactions, and toxic reactions. Metabolic (body chemistry) changes may affect drug absorption and action in this age group. Older people are smaller than they look. Wasting muscle tissue may be masked by the substitution of fat. Due to the decrease of kidney function with age, older people do not always excrete drugs well. Alterations of central nervous system, cardiovascular and respiratory function may change the sensitivity of the target organ, altering the reaction of individual neurons, making dosage choice difficult. It is smart to start the doses low, and follow the adage, "start low, go slow." Lower doses may produce higher blood levels in this age group.[10]

As a psychiatrist, I always check with the patient's family physician or other specialists before writing prescriptions for psychiatric medications to be sure that I am aware of all the patient's physical problems and other medications. Older people also often make mistakes with their medications due to forgetfulness. Medication compliance can be a problem with senior citizens. They may not be able to afford the medication, they may forget to take the medication, or they may try to fix a problem by taking more or less medication than is prescribed. "If I take a half pill, the prescription will last longer. If one pill helped a little, perhaps two pills will do better." It is helpful to provide family supervision, try to limit the number of medications that they take, and ask their physician to write for small amounts or give them a sample package. A weekly pill dispenser may aid with compliance and medication supervision.

From time to time, new medications come on the scene promising cures. They are met with much fanfare by the pharmaceutical industry, other medical organizations and even physicians themselves. Are we promising too much? Are the new treatments reliable and consistent? Will time show them to be the best choice? Henry A. Nasrallah, MD, editor-in-chief of the psychiatric journal, *Current Psychiatry*, warns that we may be promising too much and not looking at the bigger historical picture and what it shows. He maintains that in spite of new tools, most medical specialties still just manage and not cure their patients or restore function completely. He warns that physicians should "move forward with caution" and be "judicious and guided by evidence" when selecting new treatments for their patients.[11]

I certainly agree. Time and experience are the answer that allows you to put these treatment advances and new medications in perspective. Some treatments may be praised today and discredited tomorrow. I can remember, once while doing a double-blind research study in my office for a new antidepressant, on a small sample of patients (in the 1980s chief investigators would farm out small samples of research to many private practice psychiatrists in the area), I was astonished at the quick positive results that I was obtaining from my volunteers. Rather than the usual two- to four-week wait to start to see improvement, people were feeling better within one week. Miraculous! However, time showed that there was a problem. Three months after the new medication was placed on the market, it was withdrawn because it was found to be an amphetamine product, which explained the quick positive results.

Sometimes what is old and proven is better than new. Many times, in practice, I would fall back to an older product, with which I had often had good results, to treat a problem patient, who was not responding or could not tolerate a second-generation medication. The results were usually good.

Marketing companies often pose these questions to physicians, "If a new product comes on the market, will you be the first to try it? Will you wait until many of your colleagues have tried it before you try it for your patients? Will you wait until it has been out for some time before you try it?" I would hope that your physician is conservative and says that he will wait until the new medication's true worth becomes evident in journal articles, reports from respected colleagues, and other reliable sources of information. I hope that they remember that they took the Hippocratic Oath to do no harm.

For mental health problems, I am a firm believer in looking at the whole person and responding to as many of the biopsychosocial problematic areas as possible. I certainly prescribed medication for my patients where necessary and appropriate. However, I would not just reach into my desk drawer and hand the patient whatever came up from this treasure trove of medication samples, many of which were new products. I wholeheartedly believe in the therapeutic value of psychiatric therapy. I believe in Andrew Taylor Still's osteopathic philosophy that "the body has the inherent ability to cure itself." I hope that your physician aids this process by listening to you, remembering his own limitations, and is there for you. I hope that he continues to educate himself in his field and uses the best treatment modalities that he knows. Lastly, I hope that he helps you improve the quality of your life and has a positive attitude.

The three previous chapters have looked at what your physician or psychiatrist can do for you in reference to your mental health problems late in life. Now let's look at some coping skills that may help you take a more active role in your emotional recovery and improve your situation during retirement and aging.

V

Coping Skills

16

STAY ACTIVE

Successful people are active people. They set goals and work consistently and patiently toward their achievements. Their lifestyle is oriented toward being proactive and dynamic. "Be active" is an important motto to live by, particularly when you retire and as you get older. Remember, alive is a synonym of active. Take a problem-solving approach to life. Too many people lead their lives passively and just take what comes along. Often, they assume the role of the victim and constantly complain. Les Brown, American author, entrepreneur, and motivational speaker, had the right idea when he said, "We must look for ways to be an active force in our own lives. We must take charge of our own destinies, design a life of substance and truly begin to live our dreams."[1] Don't sit around and presume that others will automatically just know what you want and give it to you. You will be sitting still, alone, and unfulfilled for a long time. Make things happen. Gather information and be sure that your goal is realistic. Then reach out and work toward fulfilling your wishes.

In my book, *The Sandwich Generation: Caught between Growing Children and Aging Parents*, I say,

> The key to a successful life is to stay involved and maintain a passion for work and other projects. Strive toward a goal and don't ever be without one. Continue to learn and grow. We all need something to look forward to, something to wake up for. Be creative and remain productive. Invest yourself in others. These characteristics can do much to add satisfaction and fulfillment to your life.[2]

These words are equally relevant to coping with late life. As with much advice, the recommendations above are more easily said than done. If you do not already have things in life about which you feel passionate, how do you discover them and add them to your life? The answer is simple: Don't be afraid to try something new. In retirement, in a way, you have to reinvent yourself.

BASIC STEPS TO ACTIVATE YOUR LIFE

Some people do not get anywhere in life, because they do not know what they want. If you do not know what choices are available, ask others for suggestions. Ask your friends and acquaintances what they do in their spare time. You might be surprised as to what you will learn. They might tell you things that you had no idea that they did. Make a list and try each one. In my late thirties, I had gotten to the point in my psychiatric practice where it was moving along satisfactorily, on its own momentum, and I didn't have to beat the bushes as much for referrals. I started to think about what else I wanted to add to my life aside from work and family. I had no clue. I decided to ask some friends what they did for relaxation, fun, or a change of pace. I tried many of the things that they told me about. The two that I stayed with were playing tennis and getting involved with my high school alumni association. Both these choices added a new dimension to my life.

If you really cannot come up with new ideas, try doing something different from your routine activities. Step outside your comfort zone. Take a first step in a new direction—any direction. Open yourself up to the unknown. Read a new magazine or talk to a new person. Visit a new restaurant or shop. Take a class or join a group. Talk to new people that you meet. I often encourage patients to play a game that I call "follow your nose." Give yourself four hours, perhaps on a weekend, to do whatever you want and follow through. Leave your usual routine behind and give yourself permission to explore the world in a new way. This exercise often allows you to get out of your comfort zone. See what happens. You might be surprised how good you can feel. One thing often leads to another. You might even come home smiling.

PHYSICAL BENEFITS OF BEING ACTIVE

Staying active can have physical benefits. It can even increase your chances of living longer.[3] Thirty minutes of moderate exercise daily can make you feel good, but can also improve your overall bodily health and resistance to disease. This may mean anything from a regular gym routine to water aerobics or swimming, yoga or dance classes, or simply taking a walk. Regular physical activity can help prevent heart disease, stroke, and high blood pressure. It can reduce the risk of developing type-2 diabetes, osteoporosis, and some cancers (colon and breast).[4]

It can help build and maintain healthy strong bones, muscles, and joints thus reducing the risk of injuries from falls.[5] It can help you maintain a healthy weight, develop muscle mass, prevent atrophy (muscle wasting), and increase flexibility. Being physically active can also help you feel stronger, boost your energy, allow you to feel more alive and better able to do day-to-day activities. The positive benefits of exercise to your body are endless. Exercise is particularly helpful in keeping your body resilient as you age or experience chronic disease.

EMOTIONAL BENEFITS OF BEING ACTIVE

Being active also pays emotional dividends. Exercise releases chemicals in your brain, called endorphins, which make you feel good. Feeling better mentally will improve your quality of life. Exercise can relieve stress and is one of the best treatments for relieving anxiety. It can also decrease anger. Doing exercise at a gym or in other group setting is a great way to meet new people. Physical activity can improve your mood, prevent depression, and boost self-esteem and confidence. It can increase motivation and mental alertness. It can aid sleep. It can improve your energy level. It can increase motivation.[6]

Being active pays benefits in another way. As a secondary benefit, it allows you to feel in charge of your situation and more in control of your life. You will find yourself standing taller and smiling more. You get a warm feeling when you have taken charge, followed through, and things have worked out well. This sense of achievement will make you feel good about yourself and allow you to be more gracious and kind to other people. Your positive mood will rub off on others and create a cycle of positive feeling. By reducing your stress, you create psychological well-being which makes you less apt to deteriorate emotionally and subsequently less prone to psychiatric illness. You will be more apt to reach out to others and allow new people into your life.

INTELLECTUAL (COGNITIVE) BENEFITS OF BEING ACTIVE

Memory decline affects everyone as they age, albeit in different degrees. Retirees may become particularly aware of their memory loss. They may joke that it takes the elevator longer to reach the top floor, but inside they feel frustrated. Remaining physically active significantly reduces the risk for cognitive decline, dementia, and Alzheimer's disease.[7] It keeps thinking, learning, and judgment skills sharp. Dr. Joe Verghese, of Albert Einstein College of Medicine in New York, found in a 2003 study that regular leisure activity resulted in a low risk of dementia. He surmised that cognitive activity may work against the onset of dementia by increasing a person's "cognitive reserve," strengthening the connections between brain cells, or encouraging new networks within the brain.[8] Motivational speaker Byron Pulsifer is also encouraging when he says, "If you believe that achievement ends with retirement, you will slowly fade away. First of all, keeping the mind active is one way to prolong your life and to enjoy life to its fullest for as long as possible."[9]

My fictitious couple, Harold and Vivienne, were not easy to motivate to work on their retirement problems. As with many older people, they were set in their ways and scared of change. Their daughter heard her mother's distress on the phone and actually took the train to New Jersey to see her parents. Both Harold and Vivienne were thrilled to see her. However, the trip was all in vain. Out of pride and not wanting to be a burden, they both told her that everything was fine and that she should not worry about them. The daughter went home feeling helpless, worried, and frustrated. She called her brother in Texas, but neither could think of a solution other than to call their parents more often.

It is difficult to deal with an unhappy retired parent. In spite of your concern, they come wrapped in a lifetime of habits or personality traits, which are hard to change or undo. Be supportive. Let them know that you care for them and still need them; however, remember that it is their responsibility to change and solve their dilemma. If mom and dad seem to be having difficulty dealing with their new freedom and extra time after retirement, there are a few things that you can suggest to them or do yourself to help.

Explore community resources. The local library may be a source of information. Your religious congregation may offer activities or suggestions. Senior centers offer daily programs. The YMCA may have a silver sneakers exercise program. Senior discounts are available for the bus and train as well as local movies and sporting events. There are outdoor groups, as well as card-playing and reading groups or clubs. Suggest that they join a group dedicated to something that they believe in, such as a fund-raising group for a medical condition, or a group that provides resources for a specific age group. Encourage them to try new things and stay engaged in the world. (See below for more activity suggestions.)

Part-time work can at times be the answer for some retirees. This can be in their own field of expertise or in something completely new. My uncle, who owned a hardware store for many years, worked part time in another store after retirement. They appreciated his expertise and work ethic. A friend of mine, who had worked all his life as a teacher, started a business driving people to the airport. Professional people, such as lawyers, physicians, and accountants, can often continue to work part time, teach, or do consulting work. Artists, painters, sculptors, musicians, and writers can continue to enjoy their craft as long as they are physically and mentally capable. Many can recycle their skills in new areas. An accountant or businessman may enjoy being a treasurer or a consultant for a small business or organization or be on the board of a fifty-five and older community.

Encourage them to volunteer. This is a wonderful way to do something for others: be with people and feel good about yourself. Hospitals, schools, and nursing homes welcome help. They often offer free lunch and a rewards luncheon yearly. Fraternal, religious, and philanthropic organizations welcome participation by people of all ages. Groups such as Food Abundance, Mitzvah Circle Foundation, and Meals on Wheels would love your help. Habitat for Humanity would appreciate their participation. Politicians such as your local congressman would value their involvement in the neighborhood office.

Stress involvement with others. Look around you. Are there possibilities right in front of you? Do your parents have a neighbor, who is also retired and who may be delighted if they said hello? Do they have a young couple next door with young children that would love a substitute grandparent? Is there a park nearby where your dad can go and watch little league games? Tell them to strike up a conversation with the mail carrier or the cashier at the store. Bookstores are often filled with people. Just being in this environment can help you feel less isolated. Encourage them to get out of the house at least once a day. Any one-to-one interaction can help them feel connected and reduce loneliness. Becoming more involved in any group activity will allow them to meet new people and be less isolated.

Increase their involvement with the family. Include them in as many family occasions and celebrations as possible. Invite them out for lunch or dinner or to your house for a meal. Let them babysit or spend more time with their older grandchildren. Put the grandchildren on the phone when you call. Encourage the older grandchildren to call or e-mail them. Encourage them to call a cousin or other relative, who they have not seen or heard from in a while. Call and visit them more often. Ask them what they need done around the house. They may be too proud to ask. Remember, they are not the same people that you knew twenty years ago; let go of old grievances and relate to them as they are today. Your time and attention is one of the best and most therapeutic gifts that you can give them.

Travel is a wonderful adventure at any age. It is something to look forward to and supplies wonderful memories. Looking at travel brochures, packing, and getting ready to leave can fill in otherwise empty hours. There is a whole world out there to explore, in which much can be learned about history and geography. Traveling is a great way to meet new people who can open up new worlds of ideas. Everyone has places that they dream about going. Now is the time to make dreams a reality. Retirees have more freedom to travel during off-peak and more affordable times of the year. Various possibilities exist for every budget. Elderhostel, the American Association of Retired Persons, and other organizations offer many group opportunities. Ask a travel agent about senior discounts. An article in the *Philadelphia Inquirer*, by Sally and John Macdonald, entitled, "Not Your Grandparents' Vacations" makes the point that adventure-tour companies offer a multitude of options for retired seniors. "They've transformed trips that . . . were only for the young and virile into experiences most of us can have no matter what our age or desire for comfort . . . better equipment has made many . . . tours easier and safer."[10]

Sometimes even though they complain, retirees may really be content in their discontent and are just venting frustration. I sometimes call this putting smoke up the chimney. If this is the case, just listen and don't try to change the situation. You can encourage, gently prod, and suggest a few alternatives. However, do not attempt to solve problems for your parents. It is their life. You may also have to accept that even though your suggestions seem excellent, your advice won't always be taken. At times, you may have to realize that even though you are concerned and care, all that your parents really may need and want is your interest and love. Just calling them or visiting them may do more than you think.

In 1978, Congress passed the Mandatory Retirement Act as part of the Age Discrimination in Employment Act (ADEA), which outlawed mandatory retirement before the age of seventy. In 1986, mandatory retirement on the basis of age was abolished altogether. In spite of these new opportunities to continue working, in 1986, Harold's father took the more traditional route and retired at age sixty-five after forty-five years as a master carpenter. He worked little at carving out a new life after retirement. He seemed content just reading his newspaper, listening to the radio, watching television, puttering around the house, and looking forward to going to Florida in the winter. Harold was forty years old when his father retired. Watching his father blend easily into his new stage of life caused Harold to be surprised that he was not content with his own life after retirement.

Harold did not realize that he and his father had very different jobs that fulfilled their needs in different ways. His father gained pleasure and self-esteem from making an attractive, well-made product. He also worked mostly by himself and was used to being alone. Harold, on the other hand, enjoyed the comradeship of his co-workers, the hustle and bustle of the workplace, and being in a leadership position. His sense of worth was predicated more on being needed and respected. Upon retirement, Harold's loss was far greater than his father's. It is not surprising that he was mildly depressed. Harold's father was used to being by himself most of the day and relying on internal thoughts or listening to the radio for stimulation. Harold, on the other hand, was used to having more external stimuli to fulfill his needs. Now he was mostly alone.

In my professional opinion, it is a good idea in marriage or a relationship with a significant other to do things together and have common interests. However, independence is also essential. It is important for each person to have activities that they do by themselves or with others outside their home. Harold and Vivienne needed to develop some of these activities that would let them develop new interests they could share together and others they would do apart. Their choice is to continue to bicker, isolate themselves, and be unhappy or to be more proactive and try something new. Here are a few suggestions of things that they and you might like to try:

Art/Drawing/Painting/Crafts/Knitting/Crocheting
Be a mentor/Tutor/Teacher's aide
Become more involved with your children and grandchildren
Cross word puzzles/ Sudoko games
Exercise: Yoga/Running/Walking/Hiking/Swimming
Get a pet
Involve yourself more in your place of worship
Join a garden club or a bowling league
Join a senior center
Learn a new language
Local politics
Movies, plays, and concerts
Music: Listening/Learn to play an instrument
Part-time job
Play cards or other games
Reading/Join a book club
Take a class at a community college or adult night school
Take golf or tennis lessons
Use e-mail to write to others or use Facebook
Volunteerism
Wii games

Pay attention to your life. Make things happen. Being active rather than passive in your approach is important in achieving goals. This is true whether it be in sports, business, or retirement. When doing therapy with a newly retired person, I will often ask them to think about things that they wanted to do in the past, but didn't have the finances or time to accomplish. Another approach is to have them make a list of all the things that they would like to add to their life, even if the ideas verge on the fanciful. This may open up a world of new opportunities. At first they may often be negative and hesitant. I tell them what author Po Bronson explains about procrastination. He says, "Don't wait until everything is just right. It will never be perfect. There will always be challenges, and less than perfect conditions. So what? Get started now. With each step you take, you will grow stronger and stronger, more and more skilled, more and more self-confident, and more and more successful."[11]

After this, I encourage them to give even one of their ideas a try. I tell them that I will ask them how they fared at our next session. Possibly, knowing that they have to show up with some answers or achievement at their next session will help further motivate them. Hopefully, with a little bit of luck and a more active approach, they will have some success. It will improve their self-esteem and start to make them feel whole again. Perhaps, they will find something that not only gives them some pleasure, but makes them feel passionate; makes them want to get out of bed in the morning. Start now. Take control of your life. Take the first step.

How you fare during retirement and aging will affect those around you including your family members. If you planned ahead, you may do better than some. No matter what, give yourself time to adjust. I have suggested three to six months as a transition period. After that, if you are still discontent and unhappy, it may be time to talk to someone about your problems. However, at all times, work at finding solutions. Don't expect others to do it for you totally. Talk about what you are feeling with others. They are probably not unusual or odd. Make use of all your resources. Engage your friends, neighbors, and relatives. Film writer and lyricist M. K. Soni got it right when she said, "Retire from work, but not from life."[12] As with any dilemma in life, keep working at it. Take a problem-solving approach. Be proactive. Try new things. Keep your eyes open. You never know what you will see or find down the road. Be optimistic. Maintain a positive attitude. An unknown author once said, "Life begins at retirement."[13] Stay active. Good things may be just around the corner.

Maintaining a positive attitude is also a helpful coping mechanism as you walk through the hills and valleys of retirement and aging. The next chapter looks at the vicissitudes of this coping skill.

17

MAINTAIN A POSITIVE ATTITUDE

A positive attitude is an important ingredient in maintaining a success-ful retirement and doing well during the aging process. Negative changes are part of this end-of-life cycle. Its spectrum includes physical and mental decline. Illnesses appear more readily. Death is lurking in the shadows. No one escapes this life cycle; however, negativity does not have to be part of this life experience. A positive outlook is a choice. The late Elizabeth Edwards in the midst of dealing with the harsh blows that life gave her was able to say, "A positive attitude is not going to save you. What it's going to do is, between now and the day you die, whether that's a short time from now or a long time from now, that every day you're going to actually live."[1]

I hope that you choose to have a positive attitude. Many retirees live happy, productive, creative, and meaningful lives. Richard Atkinson, founder and president of RA Retirement Advisors, says: "(You) have a choice. Be negative, repel others and look at the future with dread or be positive, attract like-minded people and view the future as a new and wonderful opportunity."[2] Henry David Thoreau was right when he said, "None are so old as those who have outlived enthusiasm."[3]

Several studies have shown that a positive mindset during retirement and aging has many advantages. The Ohio longitudinal study found that people with a positive attitude about growing older lived an average of seven-and-a-half years longer than those with a more negative attitude. A University of California–San Diego School of Medicine study found that optimism and the ability to cope successfully with life's challenges were more important to a positive perception than physical health. University of Texas researchers found that people who had a positive attitude were significantly less likely to become frail.[4] A realistic retirement plan coupled with a positive attitude and a little bit of good luck has a good chance of producing a rewarding retirement lifestyle experience.

Your expectations of retirement will influence your attitude. Your mindset is often influenced by how your parents and grandparents viewed retirement. Did they see retirement as the end of the line, as a time to slow down and prepare for the inevitable? Did they anticipate and focus on a decline of creativity, physical, and mental ability? Did they see it as a time of illness and the loss of friends and family members? Or, did they see it as a time to leave work behind and finally develop a new lifestyle? Were they optimistic that the future would bring new adventures, a time to reawaken lost dreams, and a time to discover new people and new places? Hopefully, you will be able to evaluate your expectations and make a conscious choice of which road to follow. Francis D. Glamser, in a paper in the *Journal of Gerontology* called "Determinants of a Positive Attitude toward Retirement" investigated the possibility that attitude toward retirement resulted from the worker's realistic appraisal of the type of retirement experience expected. His research indicated that workers who have a good foundation in terms of finances and friends are likely to have a positive attitude toward retirement.[5]

Some people are negative and have a tendency to "see the glass as half empty" rather than half full. I encourage you to look for the positive in life. It is a choice that you can make. William James said, "Human beings can alter their lives by altering their attitudes of mind."[6] There are many things that you can do to encourage a positive attitude in yourself and improve your chances of having a content life during your retirement years. First of all use self-talk and positive affirmations to keep you on a positive tract. Author Jonathan Lockwood Huie suggests the following positive affirmation: "Today I choose the higher road—the path of charity, acceptance, love, selfishness, (and) kindness."[7] Some of the other ways to build and maintain a positive attitude include the following:

1. Have a financial, emotional, physical, mental, and social plan in place before you retire—this will help you have a path to follow and help you avoid some of the pitfalls that are possible during this stage of

life. Try new activities and catch up on the things that you left behind while working. Do something to allow you to meet new people. Do not just let things happen to you. Take charge of your life. Take a problem-solving approach to life. Do not give up. Keep trying until you get what you want. Retirement is a time to explore new worlds.

2. Don't let "the committee" in your head win the battle. Everyone has an internal dialogue in their head, which I once heard a comedian call "the committee." Much of this internal dialogue is negative and affects the way people see their life on a day to day basis. "The committee" says such things as, "you will fail," "No one will accept your invitation," "You will never make the cut." Let it go. Try not to ruminate. Thinking, thinking, thinking is a waste of time and tends to reinforce a negative attitude. Try to rewrite each negative thought in a positive way.

3. Believe in yourself and your ability to accomplish what you want. Love and respect yourself. Believe that you have the ability to make things happen, that you are a good person and that you deserve success, love, and all the other pleasurable and enjoyable things in life. Be active in your approach to life. Trust that you can make it work. Everyone has limitations. Everyone has similar needs. However, on the other hand, everyone is unique. Focus on what you can do rather than on what you cannot do. Ask for help if you need it but keep moving forward.

4. Exude a positive attitude. Try to maintain a positive mindset. Share your positive attitude with others. Smile more. Articulate in a positive manner. Be friendly and complimentary. Find the humor in life. Laughter has helped defuse many a negative interaction. Things are not black and white but rather radiant shades of gray. Be fair in your evaluation of yourself and the world. Do not magnify your mistakes. Give yourself and others credit for small successes. Look for the good in people and situations.

5. Accept and make peace with who you are. Do not dwell on the past. Let go of regrets and envy. Many things are not under your control. Allow yourself to be human. Focus on what you have accomplished. Compare yourself to others of the same age and socioeconomic status. Do not just look at how many people are ahead of you. Remember, there are many people behind you.

6. Communicate positive and negative feelings. People often can be behaviorally mature and be responsible by working, paying their bills, and doing their chores. Many, however, have a lower degree of emo-

tional maturity, particularly in reference to communicating and accepting feelings of love and anger. They have difficulty saying "I love you" or accepting a compliment. They have difficulty accepting criticism or telling others that they are upset by their behavior. Tell people your feelings. For the negative ones, mix it with kindness and tell them the positive along with the negative. Often this exercise can lead to increased understanding and closeness. It also engenders positivism.[8]

Poor communication skills stood in the way initially preventing Harold and Vivienne from moving in a positive direction in retirement. Both had a negative attitude stemming from their anger that retirement had not met their expectations. Once again, if they had come to me for therapy, I would have asked each of them why they felt so angry and then asked them to articulate their expectations of what they felt would happen in retirement. Vivienne may have said that she hoped that Harold would have helped more around the house leaving them more quality time together. Harold may have said that he was looking forward to traveling and doing more things outside the house with Vivienne. Once the "secret" is out in the open, perhaps they can really communicate and move forward.

As I have said before, people cannot read your mind. People are brought up with different backgrounds. Their thoughts on any particular subject may be different. Moving forward harmoniously requires that people communicate their needs and desires and expectations. You also have to examine your assumptions. Vivienne for instance would be wrong if she just assumed that Harold wouldn't help around the house without actually asking him. At a time when they needed each other the most, their anger and poor communication skills were keeping them apart.

In his blog, "A Shift of Mind," Mel Schwartz, LCSW, says that silence is a relationship killer. This was certainly true in Harold and Vivienne's case at the beginning of their retirement. Schwartz further says that this default position speaks to "the absence of verbal and emotional intimacy . . . not only does it sabotage the lifeline of a healthy coupling, it chokes your expressive needs. . . . Problematic feelings that go unexpressed tend to percolate and boil over . . . the non-verbalization and suppression of your feelings will—over time—result in substantial resentment." Schwartz further maintains that silence can be a way to control the situation ("If they don't know what we are contemplating, then they can't possibly respond.") or used to nonverbally communicate anger and punish the other individual. He concludes that silence leaves no possibility for resolution or growth. It can lead to depression and despair. "The expressing of one's voice is life affirming."[9]

7. Take care of yourself physically and mentally. A sound mind in a sound body helps accomplish goals. Take care of your body. Watch your diet. Pay attention to nutrition and rest. Get medical treatment early before physical problems escalate. Exercise to work off aggressive energy. Don't hold things inside. Talk about what is bothering you. Lighten situations with laughter. Laughter can have psychological benefits and can often be the best medicine to deal with difficult situations.

8. Ralph Carlson, PhD, in his blog on retirement suggests developing defenses against the negative by avoiding media news reports and negative people. He suggests not being a loner but rather having people in your lives that encourage you and give you objective opinions. He further encourages reading and rereading positive books such as *The Magic of Thinking Big*, by Dr. David Schwartz; *How to Win Friends and Influence People*, by Dale Carnegie; *How to Have Confidence and Power in Dealing with People*, by Les Giblin; *How I Raised Myself from Failure to Success in Selling*, by Frank Bettger; and *Positive Personality Profiles*, by Dr. Robert Rohm.[10]

9. Stay engaged in life and all that it has to offer. Stay active physically, socially, and intellectually. Always have a goal. Try new things and be creative. Reconnect to the people in your life and try to make new friends. Take a risk and try new things. Bring meaning to your life by helping others and being active in your community. A friend of mine is a great believer in the saying, "Life is a great adventure." Enjoy the journey.

10. Review your retirement plan periodically. Physical changes and energy levels may vary as you age, requiring that you fine-tune your plan. Refocus your mind if you start to slip back into negativity. Your mind has the capacity to change negative attitudes for positive ones. Be mindful. Stay in the here and now and enjoy the moment. Share your feelings and desires. Holding it all inside can create a negative mindset. Associate with positive people. They will help you stay centered on a positive tract.

A positive attitude provides a better chance of following the road that leads to success and contentment. It is a state of mind that is well worth working toward. It takes effort and determination, but it can be obtained. Author and founder of Success Consciousness, Remez Sasson, says,

> A positive attitude helps you cope more easily with the daily affairs of life. It brings optimism into your life, and makes it easier to avoid worries and negative thinking. If you adopt it as a way of life, it will bring constructive changes into your life, and makes you happier, brighter and more successful. With a positive attitude, you see the bright side of life, become optimistic, and expect the best to happen. . . . If you look at the bright side of life, your whole life becomes filled with light. [11]

There are many transitions that can occur as you age and move forward through the retirement years. If you let them, these difficult experiences can lead you down a negative road. Financial problems can increase your worries. Physical aging and health changes can cause physical and emotional distress. Loss of family members, a spouse, and friends can all be challenging, causing emotional pain and leaving you feeling lonely. You have a choice as to how you handle these stressors. You will do better with these challenges if you can maintain a positive, accepting, and forward-looking attitude. Professional baseball player, Wade Boggs says, "A positive attitude causes a chain reaction of positive thoughts, events and outcomes. It is a catalyst and it sparks extraordinary results." [12]

As the next chapter shows, you will also do better overall in retirement if you can avoid isolation, stay engaged, and get up in the morning looking forward to completing various goals.

18

HAVE A GOAL AND STAY ENGAGED

Another key to a successful retirement and coping with getting older is to stay actively involved in life and all that it has to offer. The previous chapter was entitled "Maintain a Positive Attitude." This chapter's mandate to have a goal and stay engaged goes hand in hand with that directive. One often leads to the other. "About thirty years ago, there was a popular study among social scientists in the field of gerontology that normal aging was associated with a withdrawal from interaction with others and an increase in introversion. This became known as the disengagement theory of aging. In other words, it was thought normal for individuals to disengage from social relationships and withdraw into themselves as they grew older. This is indeed wrong."[1]

More recently, the above theory, of what is considered normal, healthy aging, has been replaced by the "activity theory." This philosophy has been embraced by and reinforced by the baby boomer generation as they move into retirement. I agree that it is important to keep busy and engaged. Continue to learn and grow. Continue to share your knowledge and teach younger generations. Look to the future with optimism. Retain a passion for work or other projects. Continue to feel needed and alive and fill your life with meaning.[2]

Live in the present. Be content with the hand that you have been dealt but optimize it by seeking out things that give you pleasure and enjoyment and give your life meaning and purpose. Do not expect to be happy every moment of every day. Contentment is a more realistic goal. Many of my patients saw their life in terms of black and white. I told them that gray is also a good color. Try to accept life as radiant shades of gray. Look for the small sparkling moments of life. They are there and you can find them if you focus. Be glad and grateful when you experience the warm glow of these positive occasions.

Isolation is the antithesis of contentment. Getting involved in the world is one of the best ways to reduce isolation. The key to a successful life, overall, and retirement and late life in particular, is to stay involved and maintain a passion for work, hobbies, and other projects. Take charge of your life and don't ever be without a goal. Everyone needs something to look forward to that can motivate them to action when they get up in the morning. Staying in your own dark, self-centered world, as illustrated by Harold and Vivienne's early retirement life, will only increase your feelings of anxiety and anger and magnify the negatives. Let the light come in.

Reach out and invest in others. Doing so will help you stop thinking about your own problems and help you gain a perspective. You will realize that you are not alone in your predicament. Talk to other retirees and other older people. You may find that they have similar problems and perhaps yours are not the worst. They may even be able to give you good advice gleaned from their own experiences. You saw this happen when Vivienne finally opened up to her girlfriends. If Harold had done the same, he might have been told to get out of the house more, allow Vivienne some space, and try to develop new interests.

Joining the bowling league with his friend John was the first step that Harold took toward reinventing himself in retirement. Prior to this, he enjoyed his vegetable garden; however, this was something that he did alone. Harold needed people. One thing did indeed lead to another. After that one evening bowling with John, they decided to join a bowling league, which led to fun interaction with others. It also gave the men a chance to ventilate on occasion their anxieties about their health problems and their similar home life concerns. Gradually, Harold moved out into the world even more by adding breakfast at a fast food restaurant with the guys and going to see a sporting event on occasion to his new routine. He seemed less disgruntled and more content in his retirement.

Vivienne's first step into a more positive retirement was opening up to her girlfriends. She started going to church more often. Being a retired teacher gave her several possibilities to work part time that she had never even considered. She tried being a grandmother aide, and found it enjoyable, but not stimulating enough in light of her former higher level employment as a third grade teacher. She therefore decided to sign up as a substitute teacher at an elementary school near her home. They liked her and valued her expertise. They usually had her working one to three days a week, which was just enough to get her out of the house and allow her to maintain her identity. Now when she and Harold did see each other, they had more to share and were happier with their interactions.

In therapy, I often asked my patients, "What do you want to add to your life?" This question can often engender a slew of possibilities and get them thinking more proactively. Even reading a newspaper each day is a way to invest yourself in the outside world and stop focusing only on your own problems. Doing something that you like outside the house will help you meet new people with common interests. You may have to try different things before you find a good fit. Take a continuing education class at the local college. Many offer "lifelong learning" opportunities. Join an outdoor club, volunteer for your church choir, or tutor children at your local elementary school or junior high.

Work part time. This is particularly helpful for those who have difficulty dealing with the loss of structure brought on by retirement. Being involved in the workforce again, even part time, can help reduce your isolation, reinforce your identity, and add to your sense of contentment in retirement. As you saw, working part time as a substitute teacher was very helpful to Vivienne personally and also her marital relationship. (See chapter 16 for more information on part-time work opportunities.)

On the other hand, it is all right to relax and enjoy the simple things in life. People who retire sometimes feel guilty that they are not being productive and working hard. Give yourself permission to enjoy your new freedom. English statesman and naturalist, Sir John Lubbock tells us, "Rest is not idleness, and to lie sometimes on the grass on a summer day listening to the murmur of water, or watching the clouds float across the sky, is hardly a waste of time."[3] For many a balance of the two, work and relaxation, is the answer. However, if you feel that you need more to do, there are many ways to give back, feel productive again, and add purpose to your life.

Daniel H. Pink, in his book, *Drive: The Surprising Truth about What Motivates Us*, discusses three things that will help you stay engaged in the workplace. These points also hold true in retirement. He maintains that to be motivated and productive you need autonomy, mastery, and purpose.[4] *Autonomy* involves the human need to direct and control one's own life. Retirement gives you autonomy; within limits, you can do anything you want with your time. You no longer have to deal with time pressure, work schedules, and demanding bosses. However, the reality is that although you have more autonomy in your life, you must still take into consideration the other people that are part of your nuclear family and world. They also need your attention.

Mastery involves the urge to get better at something that matters to you. It is important to start this process before retirement. In retirement, you may not always have the energy required to start a new hobby and follow it through to mastery. However, there are many exceptions. Feeling passionate about a task will help. Prior to retirement, I asked a friend of mine what he did with his time during retirement. He answered that he looked forward to a good meal, going out with friends, and reading a good book. I wondered if this would be enough for him in the long run. Occasionally, we would hit balls on the driving range or play nine holes of golf together. One day, another friend, who was an avid golfer, asked him to join a golf league. With this friend's encouragement, he became very involved in the game, even bought new golf clubs, and is playing better and more often than ever. He had found his passion. It can be done.

Purpose involves wanting to be part of something bigger than yourself—to do better for the world. Volunteering for a charity or community organization often will help you achieve this goal. The Epilepsy Foundation, the Alzheimer's Association, the Multiple Sclerosis Society, the Lions clubs, the Variety Club, Meal-on-Wheels, and Habitat for Humanity are just a few of the organizations that would appreciate your time and effort and allow you to be part of something bigger than yourself, bring happiness to others in the world, and have purpose in your life. Look for an organization that matches your interests and needs the skills that you have honed during your working life. Senior Corps Volunteer Program is a government-run organization that connects seniors with local and national organizations in need of volunteers.

Charity and volunteer work can pay emotional dividends and increase self-esteem. In an e-newsletter reminder that April is National

Volunteer Month, the Delray Beach Public Library included five mental and physical health benefits of volunteering:

1. Volunteering decreases the risk of depression by increasing social interaction and helping form a support system.
2. Volunteering provides a sense of purpose and fulfillment.
3. Volunteering keeps one physically and mentally active by getting you up and moving while helping others.
4. Volunteering can reduce stress levels and help you appreciate what you have.
5. Volunteering contributes enormously to the "The Happiness"—Studies show that the more you volunteer, the happier you are![5]

Volunteerism is just one way to achieve this goal. There are many ways to help others and add purpose to your life. Share the knowledge that you have accumulated over the years. Mentor a younger person. Work part time, consult, write, or volunteer in your field. You have accumulated much wisdom and knowledge over the years. You may even want to write a book or a magazine article. Make a "wish list." Try to do some of the things that you thought about when you used to say, "When I have time, I will . . ." I love that television ad that maintains, "You couldn't do it earlier in life because life got in the way. Now that the kids are grown and life has moved along write the great American novel!"

Harold and Vivienne had skills that they could have used to be more engaged in the world outside their house. Vivienne was good at crafts such as knitting and crocheting. She could volunteer at a nursing home and teach the patients how to do these crafts. She could have also found others with whom to share these talents. She could also encourage more family interaction and perhaps spend more time with her grandchildren by offering to babysit. Harold also has many skills that he had used at work that his place of worship or other organization would be delighted to make use of. In the fifty-five and older community where I live, people with different skill sets (accounting, engineering, legal, construction, etc.) are often asked to serve on the board or on a committee where their skills can be used pro bono and be helpful to the community.

As I mentioned in chapter 3, invest in relationships. Having people in your life is an important way to stay engaged in the world. Humans are social beings. Ongoing contact with others nourishes people and helps them remain mentally and emotionally healthy. I often encourage patients that if they have four friends, that they should make an effort to call each of them at least once a month. To maintain a friendship, you must show the other person that you value them and are interested in them. There are many ways to widen your social network when you retire and as you age. Reconnect with old friends from high school and college. I guarantee that they will be responsive now that they also have more time on their hands. It is a great way to socialize, keep busy, and have some fun sharing memories.

Seniors today are using e-mail, Facebook, Skype, and Twitter to keep in touch.

> According to data from the Pew Research Center's Internet and American Life Project, the seventy-four-plus demographic is the fastest growing group across Web-based social networks. Use of sites like Facebook and Twitter among Internet users sixty-five and older grew 100 percent between 2009 and 2010, from 13 percent to 25 percent. Many assisted living centers have even begun offering technology classes to get seniors online and in the social-networking loop.[6]

Most communities have senior centers which offer programs for older people. Many serve lunch for a nominal fee. Participating in their programs is a wonderful way to stay engaged. Initially there is usually resistance. Senior people may say, "I don't want to leave the house. I don't want to deal with all those old people. I don't know anyone there." I had one female patient who refused to go to the center, although she lived alone and admitted that she was lonely. The center even offered a bus to pick up participants. After some time and no change in her attitude, I asked her daughter to go with her to the program just to have lunch. After this, the patient started going to the center once a week. Before long, she was going five days a week. Don't give up. Sometimes a gentle push in the right direction is needed.

In her blog, Colleen Canney[7] explains that she feels that the key to staying engaged with life means staying hungry for life. Without this element, we become apathetic. She further says that one stays hungry for life by setting new goals, taking on new challenges, and being open to experiences. Although I certainly agree with Canney that it is important to stay motivated and engaged with life, I must underline the fact, that in my professional opinion, all people do not have the same ability to either practice this philosophy or maintain this concept over time. I would only add that people also need enough mental, physical, and emotional stimulation to remain active. Everyone does not have these ingredients. People's degree of hunger, assertiveness, and drive varies. Some may require help getting started. Some do not have enough support or stimulation. Some may need someone to run along side of them to make sure that they stay on track.

However, although I am pointing out these possible roadblocks, this does not mean that I feel that you should not keep trying. Do not give up. Keep practicing. Perhaps you need some outside help. Sometimes, it is helpful to have a mentor, therapist, clergyman, or good friend to encourage you, help keep you motivated, and keep you moving in a positive direction. If you feel that you need assistance, make the call today. Help is available. Remember, life does not usually come to you. You have to leave the house and immerse yourself in it.

A study by the Sloan Center on Aging and work at Boston College showed that most people over age fifty-five are doing well in this area. It showed that "92 percent of people ages fifty-five to sixty-four and 76 percent of respondents sixty-five or older-were involved with paid work, volunteering, care giving or educational activities." The study further showed that

> these older Americans are not just casually involved in these activities . . . they are actively engaged in them. . . . Even more important, the study discovered that this high level of engagement is directly linked to the overall well being of older adults. Those who reported being highly engaged . . . had significantly higher scores for life satisfaction and mental health than those who were relatively unengaged.[8]

Staying engaged in life doesn't mean staying aimlessly busy. There is more to it than that. The Sloan Study agreed that being involved in activities is not the key to good mental health. Engagement is required. However, the nuances involved in engagement means doing something that you feel positive about, having goals that reward you with pleasure, and allow you to feel good about yourself. It is helpful if the task also helps you to feel connected to the world and other people. As you saw above, Daniel Pink feels that autonomy, mastery, and purpose are also important ingredients.

I also suggest that you will do better engaging life if you throw away feelings of guilt and resentment about the past. Be realistic about your expectations. Don't expect to be happy every moment. Remember only you can find things that make you feel happy. Don't depend on others to do the job for you. Keep working on staying positive, active, and engaged in life. It will pay dividends in many ways including improving mental and physical health.

After retiring, most of us will have eighteen to twenty years more to live. Hopefully, people will make use of these years creatively. How you add quality to your life and obtain autonomy, mastery, and purpose in the process is an individual matter. To make the most of these years and not become bored and depressed, you have to make every effort to stay engaged and active in life. This is the most important clue to being successful. Like anything else that is worthwhile, it is hard work. You must be persistent and constantly reevaluate your goals and continue to push yourself out the door each day toward fulfillment and contentment.

Another coping method to help you deal with being retired and getting older is religious affiliation and spirituality. The next chapter takes a look at what religion and spirituality can offer to make you more content in the last stage of life.

19

RELIGIOUS AFFILIATION

When I was a young boy, religion was an integral part of the fabric of my life and those around me. My family and neighbors attended religious services regularly at the sanctuary of their choice. Many went to parochial school or attended Hebrew school after their regular public school day. The Chanukah lights shone brightly in windows, and Christmas trees and decorations gave a festive air to the area during the respective holidays. The architecture of my neighborhood was punctuated with various houses of worship. There was a Roman Catholic church, several small synagogues, and a beautiful ornate Greek Orthodox church. Each had their own rituals, traditions, and prayers. What they seemed to have in common were various degrees of pomp and circumstance, a musicality, and a warm sense of community. I realize now that they also offered their members structure, security, and so much more. The world has changed and organized religion, for some, has become less important than it once was. What a loss.

Different generations have different views on religion. A third of millennials (born after 1980) are unaffiliated with any religion. They are the least religiously connected generation in modern American history. Twenty-one percent of the generation Xers (born from 1965 to 1980) are not involved in organized religion. Fifteen percent of the baby boomers (born from 1946 to 1964) are unaffiliated compared with 9 percent of the silent generation (born from 1928 to 1945).[1] I would have to add to this list, the "old-old" generation (those over age eighty-five), who, in my experience as a psychiatrist, are generally conservative and devout and are more apt to carry forward their religious beliefs, practices, and values. However, I have found, working with patients, that as they age, many, looking for true meaning in their lives and more aware of their own mortality, come back into the fold and once again embrace their religious practices, including going to religious services.

Some people deny that they are religious but maintain that they are spiritual. What is the difference? Religion can be defined as "an organized system of beliefs, practices, rituals and symbols through which ones' relationship to God or others is nurtured and exercised."[2] Spirituality, on the other hand,

> is a distinctive, potentially creative and universal dimension of human experience arising within inner subjective awareness of individuals and within communities, social groups, and traditions. It may be intimately "inner," immanent, and personal, within the self and others, and/or as relationship with that which is wholly "other," transcendent and beyond the self. It is experienced as being of fundamental or ultimate importance and is therefore concerned with matters of meaning and purpose in life, truth, and values.[3]

It is not my purpose here to push you to practice or convert to any religion or convince you that God exists. My goal is only to make the point that, because the world is chaotic, a belief system can provide a structure that can increase security and feelings of control. I also want to point out that religious faith and spirituality can have many positive benefits as you retire and age and have to cope with change, loss, and feeling vulnerable due to physical and emotional decline. Some of these are:

Increase contentment: "Retirees who attend some form of worship, even if it is only occasionally, are more content than those who seldom or never do . . . this has as much to do with being part of a group with which you share time and values."[4] A Pew Research Center study showed that attending religious services helps increase happiness in retirement.[5]

People who have religious or spiritual beliefs are happier than those who don't, no matter what their beliefs. These principles give people a sense of meaning. It also gives them a social network and a sense of well-being or comfort. It's less about what you believe than the fact that you have a community, a church, a synagogue, a Bible-study group. It's the social support network that is fulfilling. It's the sense that you are looking after one another that matters.

Believers have a certain mindset; the power of prayer, the belief in an afterlife, the sense that someone is looking after them, that there is a higher power, and that things happen for a reason. This mindset helps people make sense of tragedy, struggle, and loss. One can believe, "I'll see this person later," or "God only gives you what you can handle," or "There is a silver lining in the suffering." Religion is about helping other people and having others looking after you. [6]

- *Encourage health and well-being/Improve health outcomes*: Religious and spiritual practices appear to have a positive benefit on health and well-being. "Studies of mortality rates among Seventh Day Adventists, for example, show that the earlier the age at entry into the religious practice, the lower the mortality rate from cardiovascular disease." [7] "Another study of adults in Alameda County, California, also has shown that people who attend religious services are less likely to smoke cigarettes in the first place; however, if those who attend did smoke at the start of the study, they were more likely than those who didn't attend services to quit smoking during the period of the study." [8]
- A 2010 Internet National Med Poll showed that 79.4 percent of healthcare professionals believed that religious faith can have a positive impact on a patient's outcome (after illness, surgery, or other medical procedure). [9]
- *Diminishes the prevalence of addiction*: Substance use and abuse are less prevalent among persons who identify themselves as highly religious or spiritual. [10] Religion and spirituality is a key factor in Alcohol Anonymous. "The heart of AA's philosophy (and twelve step program) is that addiction should be seen as a spiritual problem and that genuine recovery requires a profound spiritual awakening." [11]
- *Encourages forgiveness*: Author Anne Lamott says that one of the special gifts of spiritual faith is the message of forgiveness. She talks about having empathy for others and forgiving herself and accepting her limitations as she got older. "I have finally learned to forgive myself for most of my disappointing character traits and iffier decisions." [12] "Some of the world's great acts of forgiveness

have been motivated by a religious ethic and faith in the importance of forgiveness. For example, Martin Luther King, Jr., frequently used Christian language to preach a message of peace and forgiveness. Other great leaders inspired by religious teachings on forgiveness include Mahatma Gandhi, Nelson Mandela and the 14th Dalai Lama."[13]

- *Provides a support system*: A religious community made up of a variety of individuals, representing several generations, provides a strong sense of support and connection. A church or synagogue is a place that we can go not to be alone. The activities that they offer, such as religious services, prayer groups, singing in a choir, going on a weekend retreat, or listening to an inspirational speaker can both educate and lift you up. Participation can prevent you from being isolated and can provide courage and strength at times of need, such as the death of a parent or spouse. Clergy are available to counsel if necessary. Congregants can become good friends. Religious institutions can become a second home. They can also be a place to celebrate special occasions such as the birth of a child, a bar or bat mitzvah, a confirmation, or a wedding.

- *Provide rules for living*: Religious traditions, especially in adolescence and early adulthood, provide rules for living. For example, some religions have very particular rules about diet and alcohol use, and most faiths have beliefs about maintaining the purity of the body as the vessel of the soul. In general, religious faiths discourage self-indulgent behaviors and promote "moderation in all things," if not actual asceticism. Many spiritual and religious practices, in fact, involve the temporary and intermittent, or in some cases, lifelong denial of behaviors that are considered pleasurable by most people, such as drinking, eating meat, or having sex.[14]

- *Maintain tradition*: Tradition is the glue that binds one generation to another. In a fast-paced world where people seem to only communicate through electronic media, sharing religious practices can bring people back to the basics and be a time when they are actually physically together and communicating in person. Religion encourages this through ritual and belief. Church or synagogue services are a time for family to be together in a unique way. The older people that you may meet at a religious institution have a wealth of history to share. Time spent with grandparents can be educational. Religious education also can teach much about the past. Family togetherness at holiday times are exceptional and memorable occasions. Lighting the candles during Chanukah, attending Christmas midnight mass, or partaking in a holiday meal, are special moments to share with family and others. These moments slow down time, and allow people to take a break, for a while, from their busy lives. They allow people to share past memories, make new pleasant memories, and give an opportunity to acknowledge feelings of love for each other.

There does seem to be a connection between religious affiliation/spirituality and a satisfying retirement.

The reasons . . . mostly revolve around the awareness of one's own mortality. We see our body decline, understand there is a loss of mental sharpness as we age, watch friends and relatives die, or lose frequent contact with our grown children who may live far away. These factors naturally lead us to consider what our life has meant. We also may be looking for something to help us cope with the unimaginable: the end of our time on earth.[15]

The Bible says,

for everything there is a season, and a time for every matter under heaven: a time to be born, and a time to die; a time to plant, and a time to pluck up what is planted; a time to kill, and a time to heal; a time to break down, and a time to build up; a time to weep, and a time to laugh; a time to mourn, and a time to dance; a time to cast away stones, and a time to gather stones together; a time to embrace, and a time to refrain from embracing.[16]

As people get older they are more apt to seek a universal connection and try to answer the question, what is life all about? As mentioned above, retirees with strong religious participation seem to be happier due to a variety of factors including the social aspects of being with like-minded people. The Mormons and Amish bring many of the happiness factors together as they combine the structure of religion, lifestyle, and a tight-knit community. Freud downplayed religion, feeling that it was "a universal obsessional neurosis," and just a way to have a father figure substitute to lean on. No matter what your beliefs, having a structure and being part of a compatible community are helpful in increasing happiness and contentment in retirement and aging. This stage of life can be a spiritual journey where you can continue to grow and discover new purpose, new meaning, and new direction in life.

Religion and spirituality offer another route to carry through one of the main themes of this book. I have encouraged you to stay active and engaged with others and the community. Churches and synagogues sponsor many events that allow you to volunteer and give back to others. It may be by running a rummage sale, preparing and giving food to the poor, sponsoring educational events that are open to the public, or being available to help other members in need. There are also opportunities at any religious facility to volunteer in-house by working in the office, leading a prayer group, helping with fund-raising, or being on an administrative or board committee. All of these activities can add meaning to your life.

Religion has not always been treated with tolerance and respect. In spite of all its benefits, religious affiliation has long been associated with stigma and prejudice. At times in history people have had to hide their religious beliefs and secretly practice their rituals and prayers. During the Spanish Inquisition, Jews and Protestants and anyone not believing in and converting to Catholicism were tortured. "Christians have and continue to be persecuted in certain parts of the world. Periods throughout history have condemned Christians to death due to their religion. China and certain other nations still persecute Christians, imprisoning them for preaching or handing out bibles."[17]

There is a long history of religious prejudice. At one time, every Jew in England was expelled. Those that were left were chased into a tower that was set alight burning the Jews to death. Hitler condemned six million Jews to death in the ovens of the Nazi concentration camps during World War II, due to their religious beliefs and ethnicity. Psychiatrist Viktor Frankl says that these same beliefs helped him and his fellow prisoners in Auschwitz bear their suffering and get through the night: "It is the spiritual freedom which cannot be taken away that makes life meaningful and purposeful."[18] In the United States, where religious freedom is a given and tolerant behavior applauded, the roots of anti-Semitism still run deep.

In the world today, terrorists misinterpret the Koran and the Shaha-da (the first pillar of Islam) to justify their radical behavior and indoctrinate young people to their philosophy and cause. Because of this, the average Muslim has been unfairly condemned and stigmatized. "Often, ignorance just worsens a difficult situation. The press doesn't always help, reinforcing stereotypes and publicizing only negative stories. For example, many people are currently very concerned about Islamopho-bia (prejudice of Muslims/Islam)—Muslims are hated or distrusted, and used as scapegoats."[19]

Vivienne always thought of herself as a conservative Jewish woman. She had been raised in a traditional background where she saw her mother light Friday night candles and prepare wonderful dinners for the holidays. She did the same. However, after her mother died, she went to synagogue daily to say the Mourner's Kaddish for the first thirty days after her mother's passing. (The Mourner's Kaddish is a five-verse prayer that is recited for eleven months once a week after the first thirty days by the one observing the mourning period. The practice begins on the day of burial, for a deceased parent, sibling, child, or spouse by one observing the mourning period and then is said once a year on the anniversary of the death.)

She was impressed by the congregant's kindness and words of comfort. Many came up to her to offer their condolences. The rabbi acknowledged her loss and placed his hand on her shoulder. Vivienne was grateful for the support and love that the religious services and the synagogue members offered her in her time of need. Over the course of the month, she made several new friends. After the thirty-day mourning period, she continued to attend services regularly on Saturday morning for a fresh infusion of love and emotional support. Before long, she found herself volunteering at the synagogue and participating in more of their activities. The synagogue became an integral and important part of her life.

Religious affiliation is an individual choice. However, it can offer many benefits and help cope with life's stressors and changes, both positive and negative. These supportive attributes can be particularly helpful as you retire, age, and feel more vulnerable emotionally and physically. Having a belief system can give new meaning to life, increase sense of security and emotional strength, and allow you to feel more in control. It can add to your feeling of contentment and improve your mood. Its principles can give you a perspective and a better understanding of what life is all about. It encourages forgiveness. It can have a positive benefit on health and supply guidelines for living your life. It can discourage negative behaviors. It can help deal with loss. It can provide a road map to deal with death and the last part of life.

Religion/spirituality offers a community which can be supportive during times of need and offers a place where you can feel included and less isolated. People are there when you need help. I will never forget the night that the electricity went out in my home and the surrounding area. It was cold and snowy. We had no heat in the house. We couldn't go to my daughter's house, because the bridge was closed. There were no openings in the local hotels. My wife thought to call the synagogue, thinking that we could go over there for a few hours to warm up. To our surprise, the director called us back and gave us the name of the head of the "Hesed" (benevolent) committee, who lived in another part of the community. He immediately called us and invited us to sleep over his house in their family's guest room. We are forever grateful for his family's kindness. The next night, we were able to get a hotel room.

Houses of worship offer numerous activities that can enrich your life and allow you to give back to others. You can meet and work with like-minded people. Worship also has the potential to foster companionship and friendship. Religious services are a way to spend quality time with your nuclear family and relatives. Churches and synagogues are a place to share times of sorrow as well as joyful and festive occasions with family and friends. It is a place where you can feel at home, cared for, and included. They offer ways to cope with the inevitable changes that occur when you retire and get older.

As you can see, religious affiliation can be a true lifeline for some as they try to conquer some of the difficult situations that they have to handle later in life. The next chapter will look at another valuable, but very different, coping mechanism that can be used when dealing with the negative aspects of retirement, including problems in marital and other relationships, and the downside of aging. At these times it is often helpful to see the lighter side of things, count your blessings, and laugh. Laughter can often diffuse tense situations, and can help deal with stress and change.

20

LAUGHTER IS THE BEST MEDICINE

Although humans are no longer running away from dangerous animals in the forest, stress still seems to clutter life, regardless of age. Any difficult situation has the potential for producing a stress reaction, particularly when it threatens one's life, risk of injury, or loss of security. A changing world with new conflicts between nations and the potential for nuclear warfare, shifting climate conditions, economic issues, and loss of employment, multiple marriages and second families to deal with, and an increase in technology skills to learn increases modern stress levels.

Retiring and getting older can cause much stress for individuals as they try to cope with loss and change. Living with stress can produce symptoms of anxiety, including restlessness, heart palpitations, irritability, and tension. It can cause sadness, anger, and inadequacy, and precipitate negative acting out behaviors. It can play havoc with marriage and other relationships. Everyone needs some help at times. What can be done? Sometimes, even reducing unrealistic expectations and backing off from time pressures, solutions such as exercise, relaxation techniques, biofeedback, lifestyle changes, and psychotherapy or medication are still not enough. What else can be done? There is one additional easy option—laugh. Some suggest that laughter is the best medicine to deal with difficult situations. It affects the body and mind in a positive way. Looking at life with a sense of humor helps keep things in perspective and balance and increases one's ability to cope and feel more in control.

Many famous people, including presidents, professionals, and writers, have applauded the virtues of laughter. Abraham Lincoln admitted during the Civil War, "With the fearful strain that is on me night and day, if I did not laugh I should die."[1] Sigmund Freud theorized that laughter releases tension and "psychic energy" and is thus a good way to relax and recharge.[2] American humorist, novelist, and lecturer, Mark Twain, said "The human race has one really effective weapon, and that is laughter."[3] In 1979, Norman Cousins published his book, *Anatomy of an Illness* and told the world how he treated his chronic ankylosing spondylitis with a combination of laughter induced by watching Laurel and Hardy, Marx Brothers films, and episodes of *Candid Camera* as well as taking mega-doses of vitamin C.[4]

In the movie *One Flew over the Cuckoo's Nest*, McMurphy (played by Jack Nicholson) says, "When you lose your sense of humor, you lose your footing." Another character says about McMurphy, "He knows you have to laugh at the things that hurt you, just to keep yourself in balance, just to keep the world from running you plumb crazy." This is great wisdom from someone who lives in a psychiatric institution. Your sense of humor is one of the most potent tools you have to cope with those days when life seems determined to deal you enough stress to make you crazy.[5] Even the Bible states that "a cheerful heart is good medicine, but a crushed spirit dries up the bones."[6] Everyone could use a little more humor in their life.

Much of the evidence is anecdotal and only limited research has been done on the subject; however, laughter affects the body and can have a positive impact on physical health. People change physiologically when they laugh. Laughing causes the endothelium lining blood vessels to expand which increases blood flow.[7] It can boost immunity by increasing immunoglobulin (an antibody that helps fight upper respiratory disease), lowers stress hormones, such as cortisol, decreases and increases tolerance to pain, relaxes muscles, and prevents heart disease.[8] The muscle movements involved in laughing cause the brain to produce endorphins, which are pain relievers, stress reducers, and can make people feel better. Laughter has been shown to lead to reductions in stress hormones such as cortisol and epinephrine. Laughter also boosts the number of antibody-producing cells and enhances the effectiveness of T-cells, leading to a stronger immune system and thus may be a good defense against illness.[9]

There are also psychological benefits to laughter. Looking at life with a sense of humor helps keep things in perspective and balance, and increases one's ability to cope. A positive attitude as well as a supportive environment also helps. When I do couples or marital therapy, I always recommend that the best way to reduce spousal strife is to not let arguments escalate. One of the most effective ways to accomplish this is through humor and laughter. All couples fight. Making a joke can reduce the tension and anger of the moment and help the couple refocus and gain perspective.

Children do not always meet parents' expectations as they retire and age. Parents poured their emotions and money into raising their children and giving them everything that they could, emotionally and physically. Their assumption was that as they aged, their children would give back some of that positive attention. It does not always work out that way. Children raise their own families, have their own agenda, and their own busy lives. You are not alone. Talk to other couples and you will find that you are all in the same boat. Rather than being disappointed and resentful, laugh a little and try to join your children and grandchildren for holidays, special occasions, and some of their activities. Seeing a grandchild play sports or dance in a recital can be very exciting and satisfying. "That's my grandson," I yelled, as he rounded third base, about to make the winning run in a baseball game. Be grateful for what you have and have faith that your children will be there for you if you really need them.

Laughter is also a social phenomenon that can strengthen relationships. It connects people to others in a most intimate way. Victor Borge, Danish-born American comedian and pianist, said, "laughter is the closest distance between two people."[10] For some reason, telling a joke when with others, seems to bring them closer together, relax the situation, and humanize the relationship. Most likely another person in the group will come back with another joke. Speakers use this technique to relax their audiences. An unknown author said, "Laughter is an instant vacation." Another anonymous person stated, "Laughter is the spark of the soul." My favorite, as a psychiatrist, however, is humor magazine publisher, Arnold Glasow's comment that "Laughter is a tranquilizer with no side effects."[11] I understand that there are even laughter yoga clubs forming around the country.

Humor therapy has become a positive adjunctive treatment tool in health care. It can foster "the three c's":

1. Connectivity
2. Coping
3. Control[12]

Hospitals around the country are incorporating formal and informal laughter therapy programs into their therapeutic regimens. In countries such as India, laughing clubs—in which participants gather in the early morning for the sole purpose of laughing—are becoming as popular as Rotary Clubs in the United States.[13] Physician Patch Adams used humor and clowning to help hospitalized patients and improve health-care.[14]

Laughter therapy is a thriving business for healthcare.

> "Clown care" is part of bedside treatment, using juggling, magic tricks, and gags and making "clown rounds" with novelty store rubber chickens and other paraphernalia to promote laughter in nursing homes, cancer units, and even hospice settings. There are "laughter coaches" and seminars teaching healthcare professionals how to use humor with patients. There is even a *Chuckle Channel*, a film subscription service for hospital environments featuring humor therapy specialists such as Hawaii's Hob Osterlund, RN [alter-ego: Nurse "Ivy Push"]. . . . But then there's this question—what if nothing seems very funny and you can't find anything to laugh about? Apparently, we humans have another shot at getting laughter's benefits without relying on a bedside clown act, a laughter coach, or a DVD of a comedy monologue. We can actually "fake it 'til we make it"—in another words, just pretending to chuckle, giggle, and snort starts the process of full-blown laughter. So put down the cell phone, take a break from jumping to your next web destination, and laugh.[15]

You are never too old to laugh and use humor to cope with stress. It's never too late to improve your humor skills, even if you're past retirement age. Laughter is particularly helpful, as we retire and age, in dealing with the chronic illnesses that are common during that time. Life can change in a moment. Now you are well. Suddenly you're diagnosed with a chronic illness such as diabetes, chronic obstructive pulmonary disease (COPD)/emphysema, arthritis/osteoarthritis, or ulcerative colitis. Lightening the mood can quell some of your initial feelings of fear, sadness, and loss, and give you a perspective. Laughter can help you move forward in the direction of control, a new acceptance, and contentment.

The Montefiore Einstein Cancer Center at Montefiore Hospital in New York City runs a monthly "Strength through Laughter" therapy. It is one of several types of laughter or humor therapy being offered by medical facilities around the country for patients diagnosed with cancer or other chronic diseases.[16] Your ability to laugh at the world and its absurdities is a healthy approach to life. People who adapt by using humor minimize their problems and put them in perspective. They realize the truth that a hundred years from now, nobody will care. Humor pays off. It can help you be healthier and even live longer.[17]

There are various ways to find laughter in your life and lighten the situation:

- We have to re-capture our smiles. Although laughter and smiles are not the same, they are related and often a smile will lead to healthy, hearty laughter.
- Spoil ourselves with funny comedy movies, videos, CDs, and audiocassettes.
- Relive some of the most embarrassing moments in your life. Relate these moments to family and friends in a humorous way.
- See the humor, find the laughter even in the annoying, frustrating things that happen to you.
- Read the comics. Look for the fun things in the newspaper and TV.
- Go through photo albums and relive the fun. Add funny captions to the pictures to enhance and underscore the fun moments.
- With family members at dinner time and at business meetings, share some of the fun things that happened to you, or around you.
- When people show anger or frustration, respond to the situation with humor.
- Interject your communication with family, co-workers, and friends with humor, and encourage their funny contributions in return.
- Establish a humor buddy relationship. Someone who you share fun with and who can give you a boost when you need it.

- Share a joke. More than likely, someone will share a joke back.
- Nothing in life is that bad, or so serious that laughter won't help you through the situation.[18]

Children do it naturally. A baby laughs around three hundred times a day compared to an average adult, who laughs only around twenty times a day.[19] When they are confused or afraid, children make their problems into a game, giving them a sense of control and an opportunity to experiment with new solutions. Spend time with a youngster. Take yourself less seriously.[20] Let yourself act silly and childish at times. It is good for you. Freud encouraged such behavior and called it regression in the service of the ego. Even if it is just a distraction, give it a try. Laughter is fun. It seems to have many benefits and may help you reduce stress and deal better with difficult situations. Ecclesiastes 3:4 says that "there is a time to weep, and a time to laugh; a time to mourn, and a time to dance." Make sure that you take your opportunity to laugh. It may be therapeutic. It can give you a new perspective and improve the quality of your life. It can help you cope and give you a feeling of control.

Now that you are hopefully coping better with the stressors of retirement and aging and have things better under control, this book will conclude with some of the wisdom of life that I have learned in practicing psychiatry for over forty years, and take a look at what truly is important and gives life meaning.

CONCLUSION

The Meaning of Life—Aging Wisdom

"**W**hat's it all about Alfie?" This first line in the song written by Burt Bacharach and Hal David to promote the 1966 film, *Alfie* was also one of actor Michael Caine's famous lines in the film to illustrate his confusion about what life was all about. After years of superficiality and self-centeredness, this narcissistic womanizer finally starts to think about the love and relationships that he has missed. Today, these words have become a universal symbol illustrating the philosophical question of the meaning of life. What changes as we get older is not only our overall knowledge, but the shading and nuances that give new significance to things and helps us understand what is truly important in life.

What changes as you get older is perspective. You gain the ability to see the whole picture. A new clarity develops about what is really significant in life. You gain a new appreciation of various life components. As you age, you develop gray hair, lose hearing and eyesight, but also gain a clearer understanding of life, more self-confidence, and the power that comes with the authority of experience. Good health and freedom from emotional and physical pain is a gift that cannot always be controlled completely. However there are various attitudes and behaviors that can be modified, made part of life, and used to gain positive benefits. These experiences linger long after material goals are reached and money is spent. Aging wisdom tends to focus more on acceptance, respect, honesty, hope, tradition, meaningful, close relationships, love, and gratitude. I would have to add to this list that you tend to stay in the moment more and savor the simple pleasures of life, which can bring light into an otherwise dark day.

Everyone seems to rush through life. The young can't wait to drive a car, finish school, and get a job; some want to get married and have children; parents can't wait to see their children grow up so that they can become grandparents. Life goes by so quickly. Before you know it, you are old. Sometimes people learn too late to appreciate the moment. One evening, my wife and I attended a musical program. A woman, probably in her eighties, was led in by her aide and sat next to us. She wore a cotton pink and white dress, a light-pink sweater, and white shoes. She stared straight ahead. The members of the audience were given small tambourines, maracas, and other noise makers so that we could interact with the concert. The music started. The lady sat silently, not communicating with anyone. No emotion showed on her face. Suddenly, her right hand rose and she started to shake her maraca in perfect time to the music. Her facial expression did not change; however, she was enjoying the show and having a few moments of pleasure. What a delight to see.

Viktor E. Frankl in his book, *Man's Search for Meaning*, looks for the meaning of life through a different lens, as a prisoner in the Auschwitz concentration camp. He offers a central existential theme that says, "To live is to suffer, to survive is to find meaning in the suffering." While in the camp, he was able to find a deeper meaning and something positive in seeing a wonderful sunset, a bird fly, a light in a distant farmhouse, and the memory of his wife. He developed the theory of "Logotherapy," a meaning-centered psychotherapy. "According to Logotherapy, we can discover the meaning of life in three different ways: (1) by creating a *work* or doing a deed; (2) by experiencing something or encountering someone (*love*); and (3) by the attitude we take toward unavoidable suffering (*attitude*)."[1]

John Bogle, the founder of Vanguard, the mutual fund giant, at age eighty-four, shared the following wisdom about what is important in life, when he was interviewed by columnist, Art Carey, in the *Philadelphia Inquirer*. He said,

> Pay attention to your life. . . . [It] is solitary, poor, nasty, brutish and short. Survival depends on becoming a warrior. . . . Press on regard-

less, Try to make things happen. . . . Above all never give up your idealism No matter how dark things get, keep your eye on the brighter side of things. Never let your determination falter . . . never forget the important role of luck in your life. Never, never, never say, I did it all myself else. . . . Other than that, it comes down to pretty simple things: First, don't forget your family, because in the end that's all you really have, next be a decent human being, and don't think that you are better than anybody else.[2]

As people grow older, they grow wiser and realize that there are some other human needs that if fulfilled can also give meaning to their lives. You cannot control how others treat you; however, you can live your life based on these principles and hope that others treat you in kind. These include the following four issues:

- Acceptance and approval
- Respect and dignity
- Honesty and trust
- Hope

Acceptance and approval. Children, particularly, need acceptance and approval to grow and thrive. A kind word, a compliment, or caring gesture can help raise self-esteem and foster emotional growth. Everyone wants to be accepted for who they are, flaws and faults included. Nobody is perfect. Being human means having both positive and negative traits. If you expect everyone to be perfect you will constantly be frustrated. Have realistic expectations of others. I suggest that if you have relatives, a partner or spouse or friends that have more positive traits than negative issues that you keep them around. Work on relationships that are important to you. They must be lovingly nurtured and not taken for granted. Anesthesiologist, Charlie White, when interviewed for *Time* magazine at age 102, told the reporter that the answer to how to have a good life, equanimity, and inner peace is to separate those things that we cannot control from the things that we can.[3]

Self-acceptance is also important. For some, it is a life-long struggle. Author Anne Lamott says, "getting older has given me more comfort in not knowing all the answers. . . . I have finally learned to forgive myself for most of my disappointing character traits and iffier decisions."[4] Past American Psychiatric Association president Dilip Jeste, MD, explains research that shows psychological well-being demonstrated on a u-shaped curve that the level of happiness is the early eighties is similar to that in the early twenties.[5] He says that one of the factors causing this is "a greater acceptance of one's physical limitations, contentedness with past accomplishments, [and] reduced preoccupation with peer pressure, and a more realistic appraisal of one's strengths and limitations."

Respect and dignity. Everyone wants to maintain their self-esteem, be taken seriously, and be treated with consideration. Everyone wants to be respected for their deeds and actions but particularly for being who they are. Older people—particularly as they deal with real-life stressors, including illness, disability, widowhood, financial distress, and social isolation—desperately hold on to and value being treated with respect. A Pew Research Center Social and Demographic Trends survey on aging showed that about six-in-ten older people say that they get more respect and feel less stress than when they were younger.[6] I have found that people hold doors open for you more, get up and give you a seat and also tend to show concern and ask you "are you OK?" Your children may also start to be more solicitous and caring as you age. This is certainly a pleasant bonus of getting older.

Author and editor Cindy K. Sproles advises people to treat elderly parents with dignity.

> Today's society has lost a huge part of its compassion. The world of media brings loss, pain, and tragedy into our lives at an overwhelming rate. As a people, we've become desensitized to the core values we were taught as children. . . . When the roles reverse, remember to love and treat our aging seniors with dignity and honor—for without them, we would be nothing. Scripture instructs us to "Honor your father and mother." (Eph. 6:2–3, *NLT*). . . . Preserving the dignity of our seniors as they succumb to aging is the most important thing, we as children can offer our parents. After all, everything we learned . . . we learned from our parents. If for nothing else, they have earned the right.[7]

Honesty and trust. According to Thomas Jefferson, honesty is the first chapter of the book of wisdom. Good communication can be a buffer against stress and engender trust. Filled with shame, grief, hurt, or anger, people often worry about what to tell others about the events in their lives. Dealing with the stress of divorce, losing a job, or a child's illness, they wonder what to say. The answer is simple; hit them with reality. The easiest answer is to be straightforward and tell them the simple truth without embellishment. You will probably find that they will understand and be empathetic. They more than likely have had similar experiences or know a friend or relative who has gone through the same thing. You will realize that you are not alone.

As we get older, men particularly tend to open up and share more about their disappointments and failures. They may be more willing to talk about not having been athletic or having been bullied as a child, difficulties with their parents, or being scared in high school. This tends to bring them closer together and equalize the playing field. I can remember going to my fiftieth reunion from my all-male high school. Some of the men, whom many of us had been a bit jealous of, at age sixteen, came up to the microphone and told about memories of that time and place. Some of those, whom we had greatly admired and had seen at the time as macho, tough, and together, admitted how scared and insecure they had really felt. Amazing!

Hope. During life's difficult moments of stress, physical illness, or tragedy, everyone needs hope to keep them pointed in a positive direction and motivated. My book, *Dancing with Medusa*, which is about a patient who I knew over the course of thirty-seven years, is a story of hope. In spite of how emotionally ill she was at age twenty, when I first met her, Bella did well in life and is thus a figure of hope for those with mental illness. The late Norman Cousins, author of the book, *Anatomy of an Illness*, was a strong believer that hope is a potent weapon against disease and a vital ingredient in healing even serious illness.

In his blog, Jeff Goins writes,

> Life can seem a bit disappointing. Even the greatest lives are full of profound loss and heartbreak. It seems that pain is inevitable, and while we may say that we know good can come out of it, what hurts still hurts. . . . In the process, one can quite easily lose hope. . . . As humans, we need hope. We can't live without it. It is the lifeblood to our spiritual survival, and the only thing that pulls us out of the deep trenches of the pain and hurt of life.[8]

The late Elizabeth Edwards, in her book, *Resilience*, takes a different perspective and warns against the danger of maintaining hope about things that cannot be changed. After the loss of her son, the breakdown of her marriage to John Edwards, and her battle with breast cancer, she realized, "each time that I fell into a chasm, I had to accept that the planet had taken a few turns and I could not turn it back. My life was and would always be different, and it would be less than I hoped it would be. . . . And the longer I clung to the hope that my old life might come back, the more I set myself up for unending discontent."[9]

I have saved for last, the four things in life that I feel are really the most important of all. They are:

1. Tradition
2. Closeness to people
3. Love and affection
4. Gratitude

Maintain tradition. In a world that is chaotic and constantly changing, tradition provides a sense of stability and structure. Particularly today, when there are wide gaps between generations, sharing traditions can be a vital link between the old and the new. Grandparents have a wealth of meaningful history to share. They also have an abundance of unconditional love that can nurture and sustain their families. Not having to be a parent and set limits, they can be less judgmental and more accepting. This is a true gift for a grandchild. Include them in your lives and encourage them to be involved. The warm feelings of family at holiday times or other occasions are special moments. They can be times to get to know your grandparents but also a time to interact and become friends with your cousins and extended family. Some of these people, particularly those who are around your age, may be the only family that you will have left when you get older. They may truly be in your life after many others have died and will become part of your support system. A lifetime of memories is the glue that will hold you together.

One of my most precious memories from my own childhood were two regular family gatherings, which brought together the generations. Every Sunday, my mother's family would meet for dinner at the same restaurant. Here we all sat around a large table, both young and old. We shared our lives, laughed, and enjoyed each other's company. My grandparents' stories were a history lesson. On Friday evening, before going to synagogue to greet "the Sabbath bride," my mother always made a special dinner. My father, who often was out in the evening, was always present. His mother and father were also always there. It was a special time indeed. Therefore, I encourage you to share your childhood traditions with your children, start new traditions in your own home, and encourage your children as they get older to do the same.

Closeness to people. Intimacy or being close to another human being, with whom we can share our secrets, fears, pain, and joy can add another dimension to existence. A hug can sometimes say more that many words. If life has you down ask for a hug from your spouse or significant other. It can be very therapeutic. Human touch is important. I will never forget the day that an isolated, lonely alcoholic patient of mine came into the office. He was shaking and said that he finally was ready to go into rehabilitation. In the middle of our conversation, he tremulously reached over and touched my hand for a moment. This done, he seemed to calm down a bit. He was starved for human contact.

As people age, they realize that, in many ways, human beings are all alike, which helps them feel closer to others and allows them to be more empathetic. Author Wendy Lustbader says, "Aging becomes a profound equalizer as getting older reveals what we hold in common . . . even as whispers from an aging body reminds them of all they have in common with everyone else. . . . We recognize that we are all essentially the same when it comes to living and dying, and it is a relief."[10]

Love and affection. These gifts are appreciated at any age. Everyone needs comforting and nurturing at times. Everyone needs to know that someone cares. This knowledge can increase security and reduce anxiety. Praise can help a person blossom. Sex is only one aspect of intimacy.

Elizabeth Strout, on the last page of her novel, *Olive Kitteridge*, tells it like it is. She has Olive say, after she lost her husband and is lying in bed next to her new boyfriend that she found late in life,

> What young people don't know. . . . They did not know that lumpy, aged, and wrinkled bodies were as needy as their young firm ones, that love was not to be tossed away carelessly, as if it was a tart on a platter with others that got passed around again. No, if love was available, one chose it, or didn't choose it. And if her platter had been full with the goodness of Henry [her husband] and she had found it burdensome, had flicked it off crumbs at a time, it was because she had not known what one should know: that day after day

was unconsciously squandered . . . throughout her tired self swept waves of gratitude—and regret. [11]

Best-selling author Kristin Hannah in her novel, *Winter Garden*, concurs. "If there was one thing that she learned in all of this, it was that life—and love—can be gone any second. When you had it, you needed to hang on with all your strength and savor every moment." [12]

Gratitude. Psychiatrist Viktor Frankl says, "Look inside for self-worth and contentment rather than outside ourselves for approval and self-worth. It all begins with gratitude and self-awareness. Being thankful for who you are and what you have." [13]

March brings spring and my next birthday. I am grateful for both. I am grateful for my family and friends, the education and opportunities that I have been given and the love that has come my way. In spite of a chronic illness, I am fortunate to have the stamina and attitude that has allowed me to remain active and engaged in life. I am appreciative of what I can still do and accomplish. I am thankful for my family's love and support, the beauty in the world, good food, and companionship as well as having had a fulfilling, forty-three year career in psychiatry. I am fortunate that my interest in mental health and writing have come together in a satisfying way and allowed me to be a psychiatrist, a medical writer, lecturer, and editor. Not many are so fortunate.

Author Jule Hartman tells us what he is grateful for in retirement. He says, "Retirement has been a discovery of beauty for me. I never had time before to notice the beauty of my grandkids, my wife, [and] the tree outside my very own front door. And, the beauty of time itself." [14]

Harold and Vivienne's relationship improved over time. They started to rely less on each other to fulfill all of their needs. They also tried to pay more attention to each other. Harold had a small stroke and shuffled more when he walked. Vivienne's arthritic pain increased, which made it harder for her to do certain motions and decreased her agility. She often had to ask him to help her with a project. They both found that it was difficult to get up if they got down on their knees on the floor. They both experienced hearing loss. Somehow, these aging deficits brought them closer together. Seeing each other aging caused them both to be more empathetic toward one another. They often laughed about the changes. They cuddled at night in bed before sleep while they watched the daily news. Harold went bowling with his male friends and met them for breakfast. He worked in his garden and read the newspaper. Vivienne had lunch with her female friends and started to knit and crochet. These activities along with her normal routine of cooking and cleaning the house kept her busy and content. The children visited once a month. At times they all went out to dinner. They both tried to talk more to each other over dinner when they ate at home. They watched their special TV shows together at night. They tried to go out shopping together or go to a movie or visit friends at least once a week. Gradually, they both seemed more content.

When he was interviewed for a *Philadelphia Inquirer* story, a 101-year-old attorney, said the following about the meaning of life: "Life is not a riddle to be solved. It is an adventure to be embraced. Go forward. Try your best. Get involved in causes that matter. . . . The real secret is to be decent, to be fair, and to be forgiving. . . . And don't take yourself too seriously."[15] These are wise words indeed. Goldie Hawn, who in 2003 established the Hawn Foundation to encourage mindfulness in children, encourages us to "start to live for now, rather than for what's next or, worse, waiting for the end to come. Slow down. Enjoy this ride. It's all we've got."[16]

I hope that you enjoy your retirement years and getting older. I hope that you are resilient enough to cope with the downside of this stage of life, if and when it happens. A positive attitude will help, if life deals you health problems or emotional and physical pain. But, most of all, I hope that your life from now on is a satisfying adventure filled with love and gratitude. I wish you many meaningful relationships, good luck, good health, and contentment.

ACKNOWLEDGMENTS

Writing a book is an obsessive exercise involving creativity, dedication, and time. It is also a labor of love. Each of my nonfiction books took about two years to write, going through various drafts and titles. This book was no exception. It was originally titled *Surviving Retirement*. This became *A Positive Guide to Surviving Retirement*. On the third and fourth proposal drafts the title was changed to *A Psychiatrist's Guide to Successful Retirement and Aging: Coping with Change*. My agent kept getting rejections. The publishers felt that the proposed book had obvious merits and promised to be a solid, useful book, but they worried about it standing up against the competition.

Then along came Suzanne Staszak-Silva, executive editor at Rowman & Littlefield Publishers, who went further in her rejection e-mail and made some helpful suggestions. She said that she needed something "unique" in this crowded market. She suggested that I write something on the mental and emotional issues that are possible in retirement and aging as well as ways to handle the challenges of this period of life. There it was. So simple and obvious. I said to myself, "I am a seasoned psychiatrist. I know that I can do this." I rewrote my proposal including twelve new chapters dealing with emotional and physical issues and other mental health problems that can show themselves as people go through the last stage of life. It was accepted and Suzanne offered me a contract. I am thankful and grateful to her for her faith in me and allowing my book to find a home. I would also like to thank my agent, Anne G. Devlin of the Max Gartenberg Literary Agency in Yardley, Pennsylvania, for all her hard work, guidance, and interest in my work.

A special thank you to Katherine E. Galluzzi, D.O., CMD, FACOFP dist., who is professor and chair of the Department of Geriatrics at the Philadelphia College of Osteopathic Medicine for writing the foreword for this book. She is also director of Comprehensive Care at PCOM, as well as being well known for her research, teaching, and writing on gerontology. Her words add a new dimension to my work. I am retired, after working for forty-three years in the private practice of psychiatry. I did individual, group, and family therapy in the office, was an attending psychiatrist to people in psychiatric facilities, and did psychiatric consults at several hospitals and nursing homes. I also did psychiatric research. After all this time, I continue to be grateful for the respect and trust that most of my patients gave me. What I learned from their life stories is the fabric of my writing. In this book, none are mentioned directly. All patient references combine information and show much poetic license to make certain clinical points.

I dedicated this book to my maternal grandmother, Molly Paul, for her unconditional love. I was very lucky to have been her first grandchild. She was a simple, old-fashioned woman, involved with making traditional food dishes, baking cookies, and doing household chores. When she looked at me, her love seemed to smile through her eyes embracing me with warmth. My paternal grandmother was a good woman, who was always kind to me. I am proud of her involvement in charity and religious endeavors; however, I was one of her many grandchildren. I know that my parents loved me; however, Buba Paul gave me something different and special that has sustained me through the years.

I would like to end my acknowledgments by thanking my most precious treasure, my wife of fifty years. Alice, as well as being an excellent mother and grandmother to our two children and two grandchildren and a wonderful general practitioner who was very beloved by her patients, has always been there for me in "sickness and in health." She endured countless hours of my unavailability due to professional obligations and writing commitments. All I can say is, "Thank you. I love you."

As for myself, at the time of this writing, I am almost two years into retirement. The aging process continues and I cope the best that I can and try to live by my own advice. It is not always easy. In spite of having severe COPD, I attempt to stay engaged in life focusing on the simple pleasures, relationships, and trying new hobbies. My wife and I spend quality time visiting with our daughter, son-in-law, and two grandchildren. We keep in touch with our friends and have made some new ones. I have learned to play gin rummy. In the future, I hope to paint and start to play the piano again. Alice and I enjoy traveling, particularly taking cruises. We also spend time at the Jersey Shore. Of course, I hope to keep writing on mental health issues.

H Michael Zal
Lansdale, Upper Gwynedd, Pennsylvania

NOTES

AUTHOR'S NOTE

1. Helen Simonson, *Major Pettigrew's Last Stand* (New York: Random House Trade Paperbacks, 2011), 346.

2. http://thinkexist.com/quatations/planning.

INTRODUCTION

1. http://statisticbrain.com/retirement-statistics/ .

2. Eric Adler, "Nursing Care Decision Taking Toll on Family," *Sun Sentinel*, Sunday, February 1, 2015, Special Section—Health Report, 1.3.

3. http://www.wow4u.com/retirement/index.html .

4. http://www.quotes-positive.com/quotes/retirement/ ; Rossabeth Moss Kantor, http://www.brainyquote.com/quotes/authors/r/rosabeth_moss_kanter.html .

5. André Corpeleijn, "Many More Older People Retired in 2004," *Web Magazine*, 12 December 2006, http://www.cbs.nl/en-GB/menu/themas/arbeid-sociale-zekerheid/publicaties/artikelen/archief/2006/2006-2083-wm.htm .

6. Bobby Oshel, "Starting Next Year, 2011, Over 10,000 People in the US Will Turn 65-Years-Old Every Day," 2 July 2010, http://ezinearticles.com/?Starting-Next-Year,-2011,-Over-10,000-People-in-the-US-Will-Turn-65-Years-Old-Every-Day&id=4596234 .

7. Eric H. Erickson, Childhood and Society, 2nd ed. (New York: Norton, 1963).

8. http://www.essayempire.com/customessay/psychology-research-papers/agking-olderdevelo (October 7, 2014).

9. Elisabeth Kübler-Ross and D. Kessler, *Life Lessons* (New York: Scribner, 2001), 31.

10. H Michael Zal, "Understanding the Elderly," *Osteopathic Medical News*, vol. 3, no. 3, (1986): 47.

11. Darrell Sifford, "Mining the Pleasures of the 'Golden Years,'" *Philadelphia Inquirer* (June 28, 1990), 5-E.

1. EMOTIONS

1. http://www.integralwealth.com/EmotionallyReady.aspx.

2. http://thinkexist.com/quotations/planning/.

3. http://quotespositive.com/quotes/retirement/.

4. http://www.integralwealth.com/EmotionallyReady.aspx.

5. http:///www.wow4u.com/retirement/index.html.

6. http://www.unmass.edu/fsap/articles/retire.html.

7. http://www.umass.edu/fsap/articles/retire.html.

8. http://women.webmd.com/features/retirement-planning?page=3&print=true.

9. Art Carey, "Well Being," *Philadelphia Inquirer*, October 8, 2012, C1–2.

10. H Michael Zal, *Ten Steps to Relieve Anxiety: Refocus, Relax and Enjoy Life* (Far Hills, NJ: New Horizon Press, 2013), 189.

11. Anna Quindlen, *A Short Guide to a Happy Life* (New York: Random House, 2000).

2. NEGATIVE BEHAVIORS

1. Elizabeth Hartney, "What Are Behavioral Addictions," About.com, http://addictions.about.com/od/howaddictionhappens/f/behavioraladd.htm.

2. Char B., "You can 'grow' out of food compulsions," Growing Human(kind)ness (blog), http://growinghumankindness.com/courses/food-mother/.

3. Ryan T. Howell, "Why Do Shopping Addicts Keep Spending Their Money," *Psychology Today*, 4 August 2014, http://www.psychologytoday.com/blog/cant-buy-happiness/201308/why-do-shopping-addicts-keep-spending-their-money.

4. Gail Saltz, *Women's Today*, http://www.womansday.com/health/howtoconquer yourcompulsions-1163.

5. Ibid.

6. http://www.stop-procrastination.org/.

7. Anonymous quote.

8. John Gray, *Men Are from Mars, Women Are from Venus* (New York: HarperCollins Publishers, Inc., 1992).

9. Deanne Repich, ed., *Top 100 Inspirational Quotes for Living Anxiety-Free* (Pflugerville, TX: National Institute of Anxiety and Stress, Inc., Version 1.0, 2008), 13, http://www.ConquerAnxiety.com.

10. Darrell Sifford, "Midlife Crisis: 'The Nagging Pain of Unfulfilled Dreams,'" *Philadelphia Inquirer*, October 17, 1983, 4-F.

11. Edward M. Hallowell, *Worry: Controlling It and Using It Wisely* (New York: Random House Publishing Group, 1997).

12. Repich, *Top 100 Inspirational Quotes for Living Anxiety-Free*, 7.

3. RELATIONSHIPS

1. http://www.pewresearch.org/topics/.

2. Abigail Trafford, *My Time: Making the Most of the Bonus Decades after 50* (New York: Basic Books, 2004).

3. Sharon O'Brien, "10 Tips for Happy Retirement Living," *About.com*, http://seniorliving.about.com/od/retirement/a/retirement_livi.htm.

4. Ralph Waldo Emerson, Essays-1st series, "Friendship."

5. "43 Most Insightful Friendship Quotes," http://www.lifeoptimizer.org/2007/10/10/43-most-insightful-friendship-quotes/.

6. Mayo Clinic Staff, 5 February 2015,http://mayoclinic.org/friendships/ART-20044860.

7. David C. Borchard and Patricia A. Donahoe, *The Joy of Retirement* (New York: American Management Association, 2008), 173–74.

8. H Michael Zal, "Understanding the elderly," *Osteopathic Medical News*, vol. 3, no. 3 (March 1986): 1, 47–49.

9. Terri Akman, "Online dating, turns out, isn't only for the young," *Philadelphia Inquirer*, January 22, 2014, Section C-1, C-3.

10. Humana/National Council on Aging, http://retirementperfectedd.com/resources/blog.asp?FAID=512269.

11. Zal, "Understanding the elderly," 47–49.

12. Suzanna Smith, "The Importance of Families," Strongermarriage.org, http://strongermarriage.org/htm/married/family-relationships-in-later-life/.

13. Smith, "The Importance of Families"; H Michael Zal, *The Sandwich Generation: Caught between Growing Children and Aging Parents* (Cambridge, MA: Perseus Publishing, 1992), 179–80.

14. Leo Buscaglia, *Love* (Thorofare, NJ: Charles B. Slack, Inc., 1972).

4. PHYSICAL CHANGES

1. Wendy Lustbader, *Life Gets Better: The Unexpected Pleasures of Growing Older* (New York: Jeremy F. Tarcher, Penguin, 2011), 2.

2. http://www.seniorhealthsolutionsct.org/concerns/common.asp; and http://www.arthritis.org/conditions-treatments/disease-center/osteoarthritis/.

3. http://www.seniorhealthsolutionsct.org/concerns/common.asp .

4. http://adam.about.net/encyclopedia/infectiousdiseasses/Asthma.htm .

5. Jill Leviticus, "Breathing and Lung Problems," Livestrong.com, 16 August 2013, http://www.livestrong.com/article/358745-breathing-lung-problems.

6. Richard M. Schwartzman, "Dyspnea and Pulmonary Edema," in *Harrison's Principles of Internal Medicine*, edited by Anthony S. Fauci and Dennis L. Kasper, et al. (New York: McGraw Hill Medical, 2008), 221–24.

7. Alvin C. Powers, "Diabetes Mellitus," in *Harrison's Principles of Internal Medicine*, edited by Anthony S. Fauci and Dennis L. Kasper, et al. (New York: McGraw Hill Medical, 2008,) 2275–2304.

8. seniorjournal.com/.../20090630-Growing.

9. http://www.seniorhealthsolutionsct.org/concerns/common.asp.

10. Michael B. First, ed., *Diagnostic and Statistical Manual of Mental Disorders*, 4th edition (Washington, DC: American Psychiatric Association, 1994), 133–55.

11. http://www.urmc.rochester.edu/senior-health/common-issues/top-ten.cfm.

12. http://www.nhlbi.nih.gov/health/health-topic/topics/hbp/printall-index.html.

13. http://www.seniorhealthsolutionsct.org/concerns/common.asp.

14. http://www.urmc.rochester.edu/senior-health/common-issues/top-ten.cfm .

15. http://www.livinghealthy360.com/index.php/common-health-problems-in-old-age-78023/p.

16. Anil K. Lalwani, "Disorders of Smell: Taste, and Hearing," in *Harrison's Principles of Internal Medicine*, edited by Anthony S. Fauci, Dennis L. Kasper, et al. (New York: McGraw Hill Medical, 2008), 196–204.

17. http://www.seniorhealthsolutionsct.org/concerns/common.asp .

18. H Michael Zal, *Ten Steps to Relieve Anxiety* (Far Hills, NJ: New Horizon Press, 2013), 161–62.

5. STRESS AND ANXIETY

1. www/WebMD/anxiety/Panic/guide/20061101.

2. M. T. Eaton and M. H. Peterson, "Introduction to Dynamic Psychiatry," in *Psychiatry Medical Outline Series*, 2nd ed. (New York: Medical Examination Publishing Co., 1969), 11–154.

3. H Michael Zal, "Anxiety in the Elderly," in *Ten Steps to Relieve Anxiety: Refocus, Relax and Enjoy Life* (Far Hills, NJ: New Horizon Press, 2013), 173–181.

4. http://www.pewreasearch.org/.../the-thresgold-gener.

5. Stan Hinden, "5 Steps to Retire Happy," in *AARP Bulletin Retirement Guide*, vol. 55, no. 7 (September 2014): 14–16.

6. DEPRESSION AND GRIEF

1. Sidney I. Landau (managing ed.), *Standard College Dictionary* (Funk & Wagnalls Company, 1977), 359; 590.

2. Burness E. Moore and Bernard D. Fine (eds.), *A Glossary of Psychoanalytic Terms and Concepts* (New York: American Psychoanalytic Association, 1968), 32.

3. Elisabeth Kübler-Ross, *On Death and Dying* (New York: Macmillan, 1969).

4. Michael B. First (ed.), *Diagnostic and Statistical Manuel of Mental Disorders*, 4th edition (Washington, DC: American Psychiatric Association, 2013), 320–27.

5. "Mental Health of the Elderly," *A "Let's Talk Facts About"* pamphlet (Washington, DC: American Psychiatric Association, 1988), 2.

6. Kevin Caruso, "Elderly Suicide," Suicide.org, http://www.suicide.org/elderly-suicide.html.

7. H Michael Zal, "Depression in the Elderly Patient," in *Difficult Medical Management*, edited by R. B. Taylor (Philadelphia: W. B. Saunders Company, 1991), 193.

8. http://www.cdc.gov/aging/mentalhealth/depression.html.

9. Zal, "Depression in the Elderly Patient," 188.

10. L. F. Jarvik, "Depression: A Review of Drug Therapy for Elderly Patients," *Consultant*, 22(1982): 141–46.

11. Michael Kerr, "Elderly Depression, Depression and Aging," Health-line.com, 29 March 2012, http://www.healthline.com/health/depression/elderly-and-aging#.

12. P. Thomas, "Primary Care: Depressed Elderly's Best Hope," *Medical World News*, 13 July 1987, 39–54.

13. William R. Marchand, *Depression and Bipolar Disorder* (Boulder, CO: Bull Publishing Company, 2012), 111–13.

14. Marchand, *Depression and Bipolar Disorder*, 96–102.

15. J. H. Wright A. T. Beck, and M. E. Thase, "Cognitive Therapy," in *The American Psychiatric Publishing Textbook of Clinical Psychiatry*, edited by R. E. Hales and S. C. Yudofsky (Arlington, VA: American Psychiatric Publishing, 2003), 1245–84.

16. A. J. Giannini, H. R. Black, and R. I. Goettsche, *Psychiatric, Psychogenic, and Somatopsychic Disorders Handbook* (New York: Medical Examination Publishing Company, 1978).

7. DRUG AND ALCOHOL ABUSE

1. Hazelden Betty Ford Foundation, "Substance Abuse among the Elderly; A Growing Problem," http://www.hazelden.org/web/public/ade60220.page.

2. http://www.learn-about-alcoholism.com/alcoholism-statistics.html.

3. Michael Zal, "The Female Alcoholic," *Main Line Times*, Sunday, September 21, 1986, 26.

4. Burness E. Moore and Bernard D. Fine, eds. *A Glossary of Psychoanalytic Terms and Concepts*, 2nd ed. (New York: American Psychoanalytic Association, 1968) 29.

5. Victor E. Frankl, *Man's Search for Meaning*, 3rd ed. (New York: Simon & Schuster, 1982), 143.

6. F. P. Allen, J. A. Nieuwsma, M. I. Pollitt, and D. G. Blazer, "Recovery on Higher Ground: Spirituality in the Treatment of Substance Abuse," in *Current Psychiatry*, vol. 13, no. 2 (February, 2014): 24, 29.

7. Darrell Sifford, "How a Spouse Might Help to Heal Childhood's Wounds," *Philadelphia Inquirer*, Thursday, June 18, 1987, 4-E.

8. Ashley Fox, "Lurie's Biggest Loss," *Philadelphia Inquirer*, July 20, 2010, E-1, 4-5.

8. MARITAL AND SEXUAL ISSUES
LATER IN LIFE

1. Gail Sheehy, *Passages: Predictable Crises of Adult Life* (New York: E. P. Dutton & Co., Inc., 1974), 163–64.

2. R. C. Atchley, "Retirement: Leaving the World of Work," *Annals of the American Academy of Political and Social Science*, vol. 464 (1982), http://www.jstor.org/discover/10.2307/1043818?uid=3739864&uid=2&uid=4&uid=37392 .

3. John E. Nelson and Richard N. Bolles, *What Color Is Your Parachute? For Retirement* (Berkeley, CA: Ten Speed Press, 2010), 230.

4. Nelson and Bolles, *What Color Is Your Parachute?* 230.

5. Mel Schwartz, "Silence: A Relationship Killer," 13 January 2014, http://blog.melschwartz.com/2014/01/13/silence-a-realtionship-killer/?utm_source=Silence.

6. Kerri Anne Renzulli, "'The Talk' Get Your Spouse on the Same Page about Retirement," *CNNMoney.com*, October, 2013, 26.

7. Emanuel Fliegelman, "Sex after 60 Is Nifty," *Osteopathic IAnnals*, vol. 112, no. 2 (February 1984): 74–77, 81.

8. H Michael Zal, "Understanding the Elderly," *Osteopathic Medical News*, vol. 3, no 3 (March 1986): 47.

9. Melissa Dribben, "Sex after 50, or 75? But of Course," *Philadelphia Inquirer*, October 20, 2013, G-1 and G-7.

10. J. Evans, "Medical Ethics, 'Delicate Issues of Sexuality in the Nursing Home,'" *American Medical Directors Association Newspaper*, vol. 14, no. 4 (April 2013): 16–17.

11. http://strongermarriage.org/htm/married/family-realtionships-in-later-life/.

12. Jan Fawcett, "Bereavement and the Four Noble Truths" *Psychiatric Annals*, vol. 43 no. 6 (June 2013): 246.

13. http://strongermarriage.org/htm/married/family-realtionships-in-later-life/.

14. Terri Akman, "Online Dating, Turns Out, Isn't Only for the Young," *Philadelphia Inquirer*, January 22, 2014, C-1, C-3.

9. DEMENTIA AND ALZHEIMER'S DISEASE

1. *Webster's New World Dictionary of the American Language*, College ed. (New York: World, 1957), 389.

2. US Department of Health and Human Services, "Alzheimer's Disease Fact Sheet," https://www.nia.nih.gov/alzheimers/publication/alzheimers-disease-fact-sheet; Stacey Burling, "We're All Aging Together," *Philadelphia Inquirer*, Tuesday, 15April 2014, A4.

3. *AARP Bulletin*, vol. 56, no. 1 (January–February 2015): 15–20; H Michael Zal, *The Sandwich Generation: Caught between Growing Children and Aging Parents* (Cambridge, MA: Perseus Publishing, 1992), 192.

4. https://www.nia.nih.gov/alzheimers/publication/alzheimers-disease-fact-sheet.

5. Alice Park and Mandy Oaklander, "Medical Momentum," *Time*, vol. 184, no. 16 (27 October 2014): 12.

6. Stacey Burling, "'Everything Has Changed' in Alzheimer's Research," *Philadelphia Inquirer*, November 30, 2014, G-1, G-7.

7. S. Dorfman, "Drug Offers New Hope," *Palm Beach Post*, Boomer Health column, March 25, 2014, D-1, D-5.

8. K. L. Davis, "How to Make Progress in the Battle against Alzheimer's," *AARP Bulletin*, vol. 55, no. 40 (November 2014): 24.

9. Peter Jaret, "Would You Want to Know?" *AARP Bulletin*, vol. 55, no. 4 (May 2014): 20.

10. Nancy L. Mace and Peter V. Rabins, *The 36-hour Day: A Family Guide to Caring for Persons with Alzheimer Disease, Other Dementia, and Memory Loss in Later Life*, revised and updated ed. (New York: Grand Central Publishing, 2001), 321–32.

10. ELDER ABUSE

1. http://elder-laws.com/elder-abuse.

2. Centers for Disease Control and Prevention, "Elder Abuse: Definition," 14 January 2014, http://www.cdc.gov/violenceprevention/elderabuse/definitions.html.

3. http://aoa.gov/AoA_programs/Elder_Rights/EA_Prevention/whatIsEA.aspx.

4. California Department of Justice, "A Citizen's Guide to Preventing and Reporting Elder Abuse," December 2002.

5. http://www.hivehealthmedia.com/risk-factors-for-elder-abuse/Some.

6. http://elder-abuse.com/risk-factors-elder-abuse.html.

7. Lawrence Robinson, Joanna Saisan, and Jeanne Segal, "Elder Abuse and Neglect: Warning Signs, Risk Factors, Prevention, and Reporting Abuse," September 2015, http://www.helpguide.org/articles/abuse/elder-abuse-and-neglect.htm.

8. http://elder-abuseca.com/preventing-elder-abuse.php.

9. Nancy L. Mace and Peter V. Rabins, *The 36-Hour Day: A Family Guide to Caring for Persons with Alzheimer Disease, Related Dementing Illness and Memory Loss in Later Life*, revised and updated ed. (New York: Grand Central Publishing, 2001).

10. H Michael Zal, *The Sandwich Generation: Caught between Growing Children and Aging Parents* (Cambridge, MA: Perseus Publishing, 1992), 205–9.

11. Debbie Dunn, "Elder Abuse Laws," Ehow.com, http://www.ehow.com/about_5428021_elder-abuse-laws.html.

12. Pennsylvania Department of Aging, "Older Adults Protective Services Act," http://www.portal.state.pa.us/portal/serveer.pt?open=514&objID=616729&mode=2.

13. http://www.aging.state.pa.us/portal/server.pt/community/abuse_or_crime/17992/report_el.

11. PSYCHOLOGICAL CAREGIVER CHALLENGES

1. Eric Berne, *Games People Play* (New York: Grove Press, 1964).

2. Anda Jines, "The Rewards and Challenges of Caregiving," 27 December 2009, http://ezinearticles.com/?The–Rewards-and-Challenges-of-Caregiving&id=3484803.

12. EMOTIONAL DECISIONS AT THE END OF LIFE

1. Nell Bernstein, "Eldercare Options: Find the Eldercare Option that's Right for Your Loved One," Caring.com, http://www.caring.com/articles/elder-care-options-for-senior-living-arrangements.

2. H Michael Zal, *The Sandwich Generation: Caught between Growing Children and Aging Parents* (Cambridge, MA: Perseus Publishing, 1992), 201.

3. Nancy L. Mace and Peter V. Rabins. *The 36-Hour Day: A Family Guide to Caring for Persons with Alzheimer's Disease, Related Dementing Illnesses, and Memory Loss in Later Life*, revised and updated ed. (New York: Grand Central Publishing, April, 2001), 355.

4. Zal, *The Sandwich Generation*, 202.

5. Alice J. Zal, "The Patient at the End of Life," in *Somatic Dysfunction in Osteopathic Family Medicine* (Philadelphia: Lippincott, Williams & Wilkins, 2007), chap. 13, 181.

6. Amy Wright Glenn, "Life as They Know It" *Inside Magazine*, vol. 35, no. 2 (Fall 2014): 29–33.

7. T. A. Gonda, "Death, Dying, and Bereavement," in *Comprehensive Textbook of Psychiatry*, vol. 2, 5th ed., edited by H. I. Kaplan and B. J. Sadock (Baltimore: Williams & Wilkins, 1989), 1340–41.

8. Alice J. Zal, "The Patient at the End of Life," 181.

13. CAN A PSYCHIATRIST HELP?

1. John Gray, *Men Are from Mars, Women Are from Venus* (New York: HarperCollins, 1992).

2. http://www.unitedearth.com.au/proust.html.

3. Burness E. Moore and Bernard D. Fine, eds., *A Glossary of Psychoanalytic Terms and Concepts*, 2nd ed. (New York: American Psychoanalytic Association, 1968), 55.

4. http://www.brainyquote.com/quotes/authors/s/swami_sivananda.html.

14. THERAPY

1. Sebastian Zimmerman, "Intimate Portraits: Psychotherapists in Their Own Work Space," *Psychiatric Times*, vol. 29, no. 9 (2012): 6.

2. http://www.newretirement.com/Planning 101/Thoughts_On_Retirement.aspx.

3. http://www.guotegarden.copm/retirement.html.

4. http://thinkexist.com/quatations/planning.

5. Gail Sheehy, *Passages : Predictable Crises of Adult Life* (New York: E. P. Dutton & Co., Inc., 1974), 404.

6. Sharon O'Brien, "Planning to Retire Soon? Make a Retirement Planning Checklist," About.com, http://seniorliving.about.com/od/retirement/ss/retirechecklist.htm.

7. http://thinkexist.com/quatations/planning/.

8. H Michael Zal, *Ten Steps to Relieve Anxiety: Refocus, Relax and Enjoy Life* (Far Hills, NJ: New Horizon Press, 2013), 174.

9. Philip Polatin, *A Guide to Treatment in Psychiatry* (Philadelphia: Lippincott, 1966), 100–15.

10. National Association of Cognitive Behavioral Therapists, "Providing Outstanding CBT Training Opportunities, Onsite Trainings, Conferences, and Regional Trainings," http://www.nacbt.org/whatiscbt.htm.

11. "55+ Living," Advertising Supplement, *Philadelphia Inquirer*, April 18, 2013, R4.

12. http://www.kcet.org/shows/yourturntocare/heal/aging-well-how-to-stay-healthy-and-engaged.

13. Emilee Seltzer, "How Caregivers Can Help an Aging Adult Make Dietary Changes," Agingcare.com, http://www.agingcare.com/Articles/How-to-Help-Aging-Parents-Make-Dietary-Changes-137053.htm.

14. www.NIHseniorhealth,gov.

15. "How to Live Better Longer," http://Retiredbrains.com/Home/Health+Care/How+To+Live+Better+Longer/default.aspx.

15. MEDICATION

1. H Michael Zal, *Panic Disorder: The Great Pretender* (New York: Plenum Press, 1980).

2. *Physicians' Desk Reference*, 69th ed. (Montvale, NJ: PDR Network, LLC, 2015).

3. Mayo Clinic Staff, "Selective Serotonin Uptake Inhibitors (SRRIs)," 9 July 2013, http://www.mayoclinic.org/diseases-conditions/depression/in-depth/ssris/art-20044825.

4. Bruce Jancin, "Key Points in Managing Late-Life Anxiety," *Caring for the Ages*, vol. 15, no. 10 (October 2014): 1.

5. http://www.drugs.com/food interactions/bupropion.html.

6. "The Importance of Sleep," Charlotte-Mecklenberg Schools, http://www.cms.k12.nc.us/Jobs/benefits/health/Pages/TheImportanceofSleep.aspx.

7. Kathryn Doyle, "Mindfulness Meditation May Help Older People Sleep," Psych Congress Network, 2015, http://www.psychcongress.com/article/mindfulness-meditation-may-help-older-people-sleep-21324.

8. "Medications for Memory Loss," http://www.alz.org/alzheimers_disease_standard_prescriptions.asp.

9. Michele G. Sullivan, "Combination Drug Quells Anxiety, Aggression," *Caring for the Ages*, vol. 16, no. 1 (January 2015): 9.

10. P. V. Lee, "Drug Therapy: Avoiding the Pitfalls," *Medical World News-Geriatrics*, 1972.

11. Henry A. Nasrallah, "Editorial," *Current Psychiatry*, vol. 13, no. 6 (Parsippany, NJ: 2014): 23–24.

16. STAY ACTIVE

1. http://thinkkexist.com/common/print.asp?id=344557&quote=we_must_look_for_ways_to_ .

2. H Michael Zal, *The Sandwich Generation: Caught between Growing Children and Aging Parents* (Cambridge, MA: Perseus Publishing, 1992), 223.

3. Centers for Disease Control, "Physical Activity and Health," 4 June 2015, http://www.cdc.gov/physicalactivity/everyone/health/index.html.

4. http://www.cdc.gov/physicalactivity/everyonbe/health/index.html.

5. http://www.health.gov.au/internet/healthyactive/publishing.nsf/Content/physiocal-activity .

6. Karen Frazier, "Mental Benefits of Exercise," http://exercise.lovetoknow.com/Mental_Benefits_of_Exercise.

7. Louise Balle, "Benefits of Creative Activities for the Elderly," http://www.ehow.com/list_6329723_importance-activities-elderly-people.html .

8. http: //www.echow.com/list_7222872_mental-activities-elderly-people.

9. http://www.wow4u.com/retirement2/index.html.

10. Sally Macdonald and John Macdonald, "Not Your Grandparents' Vacations," *Philadelphia Inquirer*, January 5, 2014, N3.

11. Deanne Repich, ed., *Top 100 Inspirational Quotes for Living Anxiety-Free*, (Pflugerville, TX: National Institute of Anxiety and Stress, Inc., 2008), http://www.ConquerAnxiety.com.

12. http://www.quotegarden.com/retirement.html.

13. http://www.quotegarden.com/retirement.html.

17. MAINTAIN A POSITIVE ATTITUDE

1. http://www.brainyquote.com/quotes/keywords/positive_attitude.html.

2. Society of Certified Senior Advisors, "A Positive Retirement Attitude—An Absolute Must!" CSA Blog, 9 March 2011, http://blog.csa.us/2011/03/positive-retirement-attitude-absolute.html.

3. http://www.brainyquote.com/quotes/authors/h/henry_david_thoreau_3.html.

4. http://successsfulretirementguide.wordpress.com/2009/10/02/retirement-attitude/.

5. Francis D. Glamser, "Determinants of a Positive Attitude toward Retirement," *Journal of Gernotology*, vol. 31, no. 1 (January 1976): 104–7. http://eric.ed.gov/?id=EJ129184.

6. Art Carey, "Fighting Off Life's Inevitable Assaults," *Philadelphia Inquirer*, January 12, 2014, G-3.

7. http://www.quotes positive.com/quotes/affirmations/.

8. H Michael Zal, *The Sandwich Generation: Caught between Growing Children and Aging Parents* (Cambridge, MA: Perseus Publishing, 1992), 220–21.

9. http://blog.melschwartz.com/2014/01/13/silence-a-relationship-killer/?utm_source=Silence.

10. RALPH, "Want a Successful Retirement Plan?—Stay Positive," 12 June 2013,http://www.ralphcarlsonblog.com/want-successful-retirement-plan-stay-positive/.

11. Remez Sasson, "The Power of Positive Attitude Can Change Your Life," http://www.successconsciousness.com/positive_attitude.htm.

12. http://www.brainyquote.com/quotes/keywords/positive_attitude.html.

18. HAVE A GOAL AND STAY ENGAGED

1. http://engagedinlife.com/about/.

2. Darrell Sifford, "Mining the Pleasures of the 'Golden Years,'" *Philadelphia Inquirer*, 28 June 1990, E-5.

3. http://www.wow4u.com/retirement/index.html.

4. Daniel H. Pink, *Drive: The Surprising Truth about What Motivates Us* (New York: Riverhead Books, 2010).

5. Delray Beach Public Library, "Volunteer Opportunities," http://www.delraylibrary.org/?page_id=44 .

6. Krisha McCoy, "How to Stay Socially Engaged as You Age," 16 April 2013,http://www.everydayhealth.com/senior-health/enhancing-your-life.aspx.

7. http://ahopefulsign.com/living-to-learn/how-to-stay-motivated-and-engaged-with-life.

8. Christina Matz-Costa, "After 55, the Key Is Staying 'Engaged,'" http://www.nextavenue.org/blog/after-55-key-staying-engaged .

19. RELIGIOUS AFFILIATION

1. Paul Taylor, *The Next America: Boomers, Millennials, and the Looming Generational Showdown* (New York: Public Affairs, 2014), 30, 33.

2. K. G. Meador and H. G. Koenig, "Spirituality and Religion in Psychiatry Practice Parameters and Implications," *Psychiatric Annals*, vol. 30, no. 8 (2000): 549–55.

3. C. C. Cook, "Addiction and Spirituality," *Addiction*, vol. 99, no. 5 (2004): 539–51.

4. http://money.cnn.com/2010/02/16/pf/expert/retirement_friendship.moneymag/.

5. Walter Updegrave, "What You Really Need in Retirement: Friends," *CNN Money* (17 February 2010).

6. Sally Quinn, "Religion Is a Sure Route to True Happiness," *Washington Post*, 24 January 2014, http://www.washingtonpost.com/national/religion/religion-is-a-sure-route-to-true-happiness/2014/01/23/f6522120-8452-11e3-bbe5-6a2a3141e3a9_story.html.

7. V. Fønnebø, "Mortality in Norwegian Seventh-Day Adventists 1962–1986," *Journal of Clinical Epidemiology*, vol. 45 (1992): 157–67.

8. W. J. Strawbridge, R. D. Cohen, S. J. Shema, and G. A. Kaplan, "Frequent Attendance at Religious Services and Mortality over 28 Years," *American Journal of Public Health*, vol. 87 (1997): 957–61.

9. http://www.nationalmedpol.com/default.aspx.

10. K. S. Kendler, X. Q. Liu, C. O. Gardner, et al., "Dimensions of Religiosity and Their Relationship to Lifetime Psychiatric and Substance Use Disorders," *American Journal of Psychiatry*, vol. 160, no. 3 (2003): 496–503.

11. J. P. Allen, J. A. Nieuwsma, et al., "Recovery on Higher Ground: Spirituality in the Treatment of Substance Abuse," *Current Psychiatry*, vol. 13, no. 2 (February 2014): 39.

12. Anne Lamott, "Have a Little Faith," *AARP the Magazine* (December 2014/January 2015): 56, 58.

13. http://www.biographyonline.net/spiritual/articles/benefits-religion.html.

14. Ellen Idler, "The Psychological and Physical Benefits of Spiritual/Religious Practices," *Higher Education Newsletter*, vol. 4, no. 2 (February 2008): 1–5.

15. "Retirement and Spirituality: What's the Link?" *A Satisfying Journey: Living a Satisfying Retirement with Purpose and Joy*, 5 August 2012, http://satisfyingretirement.blogspot.com/2012/08/religion-spirituality.html.

16. Ecclesiastes 3:1–10.

17. Phil Deane, "Religious Stigma—An Opinion," *Looking over My Shoulder*, 6 May 2012, https://philipdeane.wordpress.com/2012/05/06/religious-stigmaan-opinion/.

18. Victor E. Frankl, *Man's Search for Meaning*, 3rd ed. (New York: Simon & Schuster, 1982), 75.

19. "Religious Prejudice," rsrevision.com, http://www.rsrevision.com/GCSE/christian_perspectives/prejudice/religion/index.htm.

20. LAUGHTER IS THE BEST MEDICINE

1. http://www.quotegarden.com/laughter.html.

2. M. P. Mulder and A. Nijholt, "Humor Research: State of the Art," 2002, http://web.archive.org/web/20041116165933/http://citseer.ist.pru.edu/580062.html),citeseer.ist.pru.edu.

3. http://thinkexist.com/common/print.asp?id=11505&qupte=the_human_race_has_one-rea.

4. http://www.huffingtompost.com/glenn-d-brsunstein-md/is -laughter-the-best-medicine_.

5. Paul McGhee, "Using Laughter to Cope—Laughing in the Midst of Stress," *The Laughter Remedy*, 21 December 2012, http://www.laughterremedy.com/2010/12/using-humor-to-cope-%e2%80%93-laughing-in-the-midst-of-stress/.

6. Proverbs 17–22.

7. M. Miller, C. Mangano, Y. Park, R Goel, G. D. Plotnick, and R. A. Vogel, "Impact of Cinematic Viewing in Endothelial Function," *Heart*, vol. 92, no. 2 (February 2005): 261-63.

8. http://www.hwlpguide.org/life/humor_laughter_health.htm.

9. B. Smith Lee, "Humor Relations for Nurse Managers," *Nursing Management*, 21, 86. (1990).

10. http://thinkexuist.com/common/print.asp?id=8403&quote=laughter_laughter-is-the-closest-distanc.

11. http://www.quotegarden.com/laughter.html.

12. E. E. Kane, "Laughter Benefits: The Three C's," 21 March 2008, http://www.lifescript.com/well-being/articles/l/laughter_benefits_the_three_cs.aspx?gclid=CJT2m9byqMMCFdgPgQodph0ANw&trans=1&du=1&ef_id=VE-xfQAAAXs3Xvp0:20150123004955:s.

13. http://holistic-online.com/Humor_Therapy/humor_therapy.htm.

14. Gesundheit! Institute, http://www.patchadams.org/patch-adams/.

15. Cathy Malchiodi, "Humor: The Human Gift for Coping and Survival," *Psychology Today*, 26 June 2008, http://www.psychologytoday.com/blog/the-healing-arts/200806/humor-the-human-gift-coping-and-survival.

16. Ula Ilnytzky, "Laughter Therapy Helps Them Cope with Illness," *Associated Press*, 28 November 2008, http://www.sfgate.com/health/article/Laughter-therapy-helps-them-cope-with-illness-3260307.php.

17. James A. Thorson, "Humor as Coping Mechanism," from *No Laughing's the Matter*, http://www.beliefnet.com/Health/2005/07/Humor-As-Coping-Mechanism.aspx#zaEsIb86vm8Myos5.99.

18. Gerry Hopman, "Laughter a Coping Strategy," 9 May 2012, http://ezinearticles.com/?Laughter-a-Coping-Strategy&id=7052404.

19. http://en.wikipedia.org/wiki/Laughter.

20. "Laughter the Best Medicine," Helpguide.org, http://www.helpguide.org/life/humor_laughter_health.htm.

CONCLUSION

1. Viktor E. Frankl, *Man's Search for Meaning*, 3rd ed. (New York: Simon & Schuster, 1982), 9, 51, 115.

2. Art Carey, "John Bogle's Enduring Wisdom," *Philadelphia Inquirer*, 15 September 2013, Section C. D1, D5.

3. David Von Drehle, *Time Magazine*, vol. 184, no. 9–10 (8–15 September 2014): 111.

4. Anne Lamott, "Have A Little Faith," *AARP the Magazine*, vol. 58, no. 1a (December, 2014/January, 2015): 59–60.

5. Dilip Jeste, *American Journal of Psychiatry*, vol. 70, (2013): 188–96.

6. seniorjournal.com/.../20090630-Growin.

7. Cindy K. Sproles, "Treat Elderly Parents with Dignity," *Christian Broadcasting Network*, http://www.cbn.com/family/familyadvice/treat-elderly-parents-with-dignity-sproles.aspx.

8. Jeff Goins, "The Importance of Hope in a Person's Life," *Adventure in Missions*, 11 July 2009, http://jeffgoins.myadventures.org/?filename=the-importance-of-hope-in-a-persons-life.

9. Art Carey, "Fighting Off Life's Inevitable Assaults," *Philadelphia Inquirer*, Sunday, 12 January 2014, G-3.

10. Wendy Lustbader, *Life Gets Better: The Unexpected Pleasures of Growing Older* (New York: Jeremy F. Tarcher, Penguin, 2011), 27, 30, 34.

11. Elizabeth Strout, *Olive Kitteridge* (New York: Random House Trade Paperbacks, 2008), 270.

12. Kristin Hannah, *Winter Garden* (New York: St. Martin's Press, 2010), 375.

13. Frankl, *Man's Search for Meaning*, 119.

14. http://www.quotegarden.com/retirement.html.

15. Jeff Gammage, "Lawyer Retire? At 101? Heck No," *Philadelphia Inquirer*, July 20, 2014, A1 and A4.

16. David Hochman, "Mindfulness Matters," *AARP the Magazine*, vol. 58, no. 1c (December 2014/January 2015): 62.

BIBLIOGRAPHY

"43 Most Insightful Friendship Quotes," http://www.lifeoptimizer.org/2007/10/10/43-most-insightful-friendship-quotes/.

"55+ Living," Advertising Supplement, *Philadelphia Inquirer*, 18 April 2013, R4.

AARP Bulletin, vol. 56, no. 1 (January–February 2015).

Adler, Story Eric. "Nursing Care Decision Taking Toll on Family," *Sun Sentinel*, 1 February 2015, Special Section—Health Report.

Akman, Terri. "Online Dating, Turns Out, Isn't Only for the Young." *Philadelphia Inquirer*, 22 January 2014.

Allen J. P., J. A. Nieuwsma, M. J. Pollitt, and D. G. Blazer. "Recovery on Higher Ground: Spirituality in the Treatment of Substance Abuse." *Current Psychiatry*, vol. 13, no. 2 (February, 2014).

Atchley, R. C. "Retirement: Leaving the World of Work." *Annals of the American Academy of Political and Social Science*, vol. 464 (1982): 120–31. http://www.jstor.org/discover/10.2307/1043818?uid=3739864&uid=2&uid=4&uid=37392.

Balle, Louise. "Benefits of Creative Activities for the Elderly." http://www.ehow.com/list_6329723_importance-activities-elderly-people.html.

Berne, Eric. *Games People Play*. New York: Grove Press, 1964.

Bernstein, Nell. "Eldercare Options: Find the Eldercare Option that's Right for Your Loved One." Caring.com. http://www.caring.com/articles/elder-care-options-for-senior-living-arrangements.

Borchard, David C., and Patricia A. Donahoe. *The Joy of Retirement*. New York: American Management Association, 2008.

Burling, Stacey. "'Everything Has Changed' in Alzheimer's Research." *Philadelphia Inquirer*, 30 November 2014.

———. "We're All Aging Together." *Philadelphia Inquirer*, 15 April 2014. Buscaglia, Leo. *Love*. Thorofare, NJ: Charles B. Slack, Inc., 1972.

California Department of Justice. "A Citizen's Guide to Preventing and Reporting Elder Abuse." December 2002.

Carey, Art. "Fighting Off Life's Inevitable Assaults." *Philadelphia Inquirer*, 12 January 2014. G-3.

———. "John Bogle's Enduring Wisdom." *Philadelphia Inquirer*. 15 September 2013, Section C.

———. "Well Being." *Philadelphia Inquirer*, 8 October 2012.

Caruso, Kevin. "Elderly Suicide." Suicide.org. http://www.suicide.org/elderly-suicide.html.

Centers for Disease Control. "Physical Activity and Health." 4 June 2015. http://www.cdc.gov/physicalactivity/everyone/health/index.html.

———. "Elder Abuse: Definition." 14 January 2014. http://www.cdc.gov/violenceprevention/elderabuse/definitions.html.

Char B. "You Can 'Grow' Out of Food Compulsions." Growing Human(kind)ness (blog). http://growinghumankindness.com/courses/food-mother/.

Cook, C. C. "Addiction and Spirituality." Addiction, vol. 99, no. 5.

Corpeleijn, André. "Many More Older People Retired in 2004." Web Magazine. 12 December 2006. http://www.cbs.nl/en-GB/menu/themas/arbeid-sociale-zekerheid/publicaties/artikelen/archief/2006/2006-2083-wm.htm.

Davis, K. L. "How to Make Progress in the Battle against Alzheimer's." AARP Bulletin, vol. 55, no. 9 (November 2014).

Deane, Phil. "Religious Stigma—An Opinion." Looking over My Shoulder. 6 May 2012. https://philipdeane.wordpress.com/2012/05/06/religious-stigmaan-opinion/.

Delray Beach Public Library, "Volunteer Opportunities," http://www.delraylibrary.org/?page_id=44.

Dorfman, S. "Drug Offers New Hope." Palm Beach Post, Boomer Health column. 25 March 2014.

Doyle, Kathryn. "Mindfulness Meditation May Help Older People Sleep." Psych Congress Network. 2015. http://www.psychcongress.com/article/mindfulness-meditation-may-help-older-people-sleep-21324.

Dribben, Melissa. "Sex after 50, or 75? But of Course." Philadelphia Inquirer, 20 October 2013.

Dunn, Debbie. "Elder Abuse Laws." Ehow.com. http://www.ehow.com/about_5428021_elder-abuse-laws.html.

Eaton, M. T., and M. H. Peterson. "Introduction to Dynamic Psychiatry." In Psychiatry Medical Outline Series. 2nd edition. New York: Medical Examination Publishing Co., 1969.

Emerson, Ralph Waldo. Essays-1st series, "Friendship."

Epidemiology, vol. 45 (1992): 157–67.

Erickson, Eric H. Childhood and Society. 2nd edition. New York: Norton, 1963.

Evans, J. "Medical Ethics, 'Delicate Issues of Sexuality in the Nursing Home.'" American Medical Directors Association Newspaper, vol. 14, no. 4 (April 2013).

Fawcett, Jan. "Bereavement and the Four Noble Truths." Psychiatric Annals, vol. 43, no. 6 (June 2013).

First, Michael B., Ed. . 4th edition. Washington, DC: American Psychiatric Association, 1994).

Fliegelman, Emanuel. "Sex after 60 is Nifty." Osteopathic Annals, vol. 112, no. 2 (Ferbuary 1984): 74–77.

Fønnebø, V. "Mortality in Norwegian Seventh-Day Adventists 1962–1986." Journal of Clinical Epidemiology, vol. 45 (1992).

Fox, Ashley. "Lurie's Biggest Loss." Philadelphia Inquirer, 20 July 2010.

Frankl, Victor E. Man's Search for Meaning. 3rd edition. New York: Simon & Schuster, 1982.

Frazier, Karen. "Mental Benefits of Exercise." http://exercise.lovetoknow.com/Mental_Benefits_of_Exercise.

Gammage, Jeff. "Lawyer Retire? At 101? Heck No." Philadelphia Inquirer, 20 July 2014.

Gesundheit! Institute, http://www.patchadams.org/patch-adams/.

Giannini, A. J., H. R. Black, and R. I. Goettsche. Psychiatric, Psychogenic, and Somatopsychic Disorders Handbook. New York: Medical Examination Publishing Company, 1978.

Glamser, Francis D. "Determinants of a Positive Attitude Toward Retirement." Journal of Gernotology, vol. 31, no. 1 (January 1976): 104–7. http://eric.ed.gov/?id=EJ129184.

Glenn, Amy Wright. "Life As They Know It." Inside Magazine, vol. 35, no. 2 (fall 2014).

Goins, Jeff. "The Importance of Hope in a Person's Life." Adventure in Missions. 11 July 2009. http://jeffgoins.myadventures.org/?filename=the-importance-of-hope-in-a-persons-life.

Gonda, T. A. "Death, Dying, and Bereavement." In *Comprehensive Textbook of Psychiatry*, vol. 2, edited by H. I. Kaplan and B. J. Sadock. 5th edition. Baltimore: Williams & Wilkins, 1989.

Gray, John. *Men Are from Mars, Women Are from Venus*. New York: HarperCollins, 1992.

Hallowell, Edward M. *Worry: Controlling It and Using It Wisely*. New York: Random House Publishing Group, 1997.

Hannah, Kristin. *Winter Garden*. New York: St. Martin's Press, 2010.

Hartney, Elizabeth. "What Are Behavioral Addictions?" About.com. http://addictions.about.com/od/howaddictionhappens/f/behavioraladd.htm.

Hazelden Betty Ford Foundation. "Substance Abuse among the Elderly; A Growing Problem." http://www.hazelden.org/web/public/ade60220.page.

Hinden, Stan. "5 Steps to Retire Happy." *AARP Bulletin Retirement Guide*, vol. 55, no. 7(September 2014).

Hochman, David. "Mindfulness Matters." *AARP the Magazine*, vol. 58, no 1C (December 2014/January 2015).

Hopman, Gerry. "Laughter a Coping Strategy." 9 May 2012. http://ezinearticles.com/?Laughter-a-Coping-Strategy&id=7052404.

Howell, Ryan T. "Why Do Shopping Addicts Keep Spending Their Money?" *Psychology Today*. 4 August 2014. http://www.psychologytoday.com/blog/cant-buy-happiness/201308/why-do-shopping-addicts-keep-spending-their-money.

"How to Live Better Longer," http://Retiredbrains.com/Home/Health+Care/How+To+Live+Better+Longer/default.aspx.

Humana/National Council on Aging. http://retirementperfectedd.com/resources/blog.asp?FAID=512269.

Idler, Ellen, "The Psychological and Physical Benefits of Spiritual/Religious Practices." *Higher Education Newsletter*, vol. 4, no. 2 (February 2008).

Ilnytzky, Ula. "Laughter Therapy Helps Them Cope with Illness." *Associated Press*, 28 November 2008. http://www.sfgate.com/health/article/Laughter-therapy-helps-them-cope-with-illness-3260307.php.

"The Importance of Sleep." Charlotte-Mecklenburg Schools. http://www.cms.k12.nc.us/Jobs/benefits/health/Pages/TheImportanceofSleep.aspx.

Jancin, Bruce. "Key Points in Managing Late-Life Anxiety." *Caring for the Ages* newspaper, vol. 15, no. 10 (October 2014).

Jaret, Peter. "Would You Want to Know?" *AARP Bulletin*, vol. 55, no. 4 (May 2014).

Jarvik, L. F. "Depression: A Review of drug Therapy for Elderly Patients." *Consultant*, 22(1982).

Jeste, Dilip. *American Journal of Psychiatry*, vol. 70, (2013).

Jines, Anda. "The Rewards and Challenges of Caregiving." 27 December 2009. http://ezinearticles.com/?The–Rewards-and-Challenges-of-Caregiving&id=3484803.

Kane, E. E. "Laughter Benefits: The Three C's." 21 March 2008. http://www.lifescript.com/well-being/articles/l/laughter_benefits_the_three_cs.aspx?gclid=CJT2m9byqMMCFdgPgQodph0ANw&trans=1&du=1&ef_id=VE-xfQAAAXs3Xvp0:20150123004955:s.

Kantor, Rossabeth Moss. http://www.brainyquote.com/quotes/authors/r/rosabeth_moss_kanter.html.

Kendler, K. S., X. Q. Liu, C. O. Gardner, et al., "Dimensions of Religiosity and Their Relationship to Lifetime Psychiatric and Substance Use Disorders." *American Journal of Psychiatry*, vol. 160, no. 3 (2003): 496–503.

Kerr, Michael. "Elderly Depression, Depression and Aging." Healthline.com. 29 March 2012. http://www.healthline.com/health/depression/elderly-and-aging#.

Kübler-Ross, Elisabeth. *On Death and Dying*. New York: Macmillan, 1969.

Kübler-Ross, Elisabeth and D. Kessler. *Life Lessons*. New York: Scribner; 2001.

Lalwani, Anvil K. "Disorders of Smell, Taste and Hearing." In *Harrison's Principles of Internal Medicine*, edited by Anthony S. Fauci, Dennis L. Kasper, Dan L. Longo, et al. New York, McGraw Hill Medical, 2008. 196–204.

Lamott, Anne. "Have a Little Faith." *AARP the Magazine* vol. 58, no. 1a (December 2014/January 2015).

Landau, Sidney I. (Managing Ed.), *Standard College Dictionary*, Funk & Wagnalls.

"Laughter the Best Medicine." Helpguide.org. http://www.helpguide.org/life/humor_laughter_health.htm.

Lee, P. V. "Drug Therapy: Avoiding the Pitfalls." *Medical World News-Geriatrics*, 1972.

Leviticus, Jill. "Breathing and Lung Problems." Livestrong.com. 16 August 2013. http://www.livestrong.com/article/358745-breathing-lung-problems/.

Lustbader, Wendy. *Life Gets Better: The Unexpected Pleasures of Growing Older*. New York: Jeremy F. Tarcher, Penguin, 2011.

Macdonald, Sally, and John Macdonald. "Not Your Grandparents' Vacations." *Philadelphia Inquirer*, 5 January 2014. N3.

Mace, Nancy L., and Peter V. Rabins. *The 36-Hour Day: A Family Guide to Caring for Persons with Alzheimer Disease, Related Dementing Illness and Memory Loss in Later Life*, Revised and updated edition. New York: Grand Central Publishing, 2001.

Malchiodi, Cathy. "Humor: The Human Gift for Coping and Survival." *Psychology Today*. 26 June 2008. http://www.psychologytoday.com/blog/the-healing-arts/200806/humor-the-human-gift-coping-and-survival.

Marchand, William R. *Depression and Bipolar Disorder*. Boulder, CO: Bull Publishing Company, 2012.

Matz-Costa, Christina. "After 55, the Key is Staying 'Engaged.'" http://www.nextavenue.org/blog/after-55-key-staying-engaged.

Mayo Clinic Staff. 5 February 2015. http://mayoclinic.org/friendships/ART-20044860.

———. "Selective Serotonin Uptake Inhibitors (SRRIs)." 9 July 2013. http://www.mayoclinic.org/diseases-conditions/depression/in-depth/ssris/art-20044825.

McCoy, Krisha. "How to Stay Socially Engaged as You Age." 16 April 2013. http://www.everydayhealth.com/senior-health/enhancing-your-life.aspx.

McGhee, Paul. "Using Laughter to Cope—Laughing in the Midst of Stress." *The Laughter Remedy*. 21 December 2012. http://www.laughterremedy.com/2010/12/using-humor-to-cope-%e2%80%93-laughing-in-the-midst-of-stress/.

Meador, K. G., and H. G. Koenig. "Spirituality and Religion in Psychiatry Practice Parameters and Implications." *Psychiatric Annals*, vol. 30, no. 8 (2000).

"Medications for Memory Loss." http://www.alz.org/alzheimers_disease_standard_prescriptions.asp.

Miller, M., C. Mangano, Y. Park, R. Goel, G. D. Plotnick, and R. A. Vogel, "Impact of Cinematic Viewing in Endothelial Function." *Heart*, vol. 92, no. 2 (February 2005): 261-63. "Mental Health of the Elderly." *A "Let's Talk Facts About"* pamphlet. Washington, DC: American Psychiatric Association, 1988).

Moore, Burness E. and Bernard D. Fine, eds. *A Glossary of Psychoanalytic Terms and Concepts*. 2nd edition. New York: American Psychoanalytic Association, 1968).

Mulder, M. P., and A. Nijholt. "Humor Research: State of the Art." 2002. http://web.archive.org/web/20041116165933/http://citseer.ist.pru.edu/580062.html),citeseer.ist.pru.edu.

Nasrallah, Henry A. "Editorial." *Current Psychiatry*, vol. 13, no. 6. Parsippany, NJ: 2014.

National Association of Cognitive Behavioral Therapists. "Providing Outstanding CBT Training Opportunities, Onsite Trainings, Conferences, and Regional Trainings." http://www.nacbt.org/whatiscbt.htm.

Nelson, John E., and Richard N. Bolles. *What Color is Your Parachute? For Retirement*. Berkeley, CA: Ten Speed Press, 2010.

O'Brien, Sharon. "10 Tips for Happy Retirement Living." *About.com*. http://seniorliving.about.com/od/retirement/a/retirement_livi.htm.

———. "Planning to Retire Soon? Make a Retirement Planning Checklist." *About.com*. http://seniorliving.about.com/od/retirement/ss/retirechecklist.htm.

Oshel, Bobby. "Starting Next Year, 2011, Over 10,000 People in the US Will Turn 65-Years-Old Every Day." 2 July 2010. http://ezinearticles.com/?Starting-Next-Year,-2011,-Over-10,000-People-in-the-US-Will-Turn-65-Years-Old-Every-Day&id=4596234.

Park, Alice, and Mandy Oaklander. "Medical Momentum." *Time*, vol. 184, no. 16 (27 October 2014).

Pennsylvania Department of Aging, "Older Adults Protective Services Act," http://www. portal.state.pa.us/portal/serveer.pt?open=514&objID=616729&mode=2.

Physicians' Desk Reference. 69th edition. Montvale, NJ: PDR Network, LLC, 2015.

Pink, Daniel H. *Drive: The Surprising Truth about What Motivates Us*. New York: Riverhead Books, 2010.

Polatin, Philip. *A Guide to Treatment in Psychiatry*. Philadelphia: Lippincott, 1966.

Powers, Alvin C. "Diabetes Mellitus." In *Harrison's Principles of Internal Medicine*, edited by Anthony S. Fauci, Dennis L. Kasper, DL Longo, E Braunwald, SL Hauser, JL Jameson and J Loscalzo. New York: McGraw Hill Medical, 2008. 2275–2304.

Quindlen, Anna. *A Short Guide to a Happy Life*. New York: Random House, 2000.

Quinn, Sally. "Religion Is a Sure Route to True Happiness." *Washington Post*. 24 January 2014. http://www.washingtonpost.com/national/religion/religion-is-a-sure-route-to-true-happiness/2014/01/23/f6522120-8452-11e3-bbe5-6a2a3141e3a9_story.html.

RALPH, "Want a Successful Retirement Plan?—Stay Postive," 12 June 2013, http://www. ralphcarlsonblog.com/want-successful-retirement-plan-stay-positive/.

"Religious Prejudice." rsrevision.com. http://www.rsrevision.com/GCSE/christian_perspectives/prejudice/religion/index.htm.

Renzulli, Kerri Anne. "'The Talk' Get Your Spouse on the Same Page about Retirement." *CNNMoney.com*. October, 2013. 26.

Repich, Deanne, ed. *Top 100 Inspirational Quotes for Living Anxiety-Free*. Pflugerville, TX: National Institute of Anxiety and Stress, Inc., 2008. http://www.ConquerAnxiety.com.

"Retirement and Spirituality: What's the Link?" *A Satisfying Journey: Living a Satisfying Retirement with Purpose and Joy*, 5 August 2012, http://satisfyingretirement.blogspot. com/2012/08/religion-spirituality.html.

Robinson, Lawrence, Joanna Saisan, and Jeanne Segal. "Elder Abuse and Neglect: Warning Signs, Risk Factors, Prevention, and Reporting Abuse." September 2015. http://www. helpguide.org/articles/abuse/elder-abuse-and-neglect.htm.

Sasson, Remez. "The Power of Positive Attitude Can Change Your Life." http://www. successconsciousness.com/positive_attitude.htm

Schwartz, Mel. "Silence: A Relationship Killer." 13 January 2014. http://blog.melschwartz. com/2014/01/13/silence-a-realtionship-killer/?utm_source=Silence.

Schwartzstein, Richard M. "Dyspnea and Pulmonary Edema." In *Harrison's Principles of Internal Medicine*, edited by Anthony S. Fauci, Dennis L. Kasper, Dan L. Longo, et al. New York: McGraw Hill Medical, 2008. 221–25.

Seltzer, Emilee. "How Caregivers can Help an Aging Adult Make Dietary Changes." Agingcare.com. http://www.agingcare.com/Articles/How-to-Help-Aging-Parents-Make-Dietary-Changes-137053.htm.

Sheehy, Gail. *Passages: Predictable Crises of Adult Life*. New York: E. P. Dutton & Co., Inc., 1974.

Sifford, Darrell. "Mining the Pleasures of the 'Golden Years.'" *Philadelphia Inquirer*, 28 June 1990. E-5.

———. "How a Spouse Might Help to Heal Childhood's Wounds." *Philadelphia Inquirer*, Thursday, June 18, 1987.

———. "Midlife Crisis: 'The Nagging Pain of Unfulfilled Dreams.'" *Philadelphia Inquirer*, 17 October 1983.

Simonson, Helen. *Major Pettigrew's Last Stand*. New York: Random House Trade Paperbacks, 2011.

Smith, Lee B. "Humor Relations for Nurse Managers." *Nursing Management*, 21, 86. (1990).

Smith, Suzanna. "The Importance of Families." Strongermarriage.org. http:// strongermarriage.org/htm/married/family-relationships-in-later-life/.

Society of Certified Senior Advisors. "A Positive Retirement Atitude—An Absolute Must!" CSA Blog, 9 March 2011, http://blog.csa.us/2011/03/positive-retirement-attitude-absolute.html.

Sproles, Cindy K. "Treat Elderly Parents with Dignity." Christian Broadcasting Network. http://www.cbn.com/family/familyadvice/treat-elderly-parents-with-dignity-sproles.aspx.

Strawbridge, W. J., R. D. Cohen, S. J. Shema, and G. A. Kaplan. "Frequent Attendance at Religious Services and Mortality over 28 Years." *American Journal of Public Health*, vol. 87 (1997).

Strout, Elizabeth. *Olive Kitteridge*. New York: Random House Trade Paperbacks, 2008.

Sullivan, Michele G. "Combination Drug Quells Anxiety, Aggression." *Caring For the Ages*, vol. 16, no. 1 (January 2015).

Taylor, Paul. *The Next America: Boomers, Millennials, and the Looming Generational Showdown*. New York: Public Affairs, 2014.

Thomas, P. "Primary Care: Depressed Elderly's Best Hope." *Medical World News*. 13 July 1987.

Thorson, James A. "Humor as Coping Mechanism." From *No Laughing's the Matter*. http://www.beliefnet.com/Health/2005/07/Humor-As-Coping-Mechanism.aspx#zaEsIb86vm8Myos5.99.

Trafford, Abigail. *My Time: Making the Most of the Bonus Decades after 50*. New York: Basic Books, 2004.

Updegrave, Walter. "What You Really Need in Retirement: Friends." *CNN Money*. 17 February 2010.

US Department of Health and Human Services. "Alzheimer's Disease Fact Sheet." https://www.nia.nih.gov/alzheimers/publication/alzheimers-disease-fact-sheet.

Von Drehle, David. "The Answer Issue: Everything You Never Knew You Needed to Know," *Time*, vol. 184, no. 9–10 (8–15 September 2014).

Webster's New World Dictionary of the American Language. College edition. New York: World, 1957.

Wright, J. H., A. T. Beck, and M. E. Thase. "Cognitive Therapy." In *The American Psychiatric Publishing Textbook of Clinical Psychiatry*, edited by R. E. Hales and S. C. Yudofsky. Arlington, VA: American Psychiatric Publishing, 2003.

Zal, Alice J. "The Patient at the End of Life." In *Somatic Dysfunction in Osteopathic Family Medicine*, edited by Nelson, chapter 13. Philadelphia: Lippincott Williams & Wilkins, 2007.

Zal, H Michael. *Ten Steps to Relieve Anxiety: Refocus, Relax and Enjoy Life*. Far Hills, NJ: New Horizon Press, 2013).

———. *The Sandwich Generation: Caught Between Growing Children and Aging Parents*. Cambridge, MA: Perseus Publishing, 1992.

———. "Depression in the Elderly Patient." In *Difficult Medical Management*, edited by R. B. Taylor. Philadelphia: W. B. Saunders Company, 1991.

———. "The Female Alcoholic." *Main Line Times*, September 21, 1986.

———. "Understanding the Elderly." *Osteopathic Medical News*, vol. 3, no. 3 (March 1986).

———. *Panic Disorder: The Great Pretender*. New York: Plenum Press, 1980.

Zimmerman, Sebastian. "Intimate Portraits: Psychotherapists in Their Own Work Space." *Psychiatric Times*, vol. 29, no. 9 (2012).

Web Addresses

http://adam.about.net/encyclopedia/infectiousdiseasses/Asthma.htm.
http://www.arthritis.org/conditions-treatments/disease-center/osteoarthritis/.
http://www.biographyonline.net/spiritual/articles/benefits-religion.html.
http://www.brainyquote.com/quotes/authors/h/henry_david_thoreau_3.html.
http://www.brainyquote.com/quotes/authors/s/swami_sivananda.html.
http://www.brainyquote.com/quotes/keywords/positive_attitude.html.
http://elder-abuseca.com/preventing-elder-abuse.php.
http://holistic-online.com/Humor_Therapy/humor_therapy.htm.
http://www.learn-about-alcoholism.com/alcoholism-statistics.html.
http://www.quotegarden.com/laughter.html.

http://www.quotegarden.com/retirement.html.
http://www.quotes-positive.com/quotes/retirement/.
http://www.seniorhealthsolutionsct.org/concerns/common.asp.
http://statisticbrain.com/retirement-statistics/.
http://www.stop-procrastination.org/.
http://thinkexist.com/quotations/planning.
http://www.unitedearth.com.au/proust.html.
https://www.urmc.rochester.edu/senior-health/common-issues/top-ten.aspx.
http://www.wow4u.com/retirement/index.html.

INDEX

ABOUT THE AUTHOR

H Michael Zal, D.O., F.A.C.N., F.A.P.A., Dist., retired as a psychiatrist after forty-three years in private practice. He is currently a clinical professor in the Department of Psychiatry at the Philadelphia College of Osteopathic Medicine. He is board certified, a fellow of American College of Neurology and Psychiatry, and a distinguished life fellow of the American Psychiatric Association.

Dr. Zal is a graduate of the University of Pennsylvania and the Philadelphia College of Osteopathic Medicine. He completed a three year psychiatric fellowship sponsored by the National Institute of Mental Health at the Philadelphia Mental Health Clinic and Haverford State Hospital.

He is emeritus at the Belmont Center for Comprehensive Treatment and served as president of their medical staff from 1995 to 1997. He was chairman of the Psychiatric Service at Metropolitan Hospital in Philadelphia from 1980 to 1990 and a member of the University of Pennsylvania Private Practice Research Group. He was also on the staff of Charter-Fairmount Institute, Mercy Suburban Hospital, and the Medical College of Pennsylvania.

Dr. Zal received the Albert Einstein Healthcare Foundation Physicians' Award for Excellence and the Practitioner of the Year Award, from the Philadelphia Psychiatric Society, for outstanding character, dedication, and commitment to patient care.

He is a lecturer, medical writer, and editor on mental health topics with numerous published articles to his credit. He is currently the editor of the *Journal of the Pennsylvania Osteopathic Medical Association*. He is an award-winning author who has published numerous articles as well as four books entitled *Panic Disorder: The Great Pretender* and *The Sandwich Generation: Caught between Growing Children and Aging Parents*; *Dancing with Medusa: A Life in Psychiatry: A Memoir*; and *Ten Steps to Relieve Anxiety: Refocus, Relax and Enjoy Life*.

He was the winner of the Eric W. Martin Memorial Award, presented by the American Medical Writers Association, for outstanding writing and the Frances Larson Memorial Award for excellence.

He is active in the community and has served as president of the Welsh Valley Civic Association, as a member of the board of directors of Variety Club, and president of the board of managers of the Associated Alumni of the Central High School of Philadelphia.

Dr. Zal is married to Alice J. Sheflin Zal, D.O., FACOFP, a retired family physician in Norristown, Pennsylvania, and past president of the Pennsylvania Osteopathic Medical Association. They currently live in Lansdale, Pennsylvania, and Atlantic City, New Jersey. They have two children, Michelle J. Dubin, RN, MSN, CPUR, and Fredrick H. Zal, who is a registered architect and has a master's degree in his field; a son-in-law, Steven Dublin, a CFO at a landscape architectural firm; and two grandchildren, Daniel Cory Dubin and Rebecca Haley Dubin.